Christopher Fowler is the acclaimed author of seven Bryant & May mysteries, including the award-winning *Full Dark House*. He lives in King's Cross, London.

For more information on Christopher Fowler and his books, see his website at www.christopherfowler.co.uk

PAPERBOY

Christopher Fowler

BANTAM BOOKS

LONDON · TORONTO · SYDNEY · AUCKLAND · JOHANNESBURG

TRANSWORLD PUBLISHERS
61–63 Uxbridge Road, London W5 5SA
A Random House Group Company
www.rbooks.co.uk

PAPERBOY
A BANTAM BOOK: 9780553820096

First published in Great Britain
in 2009 by Doubleday
an imprint of Transworld Publishers

This book is a work of non-fiction based on the life, experiences
and recollections of the author. The author has stated to the publishers
that, except in minor respects not affecting the substantial accuracy
of the work, the contents of this book are true.

A CIP catalogue record for this book
is available from the British Library.

Addresses for Random House Group Ltd companies outside the UK
can be found at: www.randomhouse.co.uk
The Random House Group Ltd Reg. No. 954009

The Random House Group Ltd supports The Forest Stewardship
Council (FSC), the leading international forest-certification organization.
All our titles that are printed on Greenpeace-approved FSC-certified paper
carry the FSC logo. Our paper procurement policy can be found at
www.rbooks.co.uk/environment

Typeset in Sabon by
Kestrel Data, Exeter, Devon.
Printed in the UK by
CPI Cox & Wyman, Reading, RG1 8EX.

2 4 6 8 10 9 7 5 3 1

Acknowledgements

I'd like to thank my agent Mandy Little for not thinking me mad when I told her I was writing this book, and for remaining so unfailingly enthusiastic about it. I could imagine the look on the face of Simon Taylor at Transworld when he realized I was writing a memoir. 'What? He can't stick to one genre for more than five minutes?' Luckily for me, he liked it and graciously spread his enthusiasm to others. Thanks, too, to Kate Samano for bringing some level-headed attention to detail to the occasional chaos of the prose.

Most of all, this is for my mother and brother, who were probably happy to have forgotten these events, until I had to dig them all up again. And, of course, it's for my father, whose memory grows dearer with passing time.

'My, you do like a good story, don't you?'

Sweeney Todd,
Stephen Sondheim and Hugh Wheeler

1

The First Patch of Sunlight
on the Pavement

Early one morning at the height of summer in 1960, I returned from the corner shop with a packet of Weetabix* under my arm and stopped to stare at the alien death ray that was scorching the pavement in front of me.

What I saw was a fierce yellow cone of light, ragged at the edges, smashing on to the concrete slab beside the green front gate with the power to melt a thousand suns. It was filled with sparkling, shimmering life forms that writhed and twisted like an invasive virus under a microscope.

I shrugged, navigated my way around the beam, went into the house and ate my breakfast (two Weetabix coated with snowy-white Tate & Lyle sugar and soaked in evaporated milk until they attained the consistency of rotted chipboard). Then I cut out the coupon on the back

*Breakfast cereal in tablet form that resembles roofing felt, or, when milk is added, wet roofing felt.

of the packet and sent away for a 3-D Spectroscope, so that I could view the three-dimensional animal picture card they gave away free inside.

I only needed Number 32, the Marmoset, and Number 28, the Diplodocus, to complete the set. The cereal company had no qualms about mixing dinosaurs and furry woodland creatures. Earlier that year I had sent off for the 31-in-1-o-scope, a pocket gadget with supposedly myriad uses, although I could only find about seven. It included a pocket knife that had snapped on first use and a magnifying glass that couldn't even burn an insect. Before that I had collected a Cornflakes marching band finished in red plastic, and a set of Shredded Wheat bath-time submarines propelled by baking soda.

I needed to keep an eye out for free offers. A child marooned in a London backwater with no ready cash was automatically rendered passive, a watcher-listener. At the mercy of my family, I could not go very far or do anything too unusual. My only consolation was that things were probably better than they would be as an adult, when, as my father constantly reminded me, I would have to find something useful to do, like mending carburettors, or else face a miserable fate. So I passed my childhood reading, watching, listening, and soon found that I could create something out of nothing, because the tools of imagination were everywhere I looked.

Having reached this frame of mind, I discovered that it was possible to stare at the first patch of bright sunlight on the pavement outside the house on a summery morning and see what others could not see. When I looked at the light falling through the dusty, unkempt hedge on to a section of warm grey stone flecked with mica, where ants filed past each other with shreds of leaves and ladybirds dotted the branches like shiny spots of poster paint, I was transported to a hostile jungle, a parched desert wasteland, an uncharted forest. In sparkling motes of dust, I could witness a fiery apocalypse, the scorched surface of Mars, the arrival of deadly space spores, the mistrustful eye of God, the light of salvation in ascending angels.

Born in suburban post-war Greenwich with no money, a mystifying family and an uncertain future, I was uncomfortable even entering a shop or talking to classmates, and felt that I might not survive long enough to ever be considered part of the real world. But I was sure of one thing. Imagination, in one form or another, would always provide a means of escape.

In the summer of 1960 an impoverished London was limping into unknown territory, still bearing war wounds that successive governments had not been able to heal. The re-elected Conservatives were intent on building homes and motorways, creating jobs, ending debt, changing the lives of working men and women, but nothing much seemed to be happening. The New Elizabethans' England* felt dictatorial, not democratic. 'Do Not' and 'We Know Best' were the orders of the day, as if knowledge and freedom were things to be afraid of.

London, said one radio comedian, had spent the last fifteen years tidying up after a very messy party, and the Hitlers wouldn't be invited round again. The city had swept all the debris away, shovelling the rubble of destroyed houses into vales and ditches, even managing to turn the hilly scrubland of nearby Blackheath into a great green billiard table. It had eradicated all the stubborn stains and had set about replacing the damaged ornaments with ugly, cheap-looking utility versions. Everything would soon be back to normal, even if it was all much scrappier and poorer than before. But where

---

*Faintly pretentious but peculiarly charming term chosen for those born in the reign of Elizabeth II.

on earth did the country go from here, now that the framework of the past had burned down? What was going to replace it?

1960 was not a time suited to imagining – but imagination held the key to the coming decade. The ideals of a new generation could, my parents were told, transform the country; goodbye sooty old industrialization, hello trendy young image. London's image, especially, was in line for a makeover, as a tiny handful of miniskirted dolly birds and Chelsea Set* boys in military tunics prepared to spark a revival in the capital's dying leisure spots. Their psychedelic lifestyles were specifically designed to enrage adults, and yet there was a sense that something radically new was needed. Angry letters were written to *The Times* complaining about the young sporting their parents' War medals as fashion accessories. Later, punk would democratize rebellion. London's first swingers were few in number, and only appeared among the plum-voiced children of the rich. Their antics had traditionally been tolerated with a roll of the eye until their money ran out and they grew up. This time, though the air was thick with measured outrage, even I could sense that something fresh might come of it.

Unfortunately, I would never become a part of their exciting world. I was ten years old, for God's sake, a decade and a social class down, stuck in a suburban Edwardian terraced house with a family that wasn't even peculiar enough to be classed as eccentric. My classmates never noticed me, except when I accidentally found myself in charge of the playtime goalposts and let the ball into the net three times because I was busy trying to remember

*Posh trendsetters showed their rebellious independence by spending Daddy's allowance at the Chelsea Drugstore, a groovy bar on the King's Road, Chelsea, now a McDonald's.

what Gold Kryptonite* did to Superman – then they noticed me long enough to kick me into a hedge.

My formative years were to be filled with orderly lassitude, like those of a soldier posted to a peaceful backwater. These were days of strawberry jam on white bread, the squeak of chalk in hushed classrooms, *Hancock's Half-Hour,*† cold mutton on Mondays, Shirley Abicair and her zither,‡ back-fence arguments, kicking about in the garden and walking alone through empty, silent streets. The only counter-culture I could experience was the over-the-counter culture of the local Co-op. The most exciting thing that happened that spring was the tortoise waking up. If someone bought a car, all the men in the street came out to look at it.

Barely dragged out of the threadbare fifties, South London was still sooty and pockmarked, its populace coughing and on the cadge. It was a strangely private place, divorced from what was supposedly really going on. The houses might have been in London, but London was not yet in many houses. Little of what was happening in the capital filtered through; the odd radio report was commented upon, an occasional newspaper headline was read aloud over breakfast, but apart from the scandalously unfilled bombsite at the top of the hill, the part of Greenwich where my family lived was just the same as it had been for the last thirty years.

During weekdays the men were all off at work, and

---

*It robbed Superman of his powers for ever. Needless to say, he didn't come into contact with it much.
†Seminal radio show by Galton and Simpson that changed the face of British comedy by foregrounding character. Sad, dry and hilarious if listened to with patience.
‡She sat and pinged it on her lap. An example of someone who became a TV star purely because she played an instrument no one had ever seen before.

their wives were busy waxing the lino in cool, shadowed hallways or in still, dead front rooms where even the dust hung motionless in the air. You could smell coal and lavender polish, cigarettes and steamed vegetables, mildew and fresh-cut grass. It was all so quiet and safe, full of purposefully pressed lips and chapped hands. The passing summer days were sensible, predictable and becalmed. *Housewives' Choice** was on the radio, and the choice was always the same. There was very little noise. Mangles were turned by hand, workmen dug roads with pickaxes, houses were swept with brooms. On Sundays it was so quiet that you could hear your neighbours cleaning their shoes next door.

But I felt that even here, behind the dullest daily routines, there was a dark and unruly strangeness that might somehow find a way to surface. It lay just behind a wooden fence, over a wall or through a hedge. It was hidden behind net curtains, in rooms where adults sat smoking in silhouette, in kitchens where wives washed up and whispered, in railway alleys where lovers clung guiltily to each other. It was tucked away just out of reach, on top shelves, in the backs of cupboards, deep under the stairs.

Or perhaps it lay within the pages of a forgotten book.

*Morning radio show that played slush for women trapped behind ironing boards.

2

Things to Make and Do

'You haven't seen my good trowel anywhere, I suppose?'

'I didn't know you had a "good" trowel.'

'Yes, there's my good trowel and my cheap trowel.' Bill tracked dirt into the little red scullery as he wandered in, as if shedding pieces of himself. 'It's a small house. How can things go missing?'

Kath absently wiped her husband's bootprints from the red-leaded floor. If he kept shedding and she kept wiping, perhaps there wouldn't be anything of him left one day. 'Why, what else have you lost?'

'Bricks. The gas poker. Four planks. A geranium tub. Some sheets of corrugated iron. My best pliers. One of my crash helmets. A large panel of foam rubber. And the old playpen. I was going to burn it at the bottom of the garden, but it's disappeared. And I'm sure we had a coil of rope somewhere.'

I'm sure we did, thought Kath grimly. It was probably in the back room, beside the two motorbikes Bill was taking to pieces. A working-class habit, she supposed, always aware that she had married beneath her. Her husband did not distinguish between the inside and the outside of the house, which is why the tiny front garden was filled with engine parts, why there was an upright washing machine and a mangle in the back yard, why there were two motorbikes in the back room and a third leaking oil in the hall.

'Where's the boy?' Bill plunged oil-smeared hands into luminous green Swarfega,* gooshed them about, removed them with a sucking noise and wiped them dry on Kath's only clean tea towel. To my father, I was always 'the boy'.

'He was under the kitchen table, reading *Where the Rainbow Ends* to the cat.'

Kath was cooking gammon with tinned pineapple rings and marrow, which she would cut into strips and boil until it jellified, held together by the rind. Then she would grate nutmeg over it, a mis-remembered tip from a make-do-and-mend wartime recipe book. You could eat most of her meals through a straw except for the meat, which had usually been cooked for so long that it couldn't have been tenderized with a lawn-roller.

Kath didn't approve of Bird's Eye peas or Smedley's frozen fish fingers because, being convenient, they were therefore common and eaten by people in council flats, as was Echo and Stork margarine. She experimented once with a packet of Vesta Chow Mein because it was exotic and bore the name of a Roman goddess, but didn't buy it again because it was too spicy. Spices were not kept in the Fowler larder because they were nasty foreign things that spoiled the taste of food and took the pattern off your Fablon shelf coverings. Vesta Chow Mein comprised a sachet of grey powder with dried peas and unidentifiable red bits in it, like food designed for astronauts or arctic

*Glowing lime de-greaser; could double for Green Kryptonite.

explorers, and came with a packet of little yellow strips that you emptied into a hot frying pan, and watched as they swelled up into crisp twirls. Even though it smelled like the stairwell beside Waterloo Bridge and probably contained more chemicals than the Greenwich gas manufacturing plant, I thought it was fantastic.

Bill lit one dog-end of a Woodbine* from the embers of another, flicking the first out into the yard, and peered under the table at the untidy stacks of picture books high enough to hide a small child behind. 'Well, he's not here now.'

A terrible howl of pain rose from the garden. My mother dropped a pan of water into the sink with a bang and ran outside, ready to face the sight of blood.

'Christopher, what on earth are you doing?' she screamed when she realized that I was trapped within a collapsed pyre of acrid burning wood and twisted metal. She only ever called me by my full name when I had done something terrible.

My father pulled at the flaming playpen, which had concertina'd over my legs, pinching the skin blue, and was the reason why I was shouting the place down. Gradually I was released from this homemade torture chamber and dragged aside, leaving the burning frame to belch oily smoke over the neighbours' washing. The people next door had all filed out to watch with folded arms and pursed lips.

'What on earth did you think you were building?' Bill shouted, peering forlornly through the flaming tangle of embers and metal at his blackening best pliers.

'A big dipper,' I answered, as if it was obvious.

I had attached roller-skate trucks to the base of the

---

*Rough-as-guts cancer-sticks for the working class affectionately known as 'gaspers'.

geranium tub, tied the rope to it and hauled it over steeply angled tracks consisting of the planks and sheet iron, laid on top of the playpen struts. The poker had an unusually long hose, and was attached to the red-painted gas tap in the scullery. It made a wall of flame for the coaster car to blast through – I would have constructed a water flume, but the tin tub was still used for baths in our house and I did not want to risk denting it.

I had only ever been on one Big Dipper, in the hellish death-trap that was the Sheerness* Pleasure Garden, a funfair that Kath said was run by gypsies, or at least by people with curly hair, tans, gold teeth and earrings. The front car had part of its floor missing, so you needed to keep your feet raised to avoid having them torn off in the sleepers passing below. Fairgrounds provided a rich source of horror stories for my mother. 'Mrs Reed's sister was thrown out of the chain-chair roundabout just as it hit top speed,' she told me once. 'They found her handbag over by the United Dairies . . . Your grandfather was there the night a stray spark burned the ghost train down with children still inside, and the people in the queue outside thought the screams were part of the ride . . . Your cousin Brenda won a poodle at a sideshow and used to suck it at night to get to sleep. It turned out to be made of lead, and we think that's why she went simple.'

I desperately wanted to build a funfair of my own at home.

Instead, I was carried indoors, bruised, noisy and smouldering from the conflagration in the garden, and sent to my room to recover. Luckily there was an unopened Jamboree Bag and a pile of comics up there,

---

*A 'resort' on the Isle of Sheppey that comprised a lido, a funfair, some manky beach huts, a nasty estuarine beach and the pikiest holiday-makers on the South coast.

and I took consolation in them, knowing that I would never again attempt anything involving nails, saws, gas or wood. I was not, to put it mildly, a practical boy.

In 1960, when the accident happened, I was seven years old. Born during Queen Elizabeth II's coronation, I had been presented with a heraldic mug and a crested spoon, both of which my father had used in the course of repairing his Triumph motorbike, and therefore ruined. I did not hate my father, because to hate someone you have to understand what they are up to. Rather, it seemed that Bill was wired differently from me, like a Continental plug. We had no idea about what made each other pleased or angry, and as a consequence we could only communicate through a common element: my mother, his wife. Bill had a range of subjects he felt comfortable with: car engines, the War, boats, hardware shops. When Kath spoke, it was often to continue an abstract thought that had started in her head some time earlier, so that her conversation could border on the surreal. I happily related to that.

Low-evening sunshine heated the thin curtains in my bedroom. The air outside the window was alive with mayflies. My mother said they only lived for a day, but childhood seemed intent on lasting for ever. The sunset warmed the lincrusta wallpaper above my bed to a welcoming orange. Another hot suburban day tomorrow. In my memory it was always summer, except for the bits that were like living in a bowl of filthy water – there were still smogs. In December 1952, just before I was born, the worst of them had killed four thousand Londoners.

My mother came up to see me. 'Back from Treasure Island?' I figured she was referring to Long John Silver and my possible loss of a leg, because she liked all of Robert Louis Stevenson's books except *Travels with a Donkey in the Cevennes*. 'I suppose it hurt.'

'I could have lost it.'

'It's a miracle we can find anything in that garden.'

She seated herself on the end of my bed, smoothing out the racing-car bedspread. Nobody dramatized cuts and bruises in the Fowler family; they were the medals of childhood, and not to be fussed over.

'Your father is ready to kill you. I don't know why you go so far out of your way to annoy him. Perhaps you need more fresh air. Why don't you go with Percy to Greenwich Park?'

Percy lived next door and had to walk very slowly because he had TB. He had spent part of last year in an iron lung and wasn't allowed to play cricket in case the ball hit him in the chest. Plus, he had to go through life being called Percy.

'It takes too long. By the time he gets there, the park will be closing.'

'You spend an awful lot of time indoors. You're very pale.'

'You feed me too much tinned food.'

'Your father doesn't enjoy market produce. He prefers to be constipated.' My mother knew that things in tins weren't fresh, but thought that things in jars were. Her first sighting of fresh ginger root gave her quite a fright, because she was used to seeing it floating in brown liquid. We never dreamed you could get fresh beetroot. She continued to buy tins until a scandal occurred involving poisoned tins of Fray Bentos corned beef.

'I'll cook you fresh if we can get it. It doesn't make any difference to me, I get no pleasure from eating because I have no taste buds. I damaged my mouth in a bicycle accident when I was seven. But you're a growing boy.' She narrowed her green eyes at me, preparing to sum up. 'Well, there you are, more outdoor pursuits, eat things you don't like, make some friends, try not to annoy your father.'

She straightened the cornflower-blue apron she wore

every day for the first fifteen years of her marriage, and quietly shut the door behind her. My mother had a way of closing herself off from difficult conversations.

There was a time when all lower-middle-class English families were this emotionless. I remembered seeing a Victorian cartoon in a very old issue of *Punch** magazine, in which a lady's maid was calling to her employee in great distress.

Maid: 'Oh Ma'am! I've just swallowed a safety pin!'
The lady of the house (drily): 'Oh, so that's where all my safety pins go.'

As far as I could tell, there were three classes of people living in England, sandwiched together like the flavours in a Neapolitan ice-cream brick. People who were 'not like us', 'people like us', and people who were 'not for the likes of us'.

The first lot were common; they exaggerated their vowels, especially the letter 'a' (as in 'Haaang Abaaaht!') and shouted at each other in the street. They laughed all the time, voted Labour, said rude words and drank bitter or stout. One of them, Mr Hills next door, took his teeth out and hung a teaspoon on his nose when he was tipsy.

The middle ones were bemused, genteel white-collar workers who put on airs and graces even though they didn't have two halfpennies to rub together. They helped out at Tory party headquarters and admired the royals. They were always shushing each other and worrying about being embarrassed, or 'shown up'. They were obsessed with the cleanliness of their shirt collars, and

*Occasionally humorous Victorian magazine famed for its longevity in dentists' waiting rooms.

although they moaned all the time, were pathetically grateful when posh people deigned to acknowledge them. Most middle-class men stayed in one job for fifty years, at the end of which time they were presented with a carriage clock and packed off home to die.

The ones in the top bracket liked telling everyone else what to do but were generally invisible, only appearing on fête days to talk loudly about once meeting 'the radiant Princess Margaret'.* They attended street parties for the poor, but never organized them. The ladies wore white gloves and the men never knew what to do with their hands.

Naturally, none of these groups spoke to each other unless they absolutely had to – i.e., when their houses fell down.

Class was an endless source of fascination. Another ancient *Punch* cartoon I recalled showed an upper-class young lady cutting up a hansom carriage in her motor-car at Piccadilly Circus.

Cabman: 'Sound your 'orn!'
Lady driver: 'Sound your aitches!'

It was a mysterious world all right, and better to stick with what you could understand. After nursing my wounds by removing a knee-scab with surgical precision, I lay on the bed and opened my Jamboree Bag, so-called because it had a poorly printed picture of Scouts on the cover.

Inside were:

A handful of tiny round pastels as hard and tasteless as coat buttons.

---

*Elizabeth's hard-drinking sister, a legendary royal freeloader inexplicably worshipped by the lower orders.

Two of the ugliest, most utilitarian toffees in the
world, wrapped in thin wax paper that proved
impossible to separate from the toffee.
A sherbet fountain with a bunged-up stick of
liquorice in it to act as a straw.
A toy so poorly assembled that it was impossible
to figure out whether it was a submarine or a
farmyard animal.
A joke. Sample:
Q. Where does Mr Plod the policeman live?
A. 999 Letsby Avenue.

The only quality the Jamboree Bag possessed was its
mystery, and it therefore remained far more interesting
if left unopened. Things invisible to the eye contained
hope.

My bedroom was filled with reading material: books
salvaged from dustbins, books borrowed from friends,
books with missing pages, books found in the street,
abandoned, unreadable, torn, scribbled on, unloved,
unwanted and dismissed. My bedroom was the Battersea
Dogs Home of books. Unfortunately, none of them were
books I would have chosen for myself. I did not want to
learn about dentistry, rope-making, the Museum of Bricks
or the Shropshire Evangelical Guild, and I certainly did
not want to read the Condensed Books of the Reader's
Digest, not just because the novel of the month was
usually a heartwarming chronicle of a Brooklyn family
who had relocated to the Italian countryside, but because
it was obvious that 'condensed' meant 'censored'. I rescued
them because I could not bear to see them thrown away.
It seemed wrong to leave words unread, even when they
were incredibly, staggeringly boring. I read the boring bits
first just to get them out of the way, and this proved so
arduous that I often failed to reach the good bits.

I would be left alone here until dusk, which at this point of summer was around nine p.m. I loved reading. When I was reading, I could not hear my parents sniping at one another. Kath had a subscription to the *Reader's Digest*, which was filled with snippets of triumph over tragedy, girls choking back tears, brave guide dogs, recovery from secret illness and other wholesome toss in which I had no interest.

The family also owned a set of ten blue cardboard-bound volumes from the 1930s entitled *The Arthur Mee Children's Encyclopedia*. These volumes included such fascinating and useful items as:

How to Stalk a Deer
Keeping Guinea-Pigs as Pets
The History of Tunnelling
Proficiency Badges of the Boy Scouts
The Wonderful World of the Worm
Crocheting a Pot-Holder for Empire Day*
Fun and Amusement with Stops and Commas
How to Cultivate a Monastery Garden
The Right Way to Slide
The Cheerful Black Folk of Africa
And 'What Is Wrong with this Picture?'
(Answer: 'The gentleman has buttoned his waistcoat
    incorrectly.')

In an article on 'How to Build a British House', the end photograph showed a man standing on his roof behind actual crenellations, beneath a fluttering Union Jack, clenching a pipe stem between his teeth, staring

---

*On Empire Day a grateful nation (and Canada) held inspirational speeches and lit bonfires in their back gardens. It became Commonwealth Day in 1958 in order to sound less patronizing.

pompously into the middle distance. Another article entitled 'Things to See in London' included the Inigo Jones Watergate, Adelphi (moved and forgotten), the Crystal Palace (moved and burned down) and, more obscurely, the W. T. Stead Memorial on the Embankment (Stead was a journalist and spiritualist who survived the sinking of the *Titanic*). The volumes were fascinating from an anthropological perspective, but also dusty, peculiar and vaguely offensive. I loved them.

In a house that contained so little to read, I would read anything, because I possessed no functioning critical faculties whatsoever. At breakfast I would read the Cornflakes box, and then, when it was empty, attempt to make the absurdly complicated paper sculpture of a tiger's head that Kellogg's had printed on the back of the packet. I would even read the sugar bag, although Mr Cube, the anthropomorphic lump of sugar brought in by Tate & Lyle to deliver propaganda messages against the government's plan to privatize the sugar industry, gave me the creeps, as did Mr Therm, the weird dancing gas flame who advertised cookers. When there was absolutely nothing else left to read at the breakfast table I would read my father's *Daily Express*, every front page of which featured 'Our Radiant New Queen'. In times of desperation I read my mother's knitting pamphlets.* I would read on the toilet and in the bath, and while crossing the road, which you could do because there were hardly any cars about. I read while walking along the pavement, aided by a sixth sense that kept me from vanishing down manholes or smacking into lampposts. I read just standing up for a pee, with a comic book propped on the cistern.

Ideally, I wanted to read every book in the English

---

*Most of which have now been turned into a range of smutty birthday cards suggesting that the models were rent boys or on drugs.

language, climaxing with Shakespeare, which at the moment looked like gibberish. But the only things I could afford to buy for myself were comics, and they became my literature.

More than that, they were an addiction.

The first one I ever bought was a Harvey Comic featuring Baby Huey, a stupid giant yellow duck in a nappy. When this character proved unsatisfying I switched to Hot Stuff the Little Devil, Little Dot, Casper and Wendy, Sad Sack, and Richie Rich, the adventures of a grotesquely wealthy blond boy who was forever carting around wheelbarrows full of giant diamonds. Even at an early age, I knew this comic was wrong.

But there was something bigger and better out there, and its name was Superman.

3

Not a Hoax, Not a Dream, but REAL!

'You are going to take it back.'

My mother was holding up the comic I had just bought. It wasn't that she disapproved of me reading them. She was angry because she'd given me a shilling to go and buy a sliced family loaf, and I'd come back with Superman.

'I can't take it back.' The idea was mortifying. It had been opened and *partially read*. It was like taking two bites out of a Mars bar and trying to return it to the confectioner.

When Kath stood with her right hand on her hip, she was meant to be obeyed. Her pale-blue pinafore dress and freshly lacquered helmet of tight fair curls formed the weekday uniform of a woman who intended to get things done. 'This is a lesson you need to learn, Christopher. You did a wrong thing, and you must undo it by yourself, even though it hurts. Take it back.'

I took the comic from her and headed across the road to Mr Purbrick's with shame soaking into my heart. Why

27

didn't she understand that comics were the key to the world? You could always buy another loaf, but Superman comics were hard to come by.

When the Westcombe Hill corner shop began stocking *The Man of Steel*, everything changed. On the cover of the first issue I purchased, Superman had the head of a giant red ant. It was a Red Kryptonite story, and, as was so often the case with DC Comics, the cover was a 'fanciful' – i.e., untruthful – version of the events depicted inside. Red Kryptonite was my favourite chunk of Superman's home planet because the results to exposure were unguessable, and were usually part of some convoluted and ludicrous hoax to teach Lois Lane not to be nosy.

I hated Batman, who had stupid ears and no superpowers, and I spent all of my pocket money on comic series that were doomed to failure and had zero resale value, like *The Metal Men* (robots with the properties of the element table), *The Atom* (a shrinking man who spent most of his time climbing out of Venus flytraps or fighting spiders), *The Flash* (who could run fast – big deal), *Strange Sports* (weird science-fiction sports matches), *Sea Devils* (boring underwater adventures) and *Challengers of the Unknown* (purple jumpsuited heroes without superpowers).

Purbrick's stocked comics in a rusty wire revolving rack, and I had a small window of opportunity to buy them on a Wednesday before they sold out. Certain issues became legendary, especially the tale of 'Superman Red and Superman Blue', although I later decided this was more about fetishizing two different versions of the Man of Steel's costume than about the plot. One story, called 'The Death of Superman', was endlessly plugged across the DC range ('Not a hoax, not a dream, but REAL!') and I was desperate to get my hands on it. It seemed that

DC had got themselves into this having-to-explain-it's-not-a-hoax situation because they had made their hero so invincible that his powers negated most of the more dramatic storylines.* The writers had to resort to ever more elaborate ruses for their sensational cover gambits. Virtually every plot turned out to be a trick, a hoax or a dream.

I therefore found myself fascinated by the Superman comics for all the wrong reasons. I wasn't interested in heroics or battles with space aliens. I wanted to see how much more absurd Superman's psychological gambits could become before something cracked and they all went mad.

Mr Purbrick was behind the counter, dispensing horrible-tasting cough sweets called Hacks. The logo on their bottle featured an elderly man sneezing wetly into a vast hankie. Damn, why couldn't the place have been shut for lunch?

Lois Lane and Jimmy Olsen comics were particularly instructive, I found, because they took the hoax-plot to a surreal level. The Man of Steel's two sidekicks were clearly in love with him, but he didn't love them. Lois would be humiliated, bullied, deceived and placed in danger by a man who was prepared to disguise himself under rubber masks just to 'teach her a lesson'. Her old-maid status was endlessly mocked. She would be duped by gold-digging monocled counts who turned out to be Superman (punishing her for some perceived failure of judgement), fake superheroes who were revealed as gangsters, and handsome historical figures like Robin Hood or Julius Caesar, usually as a result of hitting her

---

*Superman had one flaw: he could see across the universe but not through a sheet of lead. Presumably he never solved crimes in churches, not being able to see through their roofs.

head on a rock and thinking she'd been hurled back into the past.

I re-read these comics with an increasing sense of puzzlement. Why would a gangster pretend he had superpowers just to shut Lois Lane up? *You are a gangster, and Lois Lane is about to expose your misdeeds in the* Daily Planet. *Do you, a) shoot her in the head? Or do you, b) fly through her bedroom window on wires in tights and a cape, snog her, propose, get her into a wedding dress so she can say 'I grew tired of waiting for you, Superman, I am marrying Astro-Lad' and then dump her?*

In one issue Lois Lane spent the entire story with her head in an iron box, too ashamed to go out, because she'd been given the head of a cat. Sometimes all of Lois's friends were in on these humiliations, but could not tell her because they were *being watched from space*. When Lois finally got to the altar with Superman, it turned out to be a dream caused by her falling off a pier. Sometimes she ended up in a straitjacket, raving, and this too would be revealed as a trick.

Was adult life going to be like this, I wondered? When I grew up would I have to be on my guard every second of the day in case somebody tried to trick me? Would I wake up to discover it had all been a hoax, a dream, and not real at all?

I liked Lois Lane because she was a contrary woman with a job to do, like my mother. What I could not see, of course, was that Lois Lane comics were aimed at teenage girls, and since I did not know any girls I was not able to understand the psychology of someone who would spend a week with her head in a metal box in order to get a date.

In every issue of Lois Lane, Superman did one of three things: he turned bad, died or got married. And it always turned out to be a hoax.* The Man of Steel required his girlfriend to pass an endless series of tests; she would have to go without sleep, or remain silent, or be turned into an old hag or a baby in order to prove her loyalty. Superman demanded such terrible sacrifices from his friends that you wondered whether it was worth knowing him. He was good, so he could do no wrong. He was invulnerable, so nothing would ever hurt him. And only the people with whom he surrounded himself, ordinary flawed human beings, could ever get hurt, which is why he refused to become intimately involved with anyone. He was the opposite of Jesus: everyone else had to suffer for him.

Superman also played tricks on his pal Jimmy Olsen to punish him for using his signal watch too often, making him undergo strange transformations, like becoming a human porcupine, Elastic Lad or a giant turtle boy. I loved Superman because he was a stern finger-wagging patrician who told everyone what to do and hated anyone having fun, and was therefore unconsciously homoerotic. I wanted Superman to be my father because you always knew where you were with him. A man's most attractive quality is the ability to make a firm decision. Strictness was something my father had never managed to master.

When I got home, the ritual of comic-book reading had to be carefully organized. I would clear the small oak table in the kitchen, and place a cup of tea to my right, with a chocolate bar just below it, a Fry's Mint Cream† or Cadbury's Fruit and Nut. I would lay the first comic before me and open it, solemnly reading from cover to cover (including all the advertisements for 100 magnets

*The 1950s were a period of such stasis that no one wanted change, even in their comic books; there was an outcry among fans when Lois had her hair permed.
†Also came in fruit flavours differentiated by the dazzling colour of their fillings. Sorely missed.

or an entire civil war army) so that its world entirely enveloped me, and I could no longer hear my parents arguing. Comics provided solace and protection. Their panels were windows into a happier, safer, brighter place.

When you're a kid you only really read comics for about five years before real life intrudes upon your imagination, and your teenage years arrive. DC's storylines really began to flounder after the liberation movement of the sixties, and the Lois Lane comic got discontinued, even though she continued to crop up in Superman comics, falling off piers or out of office windows, into his waiting arms. What was wrong with the woman? Did she have some kind of balance problem? Had she thought about removing her high heels before leaning over rooftops?

DC's stern fundamentalist superheroes could only ever be on the side of the establishment. Like good Christians, they tried to win back some ground by expanding their family, but by the time they had taken on a super cat, a super horse and even Beppo the Super Monkey, I knew it was time to switch to Marvel Comics. I put up with Marvel's overwrought writing style because the lurid artwork was like a rainbow being sick across the page. The best story was Spiderman's three-issue fight with Dr Octopus, involving the first of his Aunt May's many brushes with potentially fatal illnesses. Spidey needn't have worried; the old broad had the constitution of an ox.

On his rack, Mr Purbrick also stocked shoddily re-printed collections of weird tales with surprise endings. The lead stories were always about giant creatures called Koomba or Zatuu, who were defeated by an insignificant bloke in a hat, the sole purpose of their existence being for the artist to have fun drawing them smashing up city streets.

But oh, the pleasure didn't end there. In the backs

of these comics was always a page entitled BUMPER
TREASURE CHEST OF FUN! It sold:

Trick black face soap
Worms ('They magically appear when dropped in a
    glass of water. Imagine the look of horror on your
    victim's face. Harmless.')
Onion gum
See-behind glasses
Throw your voice!
Joy buzzer
Plastic sick ('Whoops! Who's been ill? Imagine their
    faces! Hours of fun!)
X-ray spex (actually cardboard lenses with pieces
    of ribbed feather across the centre pinholes that
    created a black ghost-shape within any object
    looked at, the sort of thing people see as they're
    going blind).

Purbrick's sold Ellison's Jokes, which included tin
ventriloquists' swozzles that you were always in danger
of swallowing and choking to death on, and 'Fake Soot',
which comprised tiny specks of ground rubber. His shop
was in the middle of the parade on Westcombe Hill, a
down-at-heel middle-class suburb. There were no turds
or rubber breasts in his joke shop; the children were expected to throw fake soot at each other.

Although I much preferred American comics, I also took
all the British comics because everyone else did. *Dandy,
Buster, Topper, Lion, Beezer* and the rest were delivered
every Wednesday, along with Kath and Bill's *Daily Mail*.
My favourite stories concerned the Steel Claw, a man
with a metal hand who turned invisible (except for the
hand) whenever he was electrocuted. The strip required
its hero to walk into power cables at the same rate that

normal people crossed the road. Girls weren't allowed to read these comics. They had to make do with *Bunty*, a periodical seemingly financed by the hockey industry.

I loved the private world of comics – no adult could make sense of stories that accurately reflected the preposterous illogicalities of imaginative children. Comics were a narcotic that led to harder drugs like *Mad* magazine, with its unfunny American jokes about cars and movies and Madison Avenue, and *Famous Monsters of Filmland*, which was filled with appalling puns and blurrily reproduced stills of long-forgotten B-movie monsters. My favourite monster was the crimson creature shaped like the top of a cucumber that fired mind-controlling bats to attack the people of Earth in Roger Corman's *It Conquered the World*. It wasn't much of a stretch defeating this fearsome beast; the hero just hit it with a flamethrower and tipped it on its side. When he did, you could see the castors it moved around on sticking out from underneath.

Famous Monsters had great stuff you could send away for in its back pages, including rubber horror masks that made your face sweat, ten-foot inflatable pythons, giant weather balloons, 'sea monkeys' that were actually dried brine shrimps, despite the fact that the artwork showed them sitting in armchairs reading newspapers, 8mm reels of *The Giant Claw*,* *The Deadly Mantis* and other lousy monster movies, Aurora horror model kits,† the baby chick incubator, the Mad Doctor hypodermic needle ('everyone will faint when you plunge this needle into your victim's arm!'), spooky sound effects LPs and live monkeys. None of which my mother allowed me to send off for.

---

*Fighter jets versus giant prehistoric bird! Or rather, jets versus goggle-eyed string puppet (strings highly visible).
†You could even get accessories to pimp your models of the Wolfman and the Phantom of the Opera, like spare bats and cobwebs. Cool.

'They would have to come all the way from America,' Kath told me. 'It would cost a fortune, and nothing would survive the trip. I'm not spending all that money to have a dead monkey delivered in a box.'

Entering Purbrick's shop with the Superman comic held before me like a talisman, I waited for the newsagent to finish dispensing his weird-smelling cough sweets. When he noticed me, I launched into an elaborate, pointless lie about returning home to discover that I had already bought the comic from another shop some days before, the implication being that my philanthropy virtually kept the shops in the area afloat with my purchases, and I could be forgiven for this one rare mistake.

Purbrick saw right through me. It was as though he had sent away for the X-ray spex. He stood with his arms folded over his bulging pinstriped waistcoat, staring down at my gangly form. What he didn't understand was that I needed the comics more than heroin, and would probably break into shops for them if necessary. I had developed an elaborate system of swapping at school which could translate a coveted copy of *The Legion of Super Heroes** into its equivalent value in tubes of fruit Spangles.†

'All right,' said Mr Purbrick finally, 'I'll take it back just this once. But I'll never take another comic back from you ever again.'

And with a sigh, he went to the till to return my mother's shilling.

---

*The comic-book equivalent of a tree-house club. The super-teens met in a rocket and spent most of their time banning each other and voting for new members. Saturn Girl was really bossy. Plus, their powers were rubbish. Bouncing Boy? Q.E.D.
†Fruit-flavoured boiled sweets which, like Fruit Gums, stopped being enjoyable after the revised code of acceptable additives came into force.

4

Background Material

'We're leaving to visit your grandmother in exactly ten minutes,' warned Kath. 'You know she doesn't like to be kept waiting.'

'I can't come,' I said simply, feeling it was time to put my besocked and sandalled foot down.

'Why not? Are you feeling unwell?' It was the only excuse that would be acceptable to Mrs Fowler, and possibly not even then.

'No, I'm at absolutely the most crucial moment in the whole book.' I held up a 1930s library copy of something to do with female pirates and purloined emeralds which I had found to be pretty racy, even though it was falling apart and grubby from a thousand other readers.

'Nice try. The book will wait. Good use of "crucial". Mackintosh on, please.' My mother clapped her hands together and left the room, trying to look stern but failing this time.

In the Fowler family no one was much interested in family. Alice, my maternal grandmother, had white fluffy hair, high cheekbones and a quiet half-smile, and wore

Wedgwood cameos on black lace, but no one explained why she had no husband, and I was not old or brave enough to ask. She reminded me of the granny in Tweety Pie cartoons.

She lived in Brighton in a time machine, a mid-Victorian corner house with green wooden shutters, two front doors and a hissing copper-plated boiler. Everything about her was genteel, softly spoken and late Victorian. She disapproved of shouting and running on a Sunday, and never bought a television because she thought it would irradiate the brain and destroy the art of conversation. She also had a paid companion who stayed in the kitchen, a pinch-faced witch called 'Aunt' Mary who hoarded food in case rationing returned and counted out the milkman's change as if parting with family heirlooms. After her death, Kath found a suitcase full of tinned peaches under her bed.

The house had three smells: beeswax, lavender and suet pudding. There were metal bed-warmers and aspidistras in pots, and green velvet tablecloths with tassels, and the stillness in the hall was only disturbed by ticking clocks. The scullery had a flagstone floor, and there was different crockery for day and evening use, a vivid orange for breakfast, a calming blue for dinner. The wallpaper was 'Acanthus' by William Morris, the light was always low, and it was very, very quiet. My grandmother's world was constructed around a century of Victorian advice. Children were seen and not heard, overcoats were to be worn until the last day of May, and tea cooled you better than lemonade on a hot day, as did running your wrists under cold water, where the blood was nearest the surface. I loved her house because there were strict unbreakable rules, so you always knew where you stood.

Things were different on my father's side. Bill's mother was a terrifying old woman who didn't seem keen on being reminded that she was anyone's grandmother. It was impossible to imagine that she had ever been young. She was known only as Mrs Fowler. Nobody in the family could remember whether she had any other name. She smelled of an eye-wateringly pungent perfume called 4-7-11, wore thick black zip-up fleece-lined heavy-traction boots, a long navy-blue coat she never took off and a hat seemingly constructed from black lacquered wicker. She leaned on an ebony stick more intended for thrashing someone than walking with.

Grandfather William, her silent, skeletal husband, occasionally appeared in the kitchen like Banquo's ghost, only to disappear into the shed or the pub before imparting information. I loved my grandfather. The old man smelled of tinned tobacco, bitter and oil, and winked at me behind his ghastly wife's back. He was tanned from working outside as a tar-spreader, gaunt-faced, with thin fair hair and a rumpled forehead like his son and eventually his grandson. Deep creases ran from cheekbone to jaw, and glasses were perched on a nose that had been broken so many times the blood no longer reached the end of it. Both he and Bill were physically small, but according to Kath only her husband suffered from 'Napoleon complex', whatever that was. She insisted he had been taller when they were courting.

William and Mrs Fowler lived a few streets away from Westcombe Hill, at the leafy Royal Standard on the far side of Blackheath, and were genteelly working class, meaning William was poor but honest and lived within his means, occasionally going to church and only saying 'bugger' when he hit his thumb with a hammer. He was one of those men you saw in old photographs who looked really uncomfortable with the top button of their collar done up on a white shirt. They were only ever photographed in one of two places: squinting into the sun in their front garden or sitting on the beach fully dressed, cooking complex meals on a primus stove behind a rampart of sand and a striped windbreak. I remember Mrs Fowler once complaining that the hardest part of cooking on a primus stove on a windy beach was getting the Yorkshire Puddings right.*

Their house was neat and tiny, and had no bathroom or indoor toilet, just a big butler sink in the kitchen for washing. A single latticed bay window overlooked a neighbour's sleepy beehives. The blue staircase to the bedroom was so steep that it had a rope running beside it rather than a rail, possibly as a reminder of the nation's former status as a seafaring force. There was a three-dimensional concave ceramic plate on the lounge wall with a picture of a water wheel on it, and a brown Victorian print of a woman unravelling wool while two gentlemen in tight fawn trousers perched on bended knees to wind up the twine. It bore the caption 'Two strings to her bow' and Kath said it was a pun, but I could not see how. Surely it would have been better as 'Two beaus to her string'?

The television set had shiny wooden roller doors designed to hide the screen, as if there was something vulgar about exposing a naked cathode tube. I was sometimes allowed to watch *Torchy the Battery Boy*,[†] after which Mrs Fowler would shut the roller doors with a bang. Beside the upright piano there was a scallop-windowed cabinet full of gaudy fairground knick-knacks that I was never allowed to touch. Their house smelled of polish too, but of a cheaper, less labour-intensive sort.

---

*For international readers, a light cake of baked batter, tricky to cook at the best of times. In Kath's case, a concrete orange disc ideal for use as a paperweight or doorstop.
[†]Torchy lived on another planet with a poodle and a talking letterbox for companions. He was incredibly gay.

There was also something hidden and private about my paternal grandmother that involved tears and whispers in the kitchen, and doors firmly closed against young eyes. The lounge always felt like an offstage area to the hushed dramas that were unfolding in the main auditorium. Occasionally, neighbouring wives knocked urgently and headed for the kitchen, staying behind the door and speaking in low voices before rushing back to make their husbands' tea.

The rest of my relatives were shadowy and indistinct. Bill's sister Doreen was sweet and gentle, married to a kind, decent man and the mother of normal children, but she only met up with parts of the family at their supernaturally tidy house in Reading because Auntie Doreen and her mother 'didn't speak' over something that had happened at least twelve years ago. When Mrs Fowler argued with members of her family, she left scars on them like radiation burns.

Mrs Fowler had a sister called Carrie who also had caring eyes and some kind of secret sorrow that nobody was ever allowed to mention. Kath had lost her brother Kit to diphtheria,* whatever that was, when they were six. She had a sister, Muriel, distant, religious and grand, who had married a Glasgow city archivist and given birth to a congregation of well-behaved children with biblical names. The received wisdom was that we Fowlers didn't need them, and they didn't like the Fowlers because Bill was common. At the slightest provocation, Muriel would unlock a gigantic embossed family Bible and read out bits in a condescending voice that gave us the creeps. We would endure an occasional Sunday at their house before fleeing at the first available opportunity. As

---

*One of a range of eerie Victorian illnesses like whooping cough and the dropsy, eradicated by inoculation.

we drove off in Bill's motorbike and sidecar there was always a palpable sense of relief, and everyone could start laughing again.

Around the edges of these characters were the lost ones.

A sixteen-year-old cousin who had died after climbing under a motorbike tarpaulin to smell the petrol. An uncle who had fallen off a Thames lighter, and his brother who had dived into the fast brown waters to save him – both were wearing cable-knit sweaters and workboots, and were swiftly pulled under by the racing tide. A stillborn baby, a girl who ran away – subjects that were unthinkable to broach. There was a tiny sparrow-like aunt, loud, deaf, coarse, gurning and toothless, called Aunt Nell, whose sailor husband might have died at sea, and whose daughter Brenda was mute, 'simple' and uncomprehending. Aunt Nell lived in the basement of a damp Isle of Dogs* slum with a foul-mouthed mynah bird, and cleaned cinemas until she was eighty. I adored her.

It struck me that the War had turned all of these people upside-down; nothing was in its rightful place any more, which was why they seemed so lost. Over all of them, living and dead, lay a soft fog of mystery. No anecdote had an ending, no story was ever complete. Questions were diverted and details trailed off. Where was my other grandfather? Why didn't Mrs Fowler talk to my mother or her own daughter? What had happened to Nell's husband? How could the smell of petrol kill you? The stories remained incomplete for decades, until my well-intentioned sister-in-law decided to shine a torch on the family tree, affronting everyone in the process and accidentally closing the subject for ever. Kath, in

*Traditionally poor area of South London docks, now renovated for corporate singles.

particular, had kept her secrets close to her chest, and was mortified by the idea that her grandchildren might realize she had been born out of wedlock.

It seemed obvious to everyone that my parents did not belong together. Bill's mother got the ball rolling by failing to attend her only son's wedding and avoiding all contact with her daughter-in-law. Kath took her new husband to her mother's house in Brighton, where her nervous beau committed so many cringe-worthy faux pas that he could never bring himself to go back again. Kath then went to *his* mother's house to repair the ill-will, only to rush from the front step with her nose in a handkerchief, sobbing.

Early on, a sense of buyer's remorse settled over my parents' marriage. During their courtship Bill had presented himself as an open-hearted man of action, but he turned out to be a mummy's boy who spent three worknights out of five with his parents, leaving his wife alone at home. She, on the other hand, failed to live up to his strong-willed mother, and was considered by their side to be too high-minded. There was a general consensus that if she had Put Her Foot Down early on, things would have worked out satisfactorily. But she didn't, and they didn't, and so Kath and Bill remained padlocked together for fifty years of mutual disappointment and recrimination.

For me, this was where the early appeal of burying one's nose in a book came in.

When we reached Reynold's Place, where William and Mrs Fowler lived, my mother tidied my hair and pushed me towards the front door.

'You knock,' she said, knowing that I was awkward in formal situations. 'I'm sure your grandmother will be pleased to see you.'

I knocked and waited. A thumping sound grew inside the still house. The great black door creaked open. Balanced on an ebony stick, a great navy-blue dress and coat appeared before me, topped with a stern face and a wicker hat like an upturned bucket.

'You're late,' said Mrs Fowler, stepping aside to let me in. 'Go into the front room and don't touch a single thing, while I have words with your mother.'

She did not approve of kissing. As I passed, she snatched the book from under my arm. 'You won't be needing that,' she told me. 'It'll be full of germs and bad ideas.' She left it on the rainy step outside.

There were no books in the house at Reynold's Place because books did not look nice enough to be displayed, and in Mrs Fowler's eyes did not reveal themselves as status symbols to visiting neighbours. Books developed the imagination, and imagination was the enemy of hard work. Everyone in Mrs Fowler's family worked very hard until they dropped dead. In Mrs Fowler's experience, 'imaginative' people were usually neurasthenic girls who cried a lot and proved useless to themselves and others. They moped, or were hysterical and took to their beds on rainy days. There was a word for imaginative boys, too, but it wasn't mentioned in polite company. If I had turned up with welding equipment instead of a book, Mrs Fowler and I might have got off on the right foot.

I weaved my way carefully through the fragile knick-knacks, gewgaws and whatnots in the polish-squeaky front room, and perched on the guest chair in the corner, resigning myself to a very long afternoon. On my last visit I had dared to open the cabinet of not-very-curious curiosities to handle a china dachshund, only to watch in horror as it slipped through my fingers and snapped its head off on the floor. Balancing the head back on, I furtively replaced the guillotined dog, and there it stayed in the cabinet for years, awaiting discovery and retribution.

After that, each trip to my grandparents' house was like being put on trial for a crime you had denied knowledge of committing.

5

Free Time

Childhood was filled with agonizing afternoons spent waiting beyond the whispers, or attending bizarre rituals for the sake of my parents. The least pleasurable of these was the Cubs,* presided over by a man who looked like Central Casting's idea of a paedophile. His pressed fawn shorts were so wide at the hem and his thighs so thin that we all had to look away when he crouched down in front of us for fear of witnessing a testicular protrusion. There was a particularly trying bout of suppressed laughter in the troop after he asked whether anyone had seen his conkers during a park ramble.

Having failed to impress in Ropecraft, Woodsmanship (acts of arson involving the rubbing of sticks), Folk Dancing, Tracking or Being a Friend to Animals (due to an earlier incident involving a tethered stag beetle and a magnifying glass), I was luckily hit in the eye with a cricket ball and excused meetings long enough for the

---

*Junior version of the Scouts, designed to instil obsolete qualities like good sportsmanship and fair play.

Cubmaster to wearily assume that I was unlikely to return.

With the woggle safely discarded, the other blot on my free time was Sunday School, which involved lolling around on hard wooden benches while Miss Parker, a dumpy, well-meaning woman whose bulky undergarments showed through her cardigan like riot-gear, bowdlerized the Bible's more lurid tales into fables suitable for tiny tots. To do this she used an easel and a set of pastel-coloured Fuzzy Felt action figures. The set included stick-on halos, Jacob's ladder (like a regular painter's ladder but golden) and a boulder for removing from Jesus's tomb in order to facilitate resurrection.

Miss Parker had the kind of mind that automatically went blank whenever it was confronted with images of fornication or retribution. Consequently, her biblical world consisted solely of kind acts, good Samaritans, loving thoughts and turned cheeks. She said that Mary Magdalene was Jesus's ladyfriend and called the disciples his 'best chums'. Everyone hated her except a pigtailed girl in the front row who got to put away the Fuzzy Felt figures as a reward for perfect attendance. She died of diphtheria in her second year, and nobody wanted her seat in case it was infected.

As a child of the fifties and sixties, I had several other claims on my precious free time:

Moorfields Eye Hospital (for eye-strengthening exercises that involved overlapping chipped Victorian slides of tigers and songbirds in cages, and flesh-coloured NHS specs held together in the centre with Elasto-plast).

Inoculation queues (for Diphtheria, Tuberculosis and a variety of poxes left over from an earlier century, possibly the seventeenth). Weeks passed in a dark room with whooping cough, chicken pox and measles, when you weren't allowed to open the curtains in case you suddenly went blind, and some kind of respiratory illness which required you to spend evenings with your face suspended above a steaming enamel bowl with a tea towel draped over your head.

Visits to bombsites, the source of all major childhood injuries due to the fact that they regularly required scaling up and sliding down. ('He fell twenty feet into a pitch-black crater and nobody heard his desperate cries for help,' ran one of Kath's awful warnings. 'His voice grew fainter and fainter until it finally ceased altogether. They didn't find him until after Lent.')

The fifties was also populated with the kind of characters who turned up in Ealing comedies, and some who didn't, including:

Men in mackintoshes, who went funny during the War and were now likely to interfere with you if you were wearing short trousers.

Landladies who wore nylon blouses with their bra straps showing, and who spent their days cleaning windows with brown paper and vinegar, and red-leading their front doorsteps, or trying to whack you with a broom for playing football against the side of their houses.

Policemen who insisted on asking you where you were going, why you were covered in mud and whether that lovely mother of yours was at home during the day.

Lollipop ladies with red lipstick, orange make-up, yellow hair and white raincoats.

Bus conductors who kept up a steady stream of banter with their passengers, including the recitation of songs, jokes, bits of poetry and smut-tinged social observation, while jauntily swinging from pole to pole through their buses.

Park keepers in brown suits who carried pointed sticks for picking up litter and told you off for infringing council by-laws, a sure sign that you had been accidentally enjoying yourself.

Bleached-blonde women who ran launderettes with permanent fags dangling insolently from the corners of their mouths, and who were the conduits for all neighbourhood gossip. 'She's someone to notice,' the lady who ran the Sunbeam Launderama, Westcombe Hill, told Kath. 'Her brother's cousin's husband painted Shirley Bassey's bathroom. And that was *before* she was famous.'

Train drivers who tooted and occasionally threw lumps of coal when they recognized kids waiting to see them pass on the branch line.

Cadaverous Christmas Club men who came calling with rows of numbers neatly laid out in their account books.

People dressed as giant rabbits, foxes, superheroes, princes or astronauts, who called to ask housewives if they could answer a simple question and produce a packet of Daz washing powder in order to win five pounds.*

The man at the seaside who needed to be challenged by tapping him on the back with a rolled-up newspaper in order to claim a reward.†

Gypsies selling dishcloths and clothes-pegs from wicker baskets.

Rag-and-bone men, or totters, yelling incomprehensibly from their horses and carts, something that usually sounded like 'Ramnmnbhoooouune!' and who were still, amazingly, trundling around the neighbourhood in the internet age.

---

*They drove around in cars shaped like giant tubes of toothpaste or sausages. I wish I was making this up.
†Most memorably, the snitch killed in the opening of Graham Greene's *Brighton Rock*.

The knife grinder with slicked-back hair and a bootlace tie who had an eye for the daughter of the house across the way, and who stood around chewing a match on the street corner waiting for long-legged schoolgirls to pass by.

The Knock-Down-Ginger boys from the council estate who rang doorbells and ran away, and later got tattoos and became car mechanics before going to prison for handling dud cheques.

The woman in the pink cake shop with pink hair and a pink nylon overall and pink lipstick who pinched my face and said she'd like to eat me up, and who probably wasn't joking.

The heron-necked man with round glasses who rang the doorbell on Sundays and optimistically asked if we would like to take Jesus into our hearts, and could he leave a pamphlet? Oh no, it's you, Mr Fowler, I'll be on my way then.

The ice-cream-van man, the wet-fish man, the encyclopedia salesman, and a dozen other doorbell botherers who were likely to tip up in the course of an ordinary working day.

It was just as well we didn't have a television, or we would never have got anything done. That was the problem with being born in the fifties; there was far too much talking going on, I thought, as I locked myself in my bedroom with a copy of Jules Verne's *In Search of the Castaways** (according to the stamp, last taken out of East Greenwich Public Library in 1937).

Was it a good idea about this time to start dressing up like characters from my favourite books and films?

*In the Walt Disney version, Hayley Mills and Maurice Chevalier cook eggs and sing while stuck up a tree. Not quite how Jules envisioned it.

I thought it might help me to empathize with different heroes and villains I admired, but soon learned not to suddenly come around the corner looking like Moriarty, Im-Ho-Tep or the Beast with a Million Eyes while my mother was dressing or holding sharp objects.

My arrival was usually mitigated with a sigh of 'Oh Chris, it's *you*,' but my 'exploded head' mask from *I Was a Teenage Frankenstein* had Kath screaming the house down. Perhaps I should not have waited until a foggy, dark night to put it on. Or turned the lights out and come rushing at her with a carving knife while she was quietly cutting her toenails in the bathroom.

Vampire victims went down well, if I could keep still for long enough while clutching a sawn-off bloody tent-peg over my heart. I also donned my mother's night-dress and tried ageing myself like Ayesha stepping back into the flame of eternal life in H. Rider Haggard's *She*, achieving the wrinkled-skin effect with rubber cement, but it was difficult to get off, and I was forced to go to school the next day looking like one of the lepers from *Ben-Hur*.

Three years later I had another go at frightening my family with the aid of a pint of crimson poster paint and two ping-pong balls on elastic. Staging the moment when Ray Milland tears out his own eyes in *The Man with the X-Ray Eyes* proved to be more effective than I had expected, but it wasn't a good idea to make Bill jump, because he was soldering the lid of the tropical fish tank* at the time and dropped his iron into the water in shock, branding a guppy. Bill chased me out into the street and fell over next door's dog, breaking one of its toes. The

---

*Due to the poor quality of TV reception in the sixties everyone kept tropical fish in order to have something to stare at that wouldn't give them a headache.

terrier always bared its teeth at him after that, grimacing so broadly that it looked as if someone had wedged a coat hanger into its mouth.

This penchant for theatre continued longer than was strictly healthy. Tying a dead pigeon to my blood-spattered forehead for a re-enactment of a scene from Alfred Hitchcock's *The Birds* proved to be more unhygienic than frightening, and gave me an eye infection. After this, my impersonation fetish lay dormant right up until the release of *The Texas Chainsaw Massacre*.

For now, the best way to learn about real people, I decided, was in books, because the characters were forced to follow the course of a plot rather than shuffling aimlessly through their lives being annoying and unpredictable. It was time for some serious reading.

6

You'll Hurt Your Eyes

'Where's the boy?' called Bill. 'I need him to hold the carburettor valve in place on the Triumph while I hit it.'

'I don't know,' said Kath, unwilling to commit an act of betrayal. She did not wish to lose a son and gain a G-clamp.

'If I don't get this fixed the bike will have to stay in the hall until next week,' he threatened. 'Or possibly spring.'

'He's under the table,' Kath called back, whispering, '*Sorry, Chris.*' 'Reading again.'

'Not to the cat, because that's over here.'

'He's reading to the tortoise.'

'What's he reading to it?'

'*War and Peace.* He hasn't got very far. I said it would be beyond him at seven.'

I remembered an exchange from last week's *Hancock's Half-Hour.*

Hattie Jacques: 'Reading again, eh? You'll hurt your eyes, you will.'

Tony Hancock: 'I'll hurt yours in a minute.'

Hattie was right, of course. Reading under the bedclothes with a torch was something that would become a Problem in Later Life, just as falling asleep drunk with headphones on would eventually affect the fate of your ears. The house in Westerdale Road, Greenwich SE10 (after which I would always write 'London, England, Earth, The Universe' on letters) had a few desiccated paperbacks on the shelf, but the problem lay in working out which ones were any good. Our English teacher had told us that to be properly educated, we had to be raised within an environment of rigorously structured academic philosophy, which would prove tricky given my family's favoured reading material:

Mother

Daphne du Maurier
George Bernard Shaw
The Coronation of Edward VII Souvenir Album
Robert Louis Stevenson
The Reader's Digest Anthology of Much-Loved Novels (Condensed)
Georgette Heyer
Adventures in Conversation (Turn Idle Chatter into Talk That Sparkles!)
Sundry volumes on knitting and playing the piano (separately)
Tolstoy (*Anna Karenina*)
Agatha Christie (*The Mystery of the Seven Pipe Cleaners* or something like that)
Anna Sewell (*Black Beauty*)
Make Do and Mend: The Ladies' Home Thrift Companion
T. E. Lawrence

Mrs Beeton
The Pan Books of Horror Stories

Father

Titbits
*Reveille**
Sven Hassel†
Dennis Wheatley
Ian Fleming
Sax Rohmer
Great Naval Flags of the World
Motorcycle Mechanics
R. Lobsang Rampa (*The Third Eye*)
(NB. Rampa wrote books of mystical Tibetan
philosophy, and turned out not to be a Tibetan lama
at all, but a plumber's son called Cyril Hoskins who
had never been to Tibet. He said he'd channelled
the lama's spirit after falling on his head, and that
the book had been dictated to him by his cat, Mrs
Fifi Greywhiskers. Branded a fraud, he moved to
Canada.)

Me

Where the Rainbow Ends
The Adventures of Toby Twirl
20,000 Leagues under the Sea
Finn Family Moomintroll‡
The Swiss Family Robinson

---

*Smutty cheesecake-filled periodical.
†A Dane whose brutal first-person Nazi memoirs still spark controversy today.
‡Creepy dough-faced creatures that provided a disturbing glimpse into the Scandinavian mindset.

Down with Skool! and *How to Be Topp**
The Huckleberry Hound annual
War and Peace
Professor Branestawm
Treasure Island

My parents had differing attitudes to books. My father came from a house where there had been none, and consequently handled the few he read as if they were filled with nitro-glycerine. You could never tell if he had even opened one. My mother had always been surrounded by books, so she had a healthy disrespect for them. Most of hers looked as if they had been dropped in the bath and dried out on a paraffin stove. Once I caught her using a fishbone as a bookmark.

There was also a pile of tattered Victorian children's books which the family had inherited from elderly relatives, none of which would have been allowed anywhere near modern children. Most people can recall a happy moment from a book they read as a small child, but looking back, I can only remember horrors from mine. 'Uncle Two-Heads slowly sinks into the quicksand' read the frontispiece of a grisly work called *Tiny Tim in Giant Land*, which featured the distorted creature clawing at wet sand as it was sucked into his screaming mouth. This was deemed suitable for seven-year-olds. 'Karik and Valya trapped in the lair of the water-spider' showed two miniaturized Russian children being wrapped in slimy webbing by a gigantic eight-legged multi-eyed horror at the bottom of a pond.

The nightmare-inducing winner was the fantasy *Where the Rainbow Ends*, a book considered ideal for every

*Geoffrey Willans and Ronald Searle upset parents by creating four volumes of delightful schoolboy memoirs in ungrammatical misspelled English, 'as any fule kno'.

young child's bedroom. One illustration showed a girl being yanked into a shadowy forest by homunculi with razor-sharp claws, her pale arms striped with crimson scars. It was captioned 'Rosalind is dragged into the Black Wood by imps'. Even then, I knew what the author was getting at. It was something about not liking Darkies, as my father amiably called them. In the 1960s black men were most visible as bus conductors, in which role they attracted public approbation for introducing an element of sexy cheerfulness into a job that had usually been occupied by dodderers. In old pulp novels they still turned up as dangerous exotics who were there to test white people's self-control.

There was a grisly Steptoe-ish feel to much Victoriana, a cruel sensibility that had been exacerbated by the War and now filtered unthinkingly into daily life. One day Bill opened these books to see what I found so fascinating, tutted (not because they were gruesome but because they weren't about anything real or useful) and threw them all into his weekly garden bonfire. He liked to poke a fire with a stick.

The most obscure book I ever found in the little orange-bricked house in Westerdale Road was Maurice Richardson's *The Exploits of Engelbrecht*, the adventures of the Surrealist Sportsman's Club that included chapters on witch hunting, going ten rounds in the boxing ring with a grandfather clock and a game of rugby on Mars. So carefully did I guard this from the garden bonfire that it remained lost in the house until we finally moved.

Gradually, I came to understand the genesis of reading books:

As a child you started with Janet and John* rag-books

---

*Why didn't we have Dick and Jane like the Americans? I guess they had more Dicks.

(which my 'Aunt' Mary, who had invented the concept of 're-gifting', continued to send on birthdays until I was twelve, along with old jigsaws that had pieces missing and boxes of chocolates that had turned white with heat and time).

Then you progressed to punishment-filled fairy tales, and Babar the Elephant, Gallic tales perversely translated and printed in joined-up handwriting by publishers who clearly wanted you to become annoyed with the French at an early age.

Then you moved on to Winnie the Pooh, Finn Family Moomintroll and Toby Twirl, weirdly asexual creatures who had adventures in places that were alien to a suburban child, like woods and meadows.

Then you made your first critical decision by ditching Rupert the Bear because he was boring and wet and presumably only appealed to posh, cosseted children who looked like extras from *Brideshead Revisited*.

After that it was anything the library could provide, including Edward Lear, Professor Branestawm, Dr Dolittle and Biggles. This last one was a big jump into Boys' Adventure, and opened the world to Robert Louis Stevenson, R. M. Ballantyne, Jules Verne, H. G. Wells and anything with pirates, tigers, caves, airships or secret Chinese societies in.

Finally, I started making mental lists of words I didn't quite understand:

Incognito
Copse
Ingot
Pipette
Zeppelin
Contraband
Hottentot

Capstan
Runcible
Quartermaster
Chocks
Infidel

There seemed to be little place for the fantastic in a commuter-belt white-collar household, which was a shame because the grandfather of such tales, H. G. Wells, came from just such a cosy background. On an inaccessibly high shelf, my father kept a full set of Dennis Wheatley paperbacks, which were out of date long before I could reach to read them. These eventually faded from fashion due to their peculiar mix of Nazism, racial stereotyping and the luridly supernatural. Bill's volumes of bizarre Fu Manchu tales by Sax Rohmer were peppered with wily, snickering Orientals who planned to take over the world via Limehouse opium dens, which was surely not a very sensible idea.

I plumped for the Dennis Wheatleys. The once-ubiquitous witchcraft novels reflected the period's obsession with the idea that England might become enslaved by sinister foreigner powers. Even when they were first published, the books must have appeared archaic and stilted, rather like charming, ridiculous fairy tales, although *The Haunting of Toby Jugg*, with its monstrous fascist-empowered spider tapping the bedroom windows at night, could still keep any child awake and quaking beneath the candlewick. Wheatley's absurd frontispieces featured dire warnings of the real threats posed by witchcraft, but Bill took them as seriously as his own mother had probably taken the threat of white slave-traders. 'This is a very dangerous book in the wrong hands,' he would say, tapping the spine against his calloused palm as if discussing a bomb-making manual.

Actually, he had one of those, too. It was called *How to Make Explosives* and featured photographs of beaming housewives in Marcel waves mixing volatile cocktails from ordinary household items in Pyrex bowls, as though they were baking cakes. Bill owned this book because he had been a scientist. Once, he had worked on an explosive paint that became unstable when it dried. His colleagues painted all the Os and Ps and Qs in his newspaper with it for a joke, so that when he came home and wearily threw down the paper, the dining table blew up. Somewhere I have a photograph of Bill and his colleagues in the doorway of their science shed, wearing white lab coats and nervous smiles that suggested they had just made a discovery that would have to remain hidden for the public good.

My parents' books had their place in the dining room and never strayed from it, just as ornaments belonged in the front room, cutlery belonged in the scullery and the motorbikes belonged in the back parlour.

Many years later, I went back to Westerdale Road, Greenwich SE10, London, England, Earth, The Universe, to see the half of the street that remained. It was still very quiet, but now it was because the men were off at day-schools and the women were shuttling between Primark and Sainsbury's.

This part of Greenwich had always been the shabby end, the mucked-about-with part that was grey from lorry dust, far from the stately grandeur of the Naval College, the Observatory and the *Cutty Sark*. I turned into the street and studied the raggedy front gardens, the ashen net curtains, the dripping box hedges, the walls studded with sea shells at the front and broken bottles at the back, the terrace broken halfway along by an incongruously modern builders' yard (on the site where a single bomb had fallen on the street). The old Sunday school now sold pine furniture, but the houses looked much as they had when I was a child. The only difference was that they had mostly been bought by Indian families, who tended perfumed rose bushes and painted numbers on their dustbin lids just as generations before them had done.

Our family had moved from the street shortly after my tenth birthday. The remaining houses now looked miniature. Here, armed with broom, mop and duster, my mother had waged a lifelong battle against germs, incrementally losing as they got inside each of the neighbours in turn, killing them. Not that anyone made a fuss; front doors were quietly closed until flowers arrived, and after an appropriate period of mourning the surviving partner would reappear in the front garden, ready to prune the neglected roses.

I loved the house where I grew up, and was miserable when they demolished it. Standing at the stump of the road, it felt as though if I listened hard enough, it might once more be possible to hear my parents shouting at each other in the hallway. I had been a pretty resilient child; the sound of adults bickering on a Sunday was as much part of the background as bandleader Billy Cotton shouting 'Wakey Wakey!' on the kitchen transistor or distant choirs rehearsing for church services.

The high street comprised a densely packed corner store called Lynch's, a butcher, a baker and a chemist with giant stoppered apothecary bottles full of coloured water in its windows. The local toy shop sported a model railway that could be activated by dropping a penny through the window into a tube. A dingy furniture store sold things like Pompadour Dralon boudoir stools and the Excalibur lounge suite, its hopeful owner hovering expectantly in the front doorway. The Co-operative Society gave out tin dividend coins and had an anachronistically ancient system of metal cylinders on cables that shot back and forth across the ceiling delivering bills to the cashier. The motorway that cut the street in half required all these stores to be demolished, and tore the heart from the one place where I had been happy.

Amazingly, the East Greenwich Public Library was still there, a lone surviving piece of sturdy orange and white Edwardian architecture, tucked beneath the dank shadow of the motorway. It had loose parquet floor blocks and smelled of mildew even in midsummer. A graceful flight of wooden stairs led down an oval hole to the basement, where a handful of forbidden reference books were kept. The librarian had agreed to lower the age limit for admittance to the grown-ups' bookshelves in order that I could attend her Wednesday-night reading circle. For the whole of my childhood I had borrowed three books every two weeks, until I became more familiar with the shelves than almost anyone who worked there.

One of the first books I took out was *Down with Skool* by Geoffrey Willans. Willans's collaboration with rococo artist Ronald Searle propelled him into the blazer pocket of every British schoolboy. His hero, Nigel Molesworth, the Curse of St Custard's, rocketed to fame in four lunatic children's books. With chapters on how to avoid lessons and how to torture parents, they caused outrage because of their deliberately awful spelling, and were regarded as bad examples to set before children. The second volume *How to Be Topp*, scaled the heights of the surreal. A new term begins; 'No more dolies of William the bear to cuddle and hug, no more fairy stories at nannys knee it is all aboard the fairy bus for the dungeons.' New boy Eustace is trussed to a chair and gagged with socks. His mother rings up and is reassured. 'Eustace mater ring off very relieved cheers cheers and telephone all the other lades about it. An owl hoot and Eustace is insensible. St

Custards hav begun another term.' The roster of pupils included the ghastly Fotheringtom-Thomas, 'skipping like a girlie' and 'uterly wet', and Grabber, 'skool captane and winer of the mrs joyful prize for rafia work'. The peculiar cadences of academic lassitude were perfectly nailed, so that a recital of 'The Burial of Sir John Moore at Corunna' became a bored litany trotted out by an ADD-afflicted child: 'Notadrumwasheardnotafuneralnote shut up peason larffing as his corse as his corse what is a corse sir? gosh is it to the rampart we carried.' Willans's catchphrases like 'chiz', 'enuff said' and 'as any fule kno' passed into the English language.

Around this time, I sensed that Sir Arthur Conan Doyle was beckoning with sixty-four short stories and four novels involving the world's first consulting detective. The fascinating thing about Sherlock Holmes was that the less you knew about his character the more intriguing he was, unlike Hercule Poirot, who had as much personality as a cardboard cutout.

Conan Doyle conveyed the creeping pallor of Victorian street life, the fume-filled taverns where a man might find himself propositioned by a burglarizing gargoyle, the alleyways where he could be struck on the skull by a beetling madman, the Thames-side staircases where gimlet-eyed doxies awaited the easily duped. Even his cheerful scenes felt vaguely gruesome: shopkeepers would drape a Christmas goose around a character's neck like a boa constrictor, and the welcoming yellow light of a first-floor window could somehow suggest that its tenant was lying dead on the floor. Fog muffled murderers' footsteps and London sunlight was always watery. The Holmes adventures were virtually horror stories. People went raving mad in locked rooms, or died of fright for no discernible reason. And even when you found out how it was done or who did it, what kind of lunatic would choose to kill someone by sending a rare Indian snake down a bell-pull, for God's sake?

G. K. Chesterton's Father Brown tales offered crimes that were even more inventive, but the little Essex priest was too nice, and his adventures were simply too whimsical to stay in fashion. I found other mystery writers like Margery Allingham interesting, but virtually throttled by the frightfully English language of their times.

Moving to the Agatha Christie books, I found that the initial thrill of such plot ingenuity also created a curious sense of dissatisfaction. The characters were board-game pieces. How was I supposed to identify with any of them? Westerdale Road didn't have too many colonels, housemaids, vicars, flighty debutantes, dowager duchesses or cigar-chomping tycoons. Certainly, none of our neighbours had ever attended a country-house party, let alone found a string of bodies in the library. Nobody owned a library, and country houses were places you were dragged around on Sunday afternoons.

At least Conan Doyle's solutions possessed a kind of strange plausibility, whereas Christie's murder victims apparently received dozens of visitors in the moments before they died, and were killed by doctored pots of jam, guns attached to bits of string, poisoned trifles and knives on springs. 'It is a childishly simple affair, *mon ami*. Brigadier Hawthorne removed the letter-opener from the marmalade pot *before* Hortense the maid found the burned suicide note in the grate, *after* Doctor Caruthers hid the adder, easily mistaken for a stethoscope, under the aspidistra, *at exactly the same time* as Lady Pettigrew was emptying arsenic over the jugged hare.' The only thing I ever learned from an Agatha Christie novel was the lengths to which county people would go to show how much they hated each other.

In the East Greenwich Public Library I caught glimpses of a world beyond my experience. I loved looking at the covers of books by Dickens, Huxley, Woolf, Forster, Waugh, Wodehouse, Firbank, Faulkner, H. H. Munroe and M. R. James, but I wasn't old enough to take any of them out. It was a small library with a good librarian, Mrs Ethel Clarke, a woman of thrillingly diverse tastes who stocked her shelves with the widest possible array of books. The first time I met her she scared me with a laser stare intended to weed out time-wasters.

'If you want to join the library, you'll have to fill this out.' She slid a purplish mimeographed sheet across her desk at me. 'You'll need a reference from a friend.'

'I haven't got any friends,' I told her.

She peered over the half-moon glasses chained to her neck and pursed duck-lips at me. 'Hmm.' Looking around the library, she pointed out a pair of old ladies perusing the romantic novels. 'Go over there and *make* a friend.'

Greenwich Council should have given her a gold medal. Instead, they plotted to have the place torn down and sold off behind her back. In my mind's eye I could only ever see the library becoming emptier and emptier, as this gentle, thoughtful lady remained seated at her counter with a look of doomed hopefulness on her face. A custodian of treasures with the power to improve more young lives than any politician, I imagined her facing the forces of ill-informed darkness with a rallying cry like that of Boadicea, if Boadicea had been a suburban librarian rather than the Queen of the Iceni.*

Amazingly, the axe did not fall on the library. Over forty years later it continued to stand in the same place,

*Not buried under Platform Nine in King's Cross station as previously thought. Typical that the British should venerate a warrior who lost her most important battle.

its doors open to anyone curious enough to explore the world through the printed page.

One week before Christmas, while I was still seven, I clambered on to the enamel flap of a freestanding kitchen cabinet, tipping the whole thing over and burying myself in a heap of smashed crockery. My mother came running in, thought I was dead, screamed and gave birth to my brother on the scullery floor. He had been due on Christmas Day, so I was able to blackmail him for years to come by reminding him that if this accident had not occurred he would only be getting one batch of presents.

The baby's name was Steven. He was adorable, with a quiff of whispy blond hair and big pale-blue eyes. He was a good, quiet baby whom everyone loved, so naturally I wanted to drop a paving stone into his cot.

My mother was thrilled because the birth had been so easy. 'Not like having you,' she told me ruefully. 'That took six hours and was like passing a hot copper kettle.'

After Steven came along I saw even less of my parents, and began reading in earnest to the cat, the tortoise or anything else that showed vague signs of sentient life. If I was lonely, I was too busy hurting my eyes to notice.

7

Turning the Tables

I first sensed something was going badly wrong with my parents' marriage when, during the course of a normal Sunday lunch, my father suddenly turned the laden dining table upside-down and stormed out of the room. I offered to help my mother clear up the food and broken crockery from the floor, but she said I would cut myself, and quietly got on with the job until everything was clean and tidy again.

Up until this point I had always loved Sunday lunch. Sunday was the one day in the week when my parents could lie in, and so the morning always coalesced slowly, starting with the newspapers, tea and biscuits, drifting into a late breakfast involving beans and sausages and *Two-Way Family Favourites*, the radio show aimed at BFPOs – British Forces Posted Overseas. Most of the songs they played were drippy, and the message was always the same: 'Can't wait to see you and the kids at Christmas,' never 'The government lied to us and I've had my legs blown off.'

All along the street it was the same: fathers tinkered

and mothers cooked, while fifty wirelesses played Alma
Cogan, Nat King Cole and Tommy Steele.* Everyone
listened while they ate, so lunchtime was signalled by radio
comedy. First there was *The Clitheroe Kid*, a funereally
unfunny Northern sitcom about a schoolboy, with a lead
character who spoke in the high, eerie voice of a medium
receiving a message from beyond. There were rumours
that Jimmy Clitheroe was a dwarf who wore a boy's school
uniform to get into the role, although actually he was a
four-foot-three-inch comic who could only play children.
Then came *Round the Horne*, which the whole family
had to pretend they didn't find dirty, because otherwise it
would mean they got the jokes. I realized I was growing
up in a time of spectacular hypocrisy. Everything I heard
in adult conversation had to be translated:

'Delicate' meant pregnant or queer, depending on its
   use.
'Funny' meant queer or mentally ill.
'Fallen' meant that a girl slept around or had
   become pregnant.
'Simple' meant Down's Syndrome.
'Fast' meant sleeping around.
'More than her fair share of trouble' meant her
   husband had run off with the girl from the
   launderette.
'On edge' meant suffering with nerves.
'Suffers with her nerves' meant hysterical.
'Difficulties' meant their oldest boy had been inside.
'Doings' or 'Bits and bobs' meant having a
   hysterectomy.

---

*Strangely ageless performer, who, like Cliff Richard, Val Doonican
and Lulu, is forgotten but not gone. Tends to reappear as Scrooge at
Christmas.

'Poor love' was used after a neighbour had lost a
    breast.
'A bit niggly' meant PMT.
'Trouble downstairs' could mean anything from
    your womb drying up to Siamese twins.

Clearly, being an adult was more complicated than it
first appeared. It wasn't all mending fuses and sitting in
an armchair reading the paper until your tea was ready.
Once my father gave me a warning. I had been holding a
torch in place while he attempted to re-thread fuse wire in
its ceramic block, and had momentarily lost my concentration. 'One day when you're grown up,' he angrily told
me, 'all the lights will go out, and you won't know how to
repair a fuse, and the blackness will close in around you
and there'll be nothing you can do about it but sit in total
darkness where anything can happen.' I did not really
want to become an adult after that.

Round the Horne was the first show that made me
think about the comic possibilities of language, even
though I didn't understand what half of it meant. When
Kenneth Williams said, in his best camp voice, 'This is
our friend the choreographer, Reynard La Spoon. He can
do things with a bentwood chair that'll make your eyes
stand out like organ stops,' I fell off my chair laughing, to
the bewilderment of my parents.

Kenneth was up in the crow's nest searching for Moby
Dick. 'Avast! Avast!' he'd yell. 'What is it?' 'I don't know,
but it's pretty big.' Howls of laughter from me, clutching
my sides helplessly. 'You all think I'm a raving madam,'
said Williams. 'Madman, Kenneth, that's a misprint,' said
his foil, Betty Marsden. Tears rolled down my cheeks as I
fell off my chair again.

Stars were famous for their eyes, their lips. The singer
Alma Cogan was famous for her sequined frocks ('She

makes them all herself,' my mother would parrot every time doomed, tragic Alma came on to belt out 'Fly Me To The Moon'), but Kenneth Williams was the only star I could think of who was famous for his nostrils.

As lunch came to an end *Movie-Go-Round* started, unveiling a week's worth of new films by running audio clips. Without visuals, just clanks and bonks and booming voices, the films were more intriguing. Hidden things created curiosity.

'There's something wrong with the boy,' my father decided. 'I think he has too much *imagination*.' He made it sound like smallpox or whooping cough.

The table-turning incident came after Bill had spent every evening that week up at his mother's having poison dripped into his ears.

Mrs Fowler lived to judge others. She had never travelled further than a hop-picking holiday* in Kent, yet sat at home in her navy-blue coat, holding court with a coven of the more easily swayed housewives in Reynold's Place, Blackheath, offering advice about who to ostracize, who to shun and with whom to form an alliance.

Her husband had been made to feel unwelcome in the kitchen that doubled as her headquarters, and spent his daylight hours in the tool shed shaving unwieldy offcuts of metal into household items of quite astonishing ugliness. Although William was a fine craftsman he had no sense of design. He made a music box in the shape of a piano – not an attractive concert grand, but an upright pub Joanna. He also produced a coffin-thick clock with its fine teak finish covered in a layer of Perspex that trapped the dirt behind it, and a carved tug-boat which, he revealed with the proud flick of a switch, had port and

---

*A traditional working-class paid holiday that died out when everyone switched from bitter to lager.

starboard lights that turned it into a bedside lamp. There were many other large, riveted objects that never left his workshop for a place in their tiny house, and remained on the floor, turning rusty, where they could catch the ankles of any unsuspecting visitor.

Men always made things. Armed with a fretwork saw and reeking horse-glue, Bill also made stuff, most of it horrible. He had been a glass-blower, and filled Reynold's Place with the kind of coloured glass animals I used to see at the seaside: ducks, horses, a drunk leaning on a lamp-post, even an entire funfair carousel. Tales of Bill's former job came with dire warnings – of the new glass-blowing recruit who had breathed in instead of out, filling his lungs with molten glass, and of delicate bulbs shattering in the hands, to send vitreous slivers burrowing so deeply into the skin that you had to wait for them to circulate in your bloodstream for years before they painfully emerged from a tear-duct or from under a fingernail.

The house in Westerdale Road had nowhere for Bill to work. His only escape from Kath was to go up to his parents' house and sit smoking with William while his mother thumped about on her stick, dropping insidious criticisms designed to make him feel increasingly dissatisfied with his young wife. Everybody smoked all the time. My grandfather smoked Capstan Full Strength or some kind of bitter rough-cut tobacco with a jolly jack tar on the packet. My father smoked Woodbines. Even Kath tried Old Holborn roll-ups, and when told these were not ladylike had a brief flirtation with Consulate mentholated cigarettes – 'Cool as a mountain stream' – that were vaguely minty but still tasted like throat-searing gaspers.

It emerged that the table-turning incident was over the poverty of my mother's cooking. Kath admitted that she had very little sense of taste after the bike accident and years of smoking strong tobacco, but she also had very little money, as my father refused to give her enough for housekeeping. Bill never did anything without first checking with his mother, and Mrs Fowler had presumably vetoed the idea of him surrendering part of his pay packet each week for something so prosaic as cooked meals. I imagined her warning him on the many evenings she had him to herself: 'If your wife can't make ends meet with the money you give her, it's a sign that she's a bad housekeeper. In our day we knew how to run a household and feed our husbands steak and jam roly-poly* every night on a halfpenny.'

Since getting married and being told that she could no longer go to work, Kath had lost all confidence in her former clerical abilities. But one day Bill came home with the news that he had been fired for reasons that he would not admit in front of us children. It was clearly a source of great embarrassment; men were supposed to stay in one job until they were broken, then gratefully receive their carriage clock.

Bill's loss of employment meant that Kath was to be allowed back into the workforce. With her shorthand, quick typing speed and sharp mind, she soon found a job as the company secretary for the National Association of Retail Furnishers, a Victorian organization populated by gentlemen who looked like casket-makers. The downside was that Steven and I had to be farmed out to a daytime carer. The very short-sighted, very elderly lady to whom we were seconded was affordable mainly because she looked after a dozen unruly kids in such an offhand manner that she made Dickens's Mrs Jellyby seem like a smotherer. After our mother turned up to collect us, only to find yet another child bouncing down the stairs on

*A heavy suet dessert designed to slow husbands down and stop them wanting sex.

his head, being strangled with a skipping rope or falling out of a window, she handed in her notice at the office, even though they offered her more money and a higher position.

I felt I was to blame for the loss of my mother's potential career, but she told me not to worry. 'I'll get an evening job,' she said. 'Something not too tiring. It'll be fine.' Jobs were scarce, however, and the only available part-time work was inappropriate for a sensitive, well-spoken young woman. Kath became a cashier at Catford Greyhound Stadium, where she was nightly sworn at and spat upon by punters who failed to complete their jackpot combinations before the race bell, which made the tote operator responsible for the money rung up before the off-of-the-leg. Often she came home with an empty purse, her docked pay amounting to more than her wages, and had nothing to show for her evening other than another extravagant selection of bellowed abuse.

When she was able to stand this no longer she became a collector of bad debts on one of South London's roughest housing estates, where she was regularly threatened with physical violence. Sometimes she took me with her, because the men were less likely to attack a woman clutching a child's hand. My fastidious sensibility made me loathe the stairwells, which smelled of old vegetables, and the bright lonely corridors with hidden families shut behind chained doors.

As Kath was working, Bill took to getting his meals at his mother's, not coming home until the end of the evening. My mother's job was poorly paid – this was at a time when a wife could not take out hire purchase without her husband's approval – and one morning she opened her purse to find sixpence. 'This would appear to be our evening meal,' she said, a statement of fact rather than complaint, but the butcher found a lamb bone he had shattered while cutting, and happily handed it to her. The meat was minced and served with peas, mash and gravy, a common post-war recipe that curiously falls below the radar of even the most basic English cookery books. Money was tight everywhere. Few families had accrued savings. It seemed to matter less then, though, because there wasn't much to buy. Those who had grown up through the War were suspicious of luxury, and recipes were largely based on energy value, not taste.

While we ate in silence, we listened to a terrible BBC radio play – full of crystal accents, tinkling tea cups and ostentatiously clicked doors – although concentrating must have been a trial for my parents as I kept asking questions about the plot.

'If you're not happy with the way the story turns out,' said Kath in exasperation, 'go and write one of your own.'

I didn't. Instead, by way of compensation, I became a fabulous liar. Simple truths were exaggerated out of all proportion. The smallest exchange of neighbourhood conversation became drenched with drama. The confabulations compounded into a towering Babel of untruthfulness.

To my father, this was a sure sign that *imagination* was taking a dangerous grip on his son's brain, like bindweed. To be fair, he had been raised in a family that sent everyone out at fourteen to work like a dog until they contracted cancer. In post-war England, imagination was equated with daydreaming, an indulgence that belonged to head-in-the-sand toffs* who contributed nothing to the rebuilding of the country, and Bill couldn't afford to have

---

*Not, in fact, short for 'toffee-nose' but from 'tuft', 1851, a gold tassel worn on the cap of an undergraduate with a voting peer for a father.

a son with ideas above his station, because it would end in failure and, worse than that, *show us up*.

I wondered who it would show us up to, as we had no friends to speak of. 'You don't need anyone else when you have family,' was my father's mantra. But we didn't even have family – we were just people living under the same roof who pretended to know each other well enough to have arguments.

8

A Friend for Life

Even though our family lived in a town that set great store by community, it was decided at an early point that the neighbours weren't worth getting to know.

Percy, the boy next door, had consumption, an illness that resigned him to a living death on a deserted lump of windswept, seaweed-reeking coastline for several months of the year, 'for the sake of his health'. On the other side, Mr and Mrs Hills were as old as them. They kept half a dozen smelly, moulting, squawking chickens in their rusty Anderson shelter, and once their pond froze solid and they removed the entire six-foot block of ice from it, placing it in a tin bath to melt before the fire, where, to my amazement, the giant goldfish trapped inside thawed and wriggled free, dropping back into the water.

Not to be outdone, we bought a tortoise, a pet you could only enjoy for half of every year, and an embittered mongrel cat called Wobbles, which my father purchased from a roadside bikers' café when he stopped to get fags on the way to Brighton. Ginger cats were apparently lucky. Being from a superstitious riverside family – 'naval' would sound too grand – Bill would not allow shoes on the bed because it meant death for a household member within a year (the superstition had something to do with setting out clothes for the deceased). Budgerigars were not allowed into the house for the same reason. I had my own theory about this one: if you were called up as a sailor during the War, it was common to buy your wife a caged bird to keep her company. And you probably didn't come back, like Aunt Nell's old man, who either went down on Scapa Flow or ran off with the barmaid from the Nag's Head, depending on which family member you talked to.

The Fowlers had never been good with animals. My father insisted that a pet was a friend for life, but I couldn't see how that was true, seeing that a cat only lived for about fourteen years. A pet was a friend with a built-in grief-factor. My mother warned that some of the really old pets in the neighbourhood had been traumatized in the War, and hated anyone touching them. 'Mrs Lynch's cat is twenty-two,' she told me. 'It lost its hearing after a V2 landed in their back garden, and when her little boy went to pick it up, it tore his eye out. You never know where you are with a cat.'

Bill had once tried to help out a neighbour by mercy-killing their sick rabbit. He elected to drown it in a bucket of water, which only made it angry, so he repeatedly hit it on the back of the head with a hammer. It still managed to get away, and lived for several months in a deep hole it had dug under the garden fence, where, now brain-damaged, it nursed a psychotic grudge, occasionally popping up to snap at anyone who went near it.

The feud between Mrs Fowler and my mother escalated after the incident regarding Sandy, Mrs Fowler's beloved ginger tom, a surly yellow-eyed creature with a torn ear. When my grandmother decided to drag William to Kent for a fortnight, my mother agreed to take care of the cat, and brought it over to the house under her jumper. The moment it reached the safety of the sitting room it shot up the chimney, lodged itself behind the damper and remained there for four days.

Kneeling on all fours, Kath waved a mackerel under the flue, but nothing could be done to lure it down. Then, late one night, it dropped as suddenly as it had gone up and made a mad dash for the open yard door, hurling itself up and over the garden fence like a steeplechaser.

Kath, however, was in hot pursuit. Westerdale Road ended at an unfenced railway embankment covered in white trumpet vines, where anyone could follow the path to cross the railway line to the next street. I ran after my mother, she ran after the cat and the cat ran up the line, darting back and forth across the third rail. Kath was so scared of her mother-in-law by this point that she was prepared to risk electrocution in order to save face. I hopped about unhelpfully shouting, 'I think there's a train coming!' while she, oblivious, threw herself at the demented feline.

It was no good. The cat kept a careful distance between itself and its would-be captors. After we had waited on the embankment for several hours, the wretched creature emerged from a bush and walked down into our arms. It seemed strangely docile now, and allowed Kath to carry it home.

When Mrs Fowler returned from Kent, she opened her front door and made a huge fuss of Sandy, only to recoil immediately. 'This isn't our cat,' she exclaimed. 'Sandy has a torn left ear. And it's a boy.'

I had never heard of anyone who could tell the sex of a cat. My mother checked the ear and, mortified, confirmed its untorn state. There followed recriminations, tears, threats, and dismissal from the house. My father adopted a sullen, accusatory silence for three weeks. As if to punish all cats, he took out his bad mood on Wobbles, blowing cigarette smoke in its face and tripping it over whenever he thought no one was looking.

After being shouted at by both mother-in-law and husband, Kath stood her ground and did not cry or apologize. She started, in her own small way, to fight back. My father did not tip over any more meal-laden tables.

He took things to a more troublesome level.

9

Horror Story

My father had a problem with Christmas. Although he appears in old photographs to possess a whippy, muscular frame, he was actually a frail man, and usually managed to cause some kind of drama just before the festivities were due to begin. One Christmas Eve he drunkenly crashed his motorbike and sidecar, overturning it on to his chest, and spent the holiday in intensive care. The following year he fell through a cracked coal-hole lid and broke his leg. The year after that, he sat in the darkened front room that was saved for best (he hardly ever put the lights on) and ate an entire box of 'Eat Me' dates that he'd bought cheap in the market, the ones that came on a cream-coloured plastic branch, not realizing that they were green and furry with mildew. That Christmas, instead of having his bones reset, he had his stomach pumped.

But there was one magical moment in a string of awful Christmases.

After glass-blowing, Bill had moved into a scientific lab where he designed and built vitreous instruments. He was regarded as brilliant at his job, and once constructed a human brain in glass just to show off his skills. When the company moved to Toronto he decided not to go with them, presumably because his mother would disapprove of the move. It broke his heart to watch his colleagues leave without him, and while he was looking for a new job, the family tightened its collective belt still further. But on that freezing, penniless Christmas night, I awoke to find the old leather armchair at the end of my bed covered in twinkling red and yellow lights my father had made, which were threaded around a dozen small boxes containing what seemed at the time to be the best train set in the world. How had he managed to pay for it? There was even a box of miniature coal pieces for the tender, to which I could add rubberized soot from Mr Purbrick's shop.

Bill and Grandfather William spent the whole of Christmas Day and Boxing Day crawling around on the floor getting electric shocks. They finally decided on a suitable layout for the set, and permanently mounted it on framed hardboard that was unfortunately too big to go out of the sitting-room door, so it had to be sawn in half and put on hinges, during which Bill accidentally sawed through the coffee table. When the grown-ups grew bored with the technicalities of point-switching and went in search of brown ale, I finally got to enjoy the fun of being intermittently electrocuted.

A truce had been called, but it did not last long. My mother withdrew her money from the Christmas savings club and treated herself to a dress, flared and flowered – the only one that ever turned up in family photographs. It made her look like part of the modern world and therefore slightly weird, like a blonde Alma Cogan or a prettier Fanny Cradock.

My father went nuts. He told her she looked like a cheap tart, and that she was trying to encourage the men of the neighbourhood, only two of whom were ever visible during the day: octogenarian Mr Hills and the bloke with Down's Syndrome who sat on his front step with his trousers pulled up high, looking like a big smiling baby. Dad never allowed Kath to wear any sort of make-up. There were only two items in her side of the bedroom cupboard (there being no bathroom). One was a Pifco hair-dryer in cream Bakelite that weighed the same as a leg of lamb, and was kept in its original red satin-lined box like a school trophy. The other was a scary-looking contraption with a pink rubber bulb and red tubing attached. There was an indecent intimacy about this device, but I could not begin to imagine what it might be for, other than watering plants.

The dress brought up the question of money, and money brought up unemployment, and the vexing embers of low self-esteem began to glow bright. Bill's mother fanned the flame with her own sly whispers, and suddenly everything ignited. One night I awoke to crashes, screams, the sound of someone being pushed or falling. I looked through the banisters but the kitchen door was shut, so I crept downstairs and quietly pushed it open.

My mother was sitting on the floor, wedged into a corner, and my father was standing before her, flexing his right fist. There was broken glass and china everywhere. Kath's mother's ceramic statue of a lady in a green lace dress had lost its nose. At my appearance, the rage faded from Bill's eyes and Kath climbed awkwardly to her feet. She had been punched and slapped, but I could see that she was not scared. She simply seemed emotionless, quiet and determined.

Kath pulled on her cardigan in stoic silence and went out into the rain, and around the corner to the local police station. A portly constable came back with her and spoke quietly to my father. The copper could not have been satisfied with Bill's response, though, for he remained outside in the front garden all night, his cape wrapped against the downpour, keeping watch on the house. To be on the safe side, Kath slept with a carving knife under the bed.

In the morning, having satisfied himself that the house was at peace, the policeman quietly went away before the neighbours could spot him; it was what policemen still did in the sixties. A few days later, he came back to check on the inhabitants of Number 35 again and had a quiet word with Kath, advising her that perhaps she might like to rethink her decision to remain with her husband.

The atmosphere at home calmed but it was never the same after this, because the threat of violence had been made good, and once out, this particular demon could never be put back in its bottle. There were further fights, but they lessened in frequency. My mother was not frightened of my father; quite the reverse. She felt him to be a coward, and he gradually diminished in her eyes. It was a process neither of them could control, no matter how much Bill tried to make amends. He even had the nose on the ceramic green-laced lady replaced, but it was the wrong shape and discoloured over time, making her look like an elegant leper.

It was tempting to trace the cause of Bill's behaviour to his unemployment and loss of status in the home, but the truth was more complicated. Coming from the kind of family where conscription into the armed services was seen as an escape from poverty, he developed a strange relationship to the spending of money. Things were purchased in order to last, never because they held appeal. Christmas presents invariably came from London's Petticoat Lane market*

---

*One of the many London markets where you could watch men throwing entire dinner services into the air and catching them in feats that combined salesmanship with juggling.

at knockdown prices. Pennies were watched and pounds hoarded for no other discernible purpose than habit. Although she had no sense of materialism and was thrifty by necessity, Kath felt that meanness was a sin and would ultimately deny them happiness. There was a line where thrift crossed into something more miserly and joyless.

In a flourish of rare generosity Bill also bought a television, but TV was rubbish back then, and never worse than on a Sunday, when programmes didn't start until late afternoon and consisted of things like *The Brains Trust*, where a group of elderly men in demob suits droned on about town councils and indecency, or quiz shows with Sir Mortimer Wheeler, an archaeologist who always had a pipe gripped between his teeth. Other delights of the times included nature programmes with Armand and Michaela Denis, a pair of self-publicizing globetrotters who fascinated as much for their fabulous lifestyles as for their dubious animal knowledge. Armand was Belgian, and had supposedly married New York beauty Michaela within twelve hours of meeting her. Michaela's main item of travel equipment was her cosmetic box, and she was never seen without a thick layer of orange make-up and silver nails. We also had Mr Pastry, a peculiar old man who vaulted chairs and threw himself around like a teenage acrobat. Cartoon fun was provided by a Viking and a pirate, Noggin the Nog and Captain Pugwash respectively. They were drawn with a remedial simplicity most children could have improved upon. The worst of all children's entertainers was Harry Corbett, who always wore a suit and tie, despite the fact that he had one hand up Sooty, a dead-eyed teddy bear glove puppet that was the least anthropomorphic children's character in the history of television. Believing in Sooty required a leap of imagination that was beyond anyone over two years old. For the more mature child there were *Tales from Europe*, creepy, gaudy Eastern European folk fables put out by the BBC, who saved on dubbing by simply whacking English narration on top of the existing dialogue. This show was useful for teaching us that Europeans lived inside trees and wore dirndls. On Friday evenings there was *Crackerjack*, a sort of music hall for children without the smut. It featured singalongs, bad panto skits and a game called 'Double or Drop' in which children were forced to hold a pile of stuff without dropping it. The prize for winning was the meanest of all game-show rewards, a pencil inscribed with the word 'Crackerjack', while the loser was given a cabbage. The whole thing played out like some kind of experimental psychological torture. TV was also flirting with science fiction, though, and in 1963 *Doctor Who* arrived.

I would never understand space operas like *Star Trek*; all those life-lessons to be learned each week made it like being at school. *Doctor Who* landed at a time when England was finally freeing itself from debilitating post-war gloom. The nation of smog and rations and polio jabs was slowly fading. The English imagination, cowed by the horrors of a Europe-wide conflict, was set to return. Pop music was in its grand ascendancy. After the largely disastrous design mis-step of the Festival of Britain,* which, with the exception of the Royal Festival Hall, was all curly ironwork and atom-balls, the creative arts were budding in fresh directions. Thanks to television series like *Quatermass*, *Pathfinders to Venus* and *A for Andromeda*, the strange ideas of science fiction were stealing young minds.

*Designed to show that we had bounced back from the War, it inadvertently exposed the nation's exhaustion, except for the Skylon, an elegant slender structure with no visible means of support, like Britain.

Into this fertile innocence was planted a series of such peculiar originality that it took the nation entirely by surprise. Its hero was a crafty and somewhat sinister elderly man, its setting anywhere and everywhere, its cast of characters ever-changing, fallibly human. Although flawed by primitive monochrome technology and virtually no effects that could not be produced in polystyrene, it exhibited imagination in abundance. There was one recognizable object, although it quickly became unrecognizable as they vanished from the London streets: the blue police box, bigger inside than out – the first thing I had to grasp. Folding time and space, that was the second. Time Lords, the third. And as the series developed, through many doctors and dozens of castaway passengers, one true nemesis ruled them all.

The Daleks were unlike any alien seen before. They possessed no recognizable human features and had no redeeming qualities. Their very alien-ness made them impossible to reason with. When Daleks appeared, there was a sense that the laws of normal TV could be broken and something terrible might happen. But they were popular because any child with a sack and a sink plunger could carry off a passable imitation. Even Spike Milligan conjured up some dubious Pakistani Daleks who fried a dog and put it in their curry.

Finally, Daleks ingrained themselves deep within the national psyche. It was often stated that the English were historically a cruel race, and perhaps they found a kindred spirit in this cruellest of enemies. The poverty-row settings and props became unimportant when all you saw was encroaching alien terror. Likewise, who wondered how they coped with stairs when the Daleks had ways of getting to everyone? Which just left the fear, the need to block out the sound of those rasping voices, those futuristic but oddly sixties metal bodies that hid the slimy, pulsating deformities within.

The early shows were redolent of the grim dampness of an England now lost from view. The Doctor's companions were unwilling participants, frightened and anxious to go home. Foolish and foolhardy, they had none of the robotic common sense exhibited by American starship crews; they were students and schoolteachers hurled into dislocated situations, facing unthinkable evil. Nor could the Doctor be entirely trusted to protect them. If anything, it seemed likely he might just let them all die. It felt like I was watching my family on the screen.

Before *Doctor Who* commenced, a new type of story had already caught my interest. I had grown bored with lantern-jawed pilots and their tubby sidekicks, and instead was looking for something stranger. I discovered an elegant volume bound in thick black card, presumably belonging to my mother, called *The Fifty Strangest Stories Ever Told*, part of a series printed on porous paper that turned a brittle yellow almost as I was reading it.

These dark, discordant stories chimed with the mood of disappearing innocence in our little house. During one of the many terse verbal duels that took place downstairs, a family mystery was solved by listening intently through the banisters. I discovered why I had no maternal grandfather.

There was no such person.

My grandmother was single, and, what's more, she wasn't even Kath's mother. She was a former private nurse who had kindly agreed to adopt a number of children born out of wedlock between the wars, so Kath and her sister Muriel weren't sisters, her adored brother Kit who had died of diphtheria wasn't her brother, her real parents were no more than ciphers, and my uncles, aunts and cousins weren't kin, just a bunch of strangers.

Suddenly nobody was related to anyone on my mother's side of the family, which explained a lot when my father barked, 'Don't think you're so high and bloody mighty. At least I know who my parents are.' My family history simply unravelled, fell apart and blew away.

After hearing this, I suddenly felt comfortable with the idea of opening an anthology of disturbing stories.

In the front of the book was a handwritten quote. It said:

A writer must find a direct line into the perverse nature of the human heart.

It seemed to me that horror stories were ideally suited for doing just that.

For three-quarters of the twentieth century, virtually every respected writer wrote at least one such tale. According to the introduction, the illustrious history of the horror story had begun with Christopher Marlowe, John Webster, Jane Austen and Mary Shelley. By glancing at the contents page, I could see that just about everyone had turned their hand to the genre: Dickens, Conrad, Forster, Du Maurier, 'Saki' and Conan Doyle, inevitably, but also Muriel Spark, William Faulkner, Elizabeth Bowen, W. W. Jacobs. The ability to create a frisson of fear seemed to be a rite of passage for most writers.

It wasn't hard to see the appeal of a category that set its authors the task of naming the unnameable, of imagining fates worse than death in an attempt to respond to our most deep-rooted anxieties. Wasn't identifying a discomfort the first step towards controlling it? I had always been fearful, convinced that all worst possible scenarios would eventually present themselves in my life. Whenever my parents took a Sunday trip to the coast and walked along the beach, I spent most of my time checking tide tables and imploring them to turn back in case the sea swelled up and cut us off, drowning the entire family. I knew all about horror stories because I had already played most of them out in my head.

Horror's golden age had arrived between terrifying wars at a time when the world stopped making sense. Although the traditional horror story eventually vanished the way of the locked-room mystery and the country-house murder, as forgotten by the general public as John Dickson Carr's mad, wonderful conundrums, it remained a nostalgic reminder of a simpler age, when fears were easier to define and tales of terror operated under a strict set of literary rules. I loved rules.

My mother's book was filled with horror stories of the twenties and thirties, and of a very specific type. Many of them began with a sturdy chap knocking out his pipe on the mantelpiece, pouring two large brandies and retiring to an armchair to tell his clubbable companion an eerie tale by firelight. This technique had the odd effect of simultaneously making the story more real (he was hearing it directly from a friend of the family who had come to dinner – not that the Fowlers ever had anyone to dinner, or had any friends) and more distant (it was told at one remove, a 'friend of a friend' story). Such tales usually ended with the raconteur replacing his pipe in his mouth and saying something like 'And from that day on, he *never spoke another word to anyone again.* Another snifter, old chap?'

Even I could tell that many of the stories were pretty tame and often rather reactionary, but some of those from the pen of H. G. Wells were never bettered.

The book was considered only suitable for adults – it was unthinkable that such a forbidden tome should fall into the hands of a child. Yet the adult authors were themselves Edwardian children raised on spectacularly

macabre tales and thinly disguised right-wing warnings
(Rudyard Kipling was regarded by George Orwell – a
little simplistically, perhaps – as a rabid fascist). Many of
these early stories dealt with fears that were thankfully
receding in the public imagination: fear of starvation,
poverty, foreignness, the cruelties of changing fate and
falling fortune. Others were about madness and the
fear of going insane. It was hardly surprising when you
considered the number of lunatic asylums still operating
in and around London. I once saw an old asylum
admittance slip stating that the patient was suffering
from 'Hereditary Disappointment'. No wonder people
feared doctors.

Feeling as guilty as a shoplifter, I removed the book
from its high shelf and lugged it up to my bedroom, to
be consumed in shiversome chunks, story by story, and
stored under the bed in the times between.

In the early 1960s, the horrors of atomic warfare,
sexual and social liberation changed the expectations of
readers. What were ghosts and monsters compared to the
threat of global annihilation, the perils of promiscuity,
the uncontrolled power of being free and young?

In the giant story book, a number of authors tapped
into the feelings of the times, acknowledging the world's
loss of innocence. Ray Bradbury caught the sense of
change within small-town communities. The wonderfully
imaginative EC horror comics – the 'E' was for
'Entertaining' – sometimes adapted literary stories like
Bradbury's. Lately, however, they had been removed from
Mr Purbrick's comic-book rack, having been attacked for
damaging the development of children's minds by one Dr
Fredric Wertham, in one of America's periodic piques
about the moral disintegration of the nation's youth.
Wertham described comic books as 'cheap, shoddy,
anonymous. Children spend their good money for bad

paper, bad English and . . . bad drawing'. But then he also thought that Wonder Woman's independent streak made her a lesbian. Kath happily gave such books house-room because, although they looked fabulously disreputable, they bore Bradbury's illustrious name on their covers.

Ray Bradbury blurred the line between fantasy and reality, the boys in his tales hovering in that soon-lost golden period of waiting and longing. Between the fulfilment of wishes and the failure of dreams, a melancholy sense of things lost mingled with a calming warmth that I could feel rising from the page to heat my hands. But Bradbury dealt in nightmares as well, and I needed to find them. The collecting and cataloguing gene, so often prevalent in young males, was kicking in. Soon there would be index cards, alphabetical shelves, thematic indices and all the other codifying hobbies commonly found among boys without sex lives.

Horror stories were not stocked at East Greenwich Public Library. I had to start haunting the second-hand bookshops for those. Over the next few years I discovered a wealth of beautifully written short stories hidden behind tacky covers. Some of them were so sublime and intuitive that when I read them, I felt that the authors could somehow see directly into my mind.

I discovered a chain of fantastically seedy South London second-hand book stores called the Popular Book Centres. They stamped their smudged triangular logo inside all their books, and made enough money from thrusting, pointy-breasted top-shelf smut to keep racks of yellowing, soon-to-be-lost, dirt-cheap paperbacks going for real readers. In this way, they were every bit as useful as public libraries.

The Popular Book Centre in Greenwich was presided over by a gimlet-eyed man with black fingernails and the complexion of an old haddock. He looked as though he had been cast to play a lecherous plumber in a porn movie. The great thing about the shop was that I could always find something rare and wonderful lurking in the racks, and as everything was 1/6d I could afford to take a chance on the dodgiest-looking books.

The library had been good to me, but now I temporarily deserted it for something grubbier and more delinquent. Alfred Hitchcock had put his name to a series of dog-eared anthologies that were wonderful assorted literary ragbags, and from these I started making informed decisions about the writing I enjoyed most. It was important; I did not play sports or 'join in', as my mother called it, and reading was, by its nature, an unsocial occupation.

I made my first list of favourite short stories:*

'The Cone' – H. G. Wells
'Leiningen versus the Ants' – Carl Stephenson
'Camera Obscura' – Basil Copper
'Evening Primrose' – John Collier
'The Man Who Liked Dickens' – Evelyn Waugh
'The Fly' – George Langelaan

In time I discovered a wealth of beautifully written stories, most of which are now lost from view. In my head I built the ultimate anthology. Dino Buzzati's story 'Seven Floors' was a heart-rending study of our fear of illness, while his tale 'Just the Very Thing They Wanted' chilled because it denied its characters the rights to their most basic needs – the right to sit down, to be calm, to drink a glass of water. John Collier's 'Evening Primrose' concerned a man who moved into a department store to live among the mannequins, because he could not cope

---

*The only common denominator I can find in this list is that none of the stories plays by the traditional rules of the genre.

with urban life. Tennessee Williams wrote of searching a cinema for companionship and discovering a ghost in 'The Mysteries of the Joy Rio', as did Graham Greene in the classic 'A Little Place off the Edgware Road'.

Meanwhile, *The Fifty Strangest Stories Ever Told* remained under my bed until every story was digested. When the supply of new stories dried up, I headed back to the Popular Book Centre like an itchy drug addict, creeping shamefully past the soft porn in the window to root about in the barely fingered fiction section. Here, the Pan Books of Horror provided the next benchmark that all other collections had to reach. Their anthologist, Herbert Van Thal, edited the first twenty-five volumes, but as the tales became more explicitly gruesome they lost much of their power; heavier shocks were clearly required in jaundiced times. The darkest shadows are found in brightest sunlight, so it's natural to discover them in childhood, but I still felt guilty about my nascent literary tastes. Other kids in my neighbourhood weren't even reading, or if they were, they stuck to pilots and pirates. They weren't checking out worst-case scenarios by trawling through horror stories, hoping to find survival tips.

Suddenly I felt sure that my mother had bought her anthology as a survival manual for her marriage. In several stories, a bullying husband would cruelly mistreat his innocent wife, or perhaps his son, only to finally receive a shocking comeuppance. An awful lot of the tales involved madness, death or everlasting purgatory. Even more involved the careful planning of a long, slow-nurtured revenge. Quite a few had clearly been written by downtrodden Edwardian ladies acting out wish-fulfilment fantasies.

It was as good an introduction to human nature as any.

10

Between the Lines

By 1960, I had learned that the nostalgic clichés of child-hood were largely true.

The week was indeed organized around the lynchpin of Sunday lunch – in our case, lamb, beef and pork in orderly rotation, with the odd chicken that looked as if it had spent its formative years locked in solitary confinement without sunlight or exercise, before being executed – or finally allowed to expire – in time for a special holiday. My mother cooked the meat, sliced it and cooked it some more, until it grew small, dried-out and as leathery as a posing pouch, when she would pour elasticated Bisto filled with tumorous lumps over it. Dessert was always Libby's tinned peaches in a nasal-slime syrup, tinned pineapple chunks or tinned pears. By now, though, the meals were taking place in an atmosphere of distant resentment, with only the wireless or the sound of next door's toilet being flushed to break the silence.

Children did indeed make their own amusement, and tended to be absurdly well spoken and polite. In my case, indoor pastimes included:

Using the Bayko building set to make boring miniature suburban houses with bay windows and porches. Most building kits involved the handling of many knife-sharp parts that would either give you a bloody gash or a black man's pinch.

Magic Robot – a green robot which would spin around on a circular mirror and point to answers with a wand when you asked it questions. I took it to bits to find out how it worked, after which it never worked again.

Flounders, a dice game that allowed you to build fish, and another called Beetle Drive, which let you build huge insects. These games felt like zoo-based dominoes designed by a particularly creepy aunt.

Tell Me, another question-and-answer game, involving the rapid naming of items starting with an initial chosen by a spinning wheel. Typical question: 'Name a major municipal building'. (It would be interesting to hear ten-year-olds' answers to that question now.) The source of most family shouting matches.

'Double Your Money – The Board Game Based on the Popular Hughie Green Show!' A matter of opinion, clearly.

Spirograph, the plastic-wheel system for drawing complex fractals. It was fun until you realized that it allowed everyone else to do them as well, so no one would ever say, 'Aren't you clever!'

Escalado, a horse-race game which comprised a green baize strip, a G-clamp, six poisonous lead horses and a ratchet to make said strip shiver back and forth, stimulating forward movement in the steeds, although what actually happened was that they fell over (and presumably had to be shot).

The Dan Dare Space Communicator – a red plastic spaceship console that looked like something BBC engineers might have used in the early, heady days of

Alexandra Palace, which could transmit thought waves across galaxies or possibly into the next room, if you'd only remembered to buy giant batteries for it.

Making things from smelly corrugated sheets of plasticine.

Paper-sculpture books with punch-out parts that required the use of a razor-blade to make the pieces fit together. Cue the home first-aid kit.

Building balsa-wood* gliders with brain-fuddling spirit-soaked and varnished paper wings. An introduction to the power of narcotics.

The John Bull Printing Outfit, a typesetting kit with a smeary ink pad and thousands of tiny rubber pieces a baby could choke to death on. Fact: nobody ever put together more than four words before becoming extremely irritable.

Airfix models including the Hovercraft, a miraculous sixties transporter that was too ugly to catch on, but continued its popularity in toy form for years.

The Chad Valley Give-a-Show Projector, basically a century-old Victorian slide projector given a yellow plastic makeover.

The Viewmaster 3-D viewer, which came with circular discs that, rather oddly, presented rubber-toy versions of movie scenes. The only discs I had were:

Pope Pius XII, Memorable Moments, Rome (Belgian issue)
The People of Lima, Peru
Ramsgate to Herne Bay, Kent!
Huckleberry Hound in 'Pop Goes Yogi'

*This miraculously light material grows in South American rainforests. Its seeds are carried like a dandelion's. It is still used to build gliders.

Plaster moulding kits. Pour the plaster into a red condom-shaped mould to produce British monarchs and squirrels that you could then hand-paint. Figures were always depicted standing against a tree stump, in order to strengthen their little plaster legs.

Cap bombs, spud guns, Bowie knives, sweet cigarettes, chemistry sets and other great stuff that wouldn't be allowed anywhere near a child today.*

And reading, reading, reading, reading.

I was not allowed to mix with the kids from the next street because they lived above shops and were therefore 'common'. My mother had a peculiar sense of what constituted commonness. Heinz Baked Beans, football, margarine, Spam, the *Daily Mirror*, council flats, motorbikes, public displays of emotion, playing in the street, television, tattoos, dyed hair, shouting, swearing, braces, the Labour Party, plimsolls worn with trousers, over-familiarity, and failure to hold a knife and fork properly were unconscionable to someone who had been raised in a household that had only allowed reading, praying and going for brisk walks on the Sabbath. She didn't like loud coughing either, although she was prepared to excuse Mr Hills next door, who had a cough like a duck's death-rattle, because he had contracted it in the trenches. The fact that my mother did not know who her parents were was immaterial; it was how you were raised, nurture over nature, that was important. Grace, silence, acquiescence and politeness were everything, as was knowing your place and staying in it. Her own mother might have been a prostitute for all she knew, but it did not excuse going out on the Sabbath without

---

*I don't mean this to sound as if I prefer the toys of the past. I would have given my right eye for an iPod.

gloves, or switching to a decent overcoat on the first of November.

The neighbours really did spend much of their time out on the street, gossiping. Summers were passed almost totally outside, seated on the pavement, sharing endless cups of tea, washing or polishing the front steps, complaining of the heat. Fiery sunlight, cadmium yellow and faintly dusty, forever warmed the orange brick sides of the houses. Bedtimes were proscribed by the height and rotation of the sun.

This past really is another country. How different were the children? Well, on Saturday mornings a children's record-request radio show was run by the avuncular and rather stern 'Uncle Mac'. The selection of music chosen by the boys and girls of England remained fixed for years, including patter songs like 'Nellie The Elephant', 'The Railway Runs Through The Middle Of The House' and horrible catchy, stirring military tunes like 'The Dam Busters March'. For any man over forty, it's probably still impossible to hear the opening notes of 'The Theme From 633 Squadron' without putting your thumbs to forefingers, upturning them over your eyes like a Spitfire pilot's goggles and going 'Nyeeeooour!' The War was still fresh enough in our fathers' minds for them to impress its importance on their offspring, but that didn't explain the popularity of Max Bygraves* singing 'I'm A Pink Toothbrush, You're A Blue Toothbrush'.

Although the house on Westerdale Road was minuscule, it afforded a few pleasures. I could dig in the rubbish-dump of a garden, where the neighbour's dog planted crumbly white turds and Kath grew a handful of

---

*Mr Bygraves told me that he tried in vain to vary his repertoire when appearing in variety halls, but all the old ladies always yelled 'Sing "You Need Hands!"' (one of his more sentimental hits).

carefully nurtured but doomed plants. I could play forts within the knife-sharp shards of the collapsing Anderson shelter.* I could torture daddy-long-legs in the outdoor toilet where we kept the boring comatose tortoise. I could try to keep sticklebacks in the brackish drainage ditch my father laughingly called a pond. I could creep through my parents' bedroom digging secrets from their utility wardrobe (this room possessed my father's one nod to decadence: black wallpaper decorated with oriental faces and silky sampans). But mostly I read, swapping and buying so many books that I became fearful for their existence, and took to hiding them behind grates and flues.

I had the distinct impression that our family ranked fairly low in the street's subtle and complex class table, especially since Percy next door was given a bike for Christmas and *that was just one of his presents*, Percy's mother proudly told Kath. I chanced my arm and asked for a typewriter, but Bill was currently out of work, and so instead I was publicly – and humiliatingly – presented with a blackboard, which in my father's eyes was just as good a writing accoutrement. Years later, I saw old monochrome footage on TV of children playing happily in the street with sticks and tyres, and thought with incredulity, *That was us, that's how we were*. Just as you will one day.

Our garden was particularly disgusting, a lumpy coagulation of dry, dead earth, rampant weeds, house bricks, bits of rusty iron and the odd fistful of rock-hard rabbit pellets. Londoners had become so inured to the sight of bomb damage, rubble and sooty derelict

---

*Corrugated-iron bomb shelters that accommodated up to six people. So strong that you still see them in allotments and back gardens. Ours fell down (not put together properly).

buildings remaining fifteen years after the War that they seemed not to concern themselves with gardening. My father would think nothing of having a pee against the collapsed remains of the Anderson shelter if he thought no one was looking.

Television was considered antisocial, so children formed their own social groups which roughly explored their parents' divisions, without yet feeling the need to create issues of tribal respect. The only real dividing line was class. I knew my parents were poorer than the neighbours ('But more respectable,' my mother assured us) and it only made a difference in the way in which I amused myself. Rich kids were always away somewhere; the poor ones stayed at home.

'You have to make an effort,' my mother would say, which I knew was her way of suggesting that it might be nice to put down my book once in a while and form a friendship with someone, anyone.

By the age of ten I had outgrown cuteness to become an unprepossessing sight. Skinny, gangling and bookish, as pale as a blank page, with a domed forehead and sticking-out ears, a pudding-basin haircut, sticky-taped glasses, a narrow chin and large brown eyes that easily reflected fright and surprise, I was nobody's idea of an appealing child. My weight was outstripped by my height, and I was all knees and elbows, so that when perpendicular I looked as awkward as a straightened chicken, and was better suited to lying on my stomach with a novel.

Much of my time was spent traipsing along the deserted suburban streets with an armful of library books, rain matting my hair and steaming up my lenses. At some point reading replaced doing anything else, so that I lived life as an outsider, an observer on the sidelines. In doing so, I was unconsciously copying my father.

I had a few street friends, kids who would play outside

until the second it got dark, like vampires in reverse – no one was ever allowed to play out after that because it was another sign of commonness. Lawrence was ginger-mopped, with ginger freckles and what appeared to be purple eyes. He always made up his mind about something without getting all the facts – I found out years later that he had become a vicar. There was an arrogant rival from my class called Peter who was so incredibly bright that he had a nervous breakdown on his first day of senior school, much to his mother's horror and everyone else's glee, and he was good fun to hit.

There was also Pauline Ann Ward from across the road.

She had a glossy dark bobbed haircut and wore yellow summer dresses and sandals long after everyone else had moved on to jeans. She wore cardigans and Alice bands and had eyes the colour of an August sky. I supposed I was in love with her. One day, purely in the interests of exploration, she offered to take her knickers off for me, even though we were in her garden and it was snowing, but I declined her offer because I was trying to build a sledge. Even so, her proposal was disturbing enough to make me step back through the ice of her father's frozen goldfish pond.

Girls like Pauline were far more bothersome than books. You always knew where you were with a book. A girl would laugh at your jokes and then snub you for several days, for no apparent reason. She would go out of her way to let you know you were invisible to her, then stare at you with X-ray eyes until you paid attention. She would tease you, pull up her dress, demand to see your willy, ridicule it, then run screaming to her mother when you tried to hit her.

I didn't understand Pauline, and she wasn't even a real girl because she had thick legs like a boy and no breasts to speak of yet. Plus, she played with a Noah's Ark and kept mentioning God's Will whenever I wanted to talk about space monsters.

'Your parents are funny,' she said one day as she sat cross-legged on the floor, marshalling pairs of wooden animals into the Ark.

'What do you mean?' I asked.

'They don't like each other.'

'How do you know that?'

'Your dad said he'd like to glue your mum's mouth shut. If my dad said that, my mum wouldn't cook his dinner.'

'My mum's tried that,' I replied. 'When was the last time your dad threw something at your mum?'

'Good heavens, they don't fight,' said Pauline smugly, trotting her giraffes on board. 'They adore each other.' Checking that all the animals were safe from inundation, she raised the gangplank. 'And they love the Lord Jesus,' she added for good measure.

One evening, seated in my bedroom, I tried to work out my feelings about girls by drawing up a chart. Tables, with lists and tick-boxes, always helped to sort out complicated feelings. This one was entitled 'BOOKS VS GIRLS'.

BOOKS	GIRLS
Will show you the world.	Will show you their fannies.
Can have as little or as much of them as you want.	Can only have them on their terms, usually for too long or not long enough.
If one is boring, you can get rid of it and replace with another.	Boring ones won't go. Nice ones won't stay.

Cost very little, predictable, provide hours of fun.	Expensive, and you never know if you're going to enjoy yourself or get annoyed.
Become treasured memories.	Disturb your brain for years to come.
Silent constant friends, easy to choose according to your mood.	Noisy, need constant attention, determined to upset you with strange requests.
Can send them back to the library.	Can't send them anywhere without endless questions.

From this I concluded that books were more cost-effective and enjoyable than girls, but also more predictable and less disturbing. Finding a combination of both was probably the best solution. It wasn't first love, but it was first curiosity.

Even so, I was better off with a book than hanging around with Pauline, because she took the girl thing to some kind of extreme, like Lois Lane. I decided to return to the library, but would give up the children's section and put in a request to join the Adults', even though I was technically too young to do so. Besides, I felt sure that books could teach me everything I would ever need to know about girls, without actually having to deal with them on a regular basis.

11

Lost for Words

If there was a specific point at which the desire to read transformed itself into the need to write, it must have been here, seated at a scarred desk in the wood-damp library with an immense stack of books before me, far away from harmful sunlight and fresh air. I kept notes of everything I read and liked, along with lists of words that were inexplicably pleasing. Some words could be rolled around the mouth and savoured like melting ice cream. My current favourites were:

Peculiar
Colonial
Ameliorate
Serpentine
Paradise
Emerald
Illumination.*

*I know this because I still have the list. I made notes all through my childhood, as if there was going to be a test one day. Is this normal?

There were words I hated as well, ones with sharp edges, all Ks and Xs that dug into you and were awkward to spell. Generally, the rules of spelling and grammar were easy to follow. I could not understand why so many people made such simple mistakes. It vexed me to see the greengrocer placing signs on his fruit filled with random punctuation, like *Potato's 1/6d* or *"Finest" tomatoes*. I made fun of him so much that he threw sprouts at me.

Mrs Clarke, the librarian, allowed me to raid the reference section and read whatever I wanted, on the condition that I stayed inside the library to do so. Folding my pale bare legs beneath me, I pulled down one volume after another. One book, *Uses of Speech*, stopped me in my tracks because it turned out that there were all these devices you could use to illustrate prose. The first read:

> *Litotes – the utilization of a negated antonym to make an understatement or to strongly affirm the positive.*

There were dozens of others, each more curious and convoluted in its meaning than the last. I read down the list with a sinking heart.

Metonymy
Anthimeria
Oxymoron
Metalepsis
Antisthecon
Paragoge
Ellipsis
Synecdoche
Epenthesis

Stichomythia
*Zeugma**

What point was there in even attempting to write? If I learned one of the rules, I would need to learn them all. It was what you had to do if you were to become proficient at anything. My father had told me so. Whenever I read a copy of my mother's *Reader's Digest* I read the entire thing from cover to cover, including the adverts, even though 95 per cent of it was complete tosh.

'Christopher, can I offer you a word of advice?' said Mrs Clarke, sitting down beside me. 'You don't have to learn every single thing.' She smelled of roses and peppermints. She looked dusty and ancient, as old as the volumes bound in cracked red leather that she kept locked up in her reference section, and yet she always seemed to be fighting down a smile, as if recalling a happy memory. She was thirty-four years old, and my mother referred to her as a 'spinster'.

'I'm just looking at the rules,' I told her with a twinge of embarrassment.

'Oh, they're not rules. They're just tools, and not even important ones. You wouldn't learn how to use a spirit level before you knew what to do with a hammer.' She studied my profile, my slender hands at rest on the pages. 'You're good at English, aren't you.' It wasn't a question.

'I like books,' I said simply.

'The words or the ideas?'

'Both.'

'Like writing stories too?'

'Top of my class in essays. Bottom in arithmetic.'

'Well, nobody likes a good all-rounder. The love of books is a quiet thing. It's different to having a passion

*I still have no idea what this means.

for, say, sport. It's not a group activity.' She gestured at the shelves. 'I don't own these books, sadly. There are not many things I can give you, but there is something you can have.' She rose and returned with a slim volume. 'You can take this one away and look after it for a while. Don't worry if you find some of them hard to understand; at your age I wouldn't expect anything else. I'm giving you this so you can see how words fit together. I've had it since I was a little girl of ten, and my grandmother owned it before me.'

I studied the cover. *A Child's Garden of English Verse*. It looked really boring.

Glancing back at Westerdale Road as a young man, I saw the orange-brick terraced homes through yellow rain needles slanting in sodium lamplight, bedraggled little front gardens, the house next door with pearlized shells embedded in its front wall, the Scouts' hall, the railway line – just like millions of other English childhoods.

And yet there were oddities, like the 1930s advertisement painted on a side wall, gigantic and fading, that showed a smiling housewife pouring boiling water from her kettle on to the surface of her dining-room table; what was it advertising, and why was this demented woman so happily destroying her home?

The twisting alleyways and tunnels behind and between the houses – where today kids would lurk to smoke dope – had been unfenced and completely safe, if a little creepy, but imagining the streets as they had been then, I was impressed by the sheer *lack* of things; there were no mattress farms on street corners, no skips, no dented metal signs, no road markings, no cars, no traffic bays, no yellow murder boards, no charity muggers, no litter, no graffiti, no noise, just the huff of the occasional passing steam train, just kids and stag beetles and butterflies and sparrows. You could hear conversation in the next street, and perhaps in the street beyond that.

Despite the sense of community, which everyone said had strengthened during the War, there were still endless household secrets, drawn curtains and muffled sobs, husbands' dark whispers and wives commiserating, private sorrows, closing ranks, mothers with folded arms staring disapprovingly across the road, children whisked away to relatives because *something dreadful happened that you must never talk about*. Real life occurred behind the walls, between the casual conversations. The woman at the end of the street kept stuffed cats, twenty of them in all, and referred to them as if they were relatives. The man opposite talked constantly, even when he was alone, because during a wartime bombing raid his identical twin had run one way and he another, and his brother had been killed, and he blamed himself.

It was the age of euphemism. Nobody died of pneumonia, diphtheria or tuberculosis, they were *peaky*, then *poorly*, then *passed over*. Some adults had to be watched because they could *turn funny*. The bloke around the corner had become *less of a man* after the War. The boy in the next street had been *interfered with* behind Greenwich Park playground. I could have done with an Enigma machine to de-code our family conversations.

I picked my way over the broken triangle of litter-strewn grass at the edge of the motorway, all that remained of what had once been our family's back garden. Here, at the very tip where the crumbling, graffiti-plastered walls met, a small blackened patch of soil still remained, the spot where my father had burned old furniture and bits of wood. He had set fire to the librarian's treasured poetry book, and pinned it in the flames with a poker until its pages were blackened, muttering through his teeth that no son of his was going to read nancy stuff.

I had been too ashamed to return to the library without it. Instead of telling her what had happened, instead of even saying I had lost it myself, I had simply stopped attending.

One evening Mrs Clarke came to the house looking for me. I heard her talking with my father at the front door and desperately wanted to speak to her, if only to explain why I hadn't been to the library. Instead I waited behind the door, listening. My father made it plain that she was interrupting his evening. 'I'm sure if the boy was interested in coming back, he'd have been to see you by now,' he said, anxious to shut the door and return to his urgent rendezvous with the evening paper. 'He's probably found something more interesting to do.'

Mrs Clarke wasn't angry, just saddened. She paused on the front step and peered up the stairs, hesitant. If she was about to speak her mind she must have thought better of it, because Bill closed the door and she was sent away.

I ran up to my bedroom and looked down from the window. At the corner of the street she stopped briefly and looked back at the house. That was the last time I ever saw her.

Even now the mysteries remained. My father's fury over a book of poems, Kath's tacit support of her husband. Unspoken fears and truths, held within the walls of the little house, that had been lost in the brickwork, and finally shattered by wrecking balls.

The biggest mystery remained my mother.

12

Mother and Movies

As one indignity piled on top of another, I wondered about Kath. Why did she stay on, like Lois Lane? Why didn't she say to Bill, 'Shag this for a lark, Superman, I'm off.' Although she had never been scared of him, her new-found strength did not put her on an equal footing, or persuade her to back down. She returned to work and became more independent, but obeyed him because he was her husband.

On the day I returned to visit Westerdale Road, I noticed the proximity of the neighbourhood church and realized one thing that should have been obvious from the start: my mother was Church of England, and believed in the sanctity of her wedding vows. She had attended services twice every Sunday throughout her childhood, and always made the family say Grace before a meal. Bill was a shameless atheist, so the subject of religion was never broached at the table.

I had seen grim photographs of their big day, the depleted group of relatives in demob suits and austerity dresses, the ladies' strange fifties hats that clenched their heads like silken sea coral, the grinning elderly couple who had crept into the picture because they just happened to be passing St John's, Blackheath, on their way to the shops. My father always pointed them out because he had once done something similar, arranging to meet Kath at her friend's wedding, only to find himself in the wrong hotel suite.

'Didn't you notice?' asked Kath afterwards. 'They were celebrating Divali, you were the only non-Asian in the room.'

But Kath stayed and the marriage held, after a fashion. Presumably she found enough snippets of pleasure to keep her from burning down the house, like Mrs Danvers. 'You were lovely boys,' she would tell me and Steven in her later years. 'You were always making me laugh. You gave me the strength to stay.' It was a compliment that carried the seeds of unthinkable guilt.

Was she happy? I found it impossible to tell. She loved her children, and immersed herself in the daily running of the household, keeping too busy for rumination on such woolly concepts as happiness. Presumably she and Bill occasionally made love, even though they didn't get on with each other – the bedroom curtains in Westerdale Road stayed shut up and down the street until late on a Sunday morning, to allow time for a certain amount of fumbling beneath marital eiderdowns.* But passion remained a word you were more likely to find in a book of poetry. I supposed Kath wasn't that bothered, in much the same way that she had admitted not being able to appreciate food because she didn't think her taste-buds worked properly.

---

*I longed to use the word 'carphology' here ('delirious fumbling under bed linen'), but my editor felt it was taking the love of words a tad too far.

I had the feeling she would have liked a cuddle or an occasional word of encouragement, though.

On the nights when she wasn't working she went to the pictures alone, returning home to seat herself on the end of my bed, where she would describe, in exhaustive detail, the plots of the films she had seen. As a consequence, I had second-hand knowledge of a great many films, filtered through my mother's enthusiastic but somewhat subjective perception. Had she described them for me, or for herself? Perhaps she had just been starved of conversation.

It wasn't until many years later, when I finally saw *2001*, that I realized it wasn't really about 'a man who uses a computer to go back in time to meet himself as a baby'. Rather, it contained the most profound surprise – that the discovery of life beyond our world would only make us feel more desperately alone than ever. Man remained at the mercy of something vast, terrifying and unknowable. The past was a puzzle, but at least it could be safely locked away. No wonder *2001* became my mother's favourite film of all time. Mind you, her number-two spot was occupied by *South Pacific*, so you had to take her enthusiasms with a pinch of salt. And a part of me liked *2001* not because it revealed the infinite majesty of the universe, but because the space station was really clean.

Kath's vivid descriptions of movies got me excited. *2001* opened in 1968, the same year as *Rosemary's Baby*, *Bullitt*, *The Thomas Crown Affair*, *The Lion in Winter* and *Witchfinder General*, all of which she saw. Weren't movies just animated versions of books? They weren't, of course, but they could deliver an entire plot in ninety minutes, which was easier than hanging around the library knowing that I had failed the one person who had shown faith in me. In this I empathized with

Mr Brownlow, who had trusted Oliver Twist to run an errand, only to be let down when the boy failed to return. It hadn't been Oliver's fault, but to me that wasn't the point at all. The idea of disappointing others filled me with shame. I resolved never to be late for anyone, ever.*

Looking around the neighbourhood at the people I most admired, I decided to emulate their finest qualities, which were being polite, keeping your nose clean, pulling your socks up, avoiding embarrassment, being on time, staying smart, not making a nuisance of yourself, never being in anyone's debt and making yourself invisible wherever possible. With these rules in place, surely I would be destined for a great future.

Meanwhile, there were more stories to be discovered, but with the library now out of bounds, the cinema seemed my best option. I wanted to go there by myself, but my mother suggested I start with Saturday Morning Pictures, where I would see some good films aimed at my age group.

So that was where I went next.

---

*If you are ever required to fill in a form listing essential leadership qualities, do not put 'punctuality'.

13

In the Dark

My nearest cinema was the Granada Greenwich, where hunchbacked, chain-smoking pensioners whiled away their afternoons because they got cheap tickets to the early shows. When they weren't noisily unwrapping boiled sweets in the quiet parts of the film, they were creeping around the toilets with bladder complaints.

It was here that I fell truly in love.

I had seen her before, watching the film at an absurd angle in the penumbral auditorium, and had felt a prickling warmth beneath her gaze, a confusion, a desire. I wanted to follow the warm red glow of her torch down the aisle, back to the little room where she waited between shows.

I sat fidgeting, waiting for the credits to roll, then looked around and saw her carefully making her way down to the front of the auditorium. She moved slowly because the floor was raked and she wore white high heels. Positioning herself between the aisles, she patiently waited for the house lights to go on. The bulb hidden in her white tray illuminated choc ices, Mivvis,* wafers, tubs, ice lollies,† and ridged plastic cartons of fluorescent orange juice, but also shrouded her face in shadow. Her proudly raised chin and disdainful air suggested that she might have been displaying ancient Egyptian artefacts, even though the effect was slightly tarnished by the fact that she was chewing gum.

Her strapped heels, her little Grecian skirt and her illuminated tray of offerings gave her the appearance of an electric goddess. Her blonde hair was fixed with a red plastic bow to keep her fringe out of her eyes, but the sides fell to her shoulders in an old-fashioned style. She wore a glittery white patent-leather belt and a short pink nylon blouse buttoned down the front. The first two buttons were undone, so that the rise of her pale breasts shone in the overhead spotlight. When I thought about undoing the remaining buttons, I could scarcely catch my breath.

Was she aware of her own perfection? Despite the fact that she had obviously been chosen by the management to entice men from their seats, she seemed not to notice her surroundings, as if her spirit was still far away in the Nevada desert, where this week's first film had been set. Would she travel with me to the South Seas for the second half of the double bill, and swim in the warm clear waters while the Swiss Family Robinson prepared for their beachside ostrich race? And why were they called Robinson if they were Swiss?

The cinema was almost empty; the double bill had been playing every Sunday for a month now. I knew I could wait until she began her walk back up the aisle of the great auditorium, but there was a risk that I might fail

---

*An ice cream clearly named before the development of market research.
†Brand name: the rather wonderful 'Drink-On-A-Stick'.

to attract her attention and my opportunity would be missed. I rose a little unsteadily from my seat, checked that I had money in my pocket and made my way to the edge of the stage.

I had bought ice creams from her many times before, but she had barely noticed me. This time, though, I felt sure it would be different. It simply took an act of courage on my part to talk to her. I waited until all her customers had been served, then presented myself before her, staring down at the selection of fiercely coloured ice-cream boxes. Caught in the low light of the tray, her eyes were lost in darkness as she chewed rhythmically, awaiting my request. Her red lips sparkled with frosted gloss.

'I'd like . . .' I began. 'I see you here every week . . .' My words emerged with awkward bluntness. 'You're so . . .' I put my money away.

'If you wanna choc ice it might 'elp if you stop staring at my tits,' she snapped. Her lips shone fiercely in the spotlight. She breathed out, a long slow sigh, clicked off her tray light and walked out of my life.

There were just three classifications of film from which to choose.

'U' certificates meant Disney animations and live-action stories of brave animals that banded together to find their way home, boring musicals, homoerotic Italian Hercules movies in which the hero would glisten while lifting fake rocks in a short red skirt, or effects-driven action films featuring giant stop-frame animated bees being poked by men with javelins.

'A' certificates admitted children so long as they could locate an adult to see them through the door, which meant hanging around on street corners to pick up strangers, like under-age rent boys touting for trade.

'X' certificates were for over-sixteens and were forbidden and scary, but you could start slipping into them if you were a tall fourteen, or like the weirdly mature Greek boy in my class, who had permanent five o'clock shadow by the time he was twelve.* I discovered that I could gain free entrance by walking in backwards while everyone else was coming out.

On Saturday mornings there were the imaginatively titled Saturday Morning Pictures, which consisted of just over a thousand children slinging things at each other for two hours. This was a proper club, for which we got spiffy orange enamel badges and our own signature song, 'The Greenwich Granadiers',† sung to the tune of 'The British Grenadiers', a military song that no one now remembers. Naturally, no girls were allowed to attend such events for fear that they would be knocked unconscious – or maybe there were girls, but I never noticed any. I once tried to get Pauline to come along, but she loftily informed me that I had absolutely no idea what girls wanted and never ever would, before returning to work on the tariff for her Ark's passengers. She wanted to be a tax lawyer when she grew up, like her father.

The experience of attending the Saturday Morning Pictures was appalling: a sea of bouncing, shrieking, caterwauling, flailing, flatulent, hyperactive kids throwing empty Jubbly cartons and rock-hard sweets from Jamboree Bags at each other. A Jubbly was orangeade frozen in a triangular carton: once you had sucked all the condensed juice from the corners and crunched them, you had to take the whole thing out and turn it upside-down, at which point you usually dropped it on the floor.

While I was doing this, a vaguely sinister man in a

---

*I think I loved him.
†Granada: a cinema chain with such faith in the British film industry that they were turned into bingo halls.

double-breasted suit called Uncle Arthur would come on stage and award sweets to children, whom he drew from the dark by shining a mirror in their faces. How Uncle Arthur picked these children was a mystery; I liked to think they were selected at random, or perhaps he picked the most intelligent-looking ones, or the ones who looked like they wouldn't tell their mothers if he touched them above the knee.

After several ineffectual pleas to keep quiet, Uncle Arthur beat a hasty retreat and was replaced by two Warner Brothers cartoons, an episode from an ancient Captain Marvel serial featuring square-shouldered men in trilbies, and a feature film – not a proper film, but wholesome tripe produced by the Children's Film Foundation.

The CFF, one of the greatest nails in English cinema's coffin, made films about perky pigtailed girls, and boys in grey flannel shorts who usually discovered counterfeiters' lairs while on hop-picking holidays, and who dispatched crooks by dropping bags of flour and hockey nets on them. Saturday Morning Pictures clubs eventually died out, but were periodically revived by do-gooders who honestly believed that modern kids wouldn't grow bored of them and start stabbing each other.

I thought I had probably been *interfered with* on the way home from one such event, but I could not be entirely sure. A man in a plastic mackintosh called to me from the narrow rain-slick street beside the cinema and asked if I could lend a hand with his bike. He said the front wheel had a puncture, but there didn't seem to be anything wrong with the tyre. While I held the bike upright so it could be checked, the man knelt beside me and allowed his hand to roam lightly to the top of my short trousers. He squeezed my inside leg a couple of times, telling me I had strong muscles, and that was it. I didn't tell my parents because there wasn't very much to tell, although of course the man might have gone on an interfering rampage after that. I remember, though, that only one of us had been nervous, and it hadn't been me. To hear parents talk, you'd have thought it was a big deal.

Life at home reached an uneasy truce. Bill finally found a job, and although it was a humiliating step down and didn't use his old skills in scientific glass technology or gas chromatography, it was at least tangentially related. He became the manager of the Elephant & Castle gas showroom, working in the hideous concrete mall where gang members were soon to start knifing each other over issues of respect. He also agreed to spend fewer evenings at his mother's house and more time with his children. I could not imagine why he wanted to be anywhere near his horrible mother when we were so much more interesting, but her shadow reached down over our little orange house like Dracula's, luring Bill away to sit with her while she peeled pomegranates* and knitted her four-thousandth shapeless cardigan of the winter.

Saturday Morning Pictures was fun in an anthropological way. It was worth going just to see how badly children behaved when locked in a big dark room together. The films were never really about anything, but were packed with enough incident to quieten the audience down from time to time. The noise level roared back up whenever there was a dialogue scene or a bit with a girl in. Books didn't just have plots, they had themes, but the only message I got from a Children's Film Foundation film was that crooks could be captured with bags of flour, and all windmills had treasure maps hidden inside them.

The funny thing about the children's films they showed at Saturday Morning Pictures was that one day, all of a

*Bitter fruit not intended to be eaten like an orange.

sudden, the thought of seeing just one more was enough to make you throw up, and you could never face going back again. It was a far cry from a world where adults paid to see Spiderman films without worrying about being considered infantile.

I thought about the shared experience of cinema-going for a while, and came up with a great idea. My mother loved films, so I would get my father to take us all to the pictures, share confectionery in the dark and become a happy family again.

Of course, it didn't quite work out like that.

14

Tea with Mother

A new world of convenience was on the horizon. Now that nobody could afford servants any more, labour-saving devices were needed at home. I once saw an advertisement in a Victorian issue of *Punch* that depicted a delighted housewife unwrapping a fireplace. The headline read: '*If you really love her, this Christmas you'll buy her a grate.*'

In the sixties, grates, gas pokers and coal scuttles ceased to be desirable gifts for loved ones.

In order to rid the world of Victoriana, everyone in the country had started covering their doors and boarding over their staircases with plywood, inadvertently preserving the original features of their houses in the process.

This DIY frenzy, which my father caught on to despite the fact that he never finished a single job in his life, was the fault of a man called Barry Bucknell, who had the first-ever makeover show on TV. Bill referred to him as 'the bodger', which was a bit rich coming from a man who couldn't hang a picture without accidentally knocking through to next door.

Bodger Bucknell was popular because there were only two TV channels, so programmes achieved astonishing ratings and were highly influential. If TV chef Fanny Cradock dyed her boiled eggs aquamarine (she was addicted to lurid food colouring) then all the women did, although nobody chose to follow her lead on the 'shave your eyebrows off and repaint them just below your hairline' front. Cradock also treated her husband Johnnie like a whipped dog, which many suburban wives must have found exciting. But then, women of the period had adopted Lady Isabel Barnet as a role model because she spoke so nicely on *What's My Line?* and wore a frilly blindfold-mask as the guests signed in. Isabel Barnet finally killed herself out of shame at being caught with a shoplifted jar of jam, which, to women of my mother's generation, seemed a decent and entirely logical reason for suicide.

I didn't bother with television because it consisted largely of windmills, puppets and pottery wheels, interspersed with elderly men smoking pipes while they discussed Harold Macmillan in Old Etonian accents. Television was worthy and posh and educational. If the members of the latest Big Brother house had been tipped on to the screen in the sixties, they would have been the subject of a condescending documentary investigating primitive cultures, or slugs.

However, the couch-potato era started here, with families sitting together on the three-piece suite of an evening, mother knitting, father reading the paper, kids quietly playing, and everyone at least half-watching television. Boys were obsessed with *Thunderbirds*, because the stories took a back seat to the nuts-and-bolts mechanical detail of each rescue. We never asked why the characters had American accents or why their heads were so disproportionately large for their bodies; we just wanted to see a monorail catch fire.

The Avengers offered stranger fare, with tales of killer rain, robots and murderous grannies, and endless shots of eerily deserted airfields and villages. The most amoral and fantastical episodes were written by Philip Levine and Brian Clemens, who also conjured the show's marvellous line-up of eccentric cameos, from deranged colonels to railway fanatics. Best of all, every episode had a simple hook that suckered you in – the town that loses an hour, the man who is killed by an invisible winged creature, the church with no parishioners and a graveyard full of coffins. The episodes were virtual blueprints for budding writers.

There was nothing like this on the BBC, though. Auntie was obsessed with the everyday. When the BBC showed a game-show challenge in which the contestants had to hack up a piano with an axe and feed it through a letterbox before a bell went off, the entire nation chopped its upright parlour pianos into matchsticks. This appealed greatly to my father, as he was very fond of destroying things. He soon dealt with the beautiful piano in the front room, hacking it into splinters and filling the summer sky with the smell of burning varnish. Another time, he boiled my lead farmyard figures down in Kath's only frying pan; the resulting poisonous metal pancake lay in our back garden for years, killing everything within a five-foot radius. When Bill wasn't practising the destructive art of DIY, he was taking his motorbikes apart and putting them back together, at which point he would find himself with several pieces left over.

But there was one room in our house that genuinely felt indoors, and didn't have bits of motorbike all over it. The front room had a three-piece brown hide sofa with farting leather cushions, a polished walnut sideboard full of unused best crockery, the tiny television, and a three-panelled mirror on a chain above a green tiled fireplace.

The room was comfortable and cosy and nobody was ever allowed to sit in it. This was because it was for guests, an idea my mother must have read about in *Woman's Realm** or heard Fanny Cradock lecturing on. The idea was that guests came to tea and you served them sherry and little sandwiches without crusts and had intelligent conversation. The only problem was that the Fowlers didn't know anybody upon whom this practice could be inflicted.

Kath tried it with the Hills next door, but they were ancient, deaf and slightly incontinent, so nobody was allowed to tell jokes or make them jump. And on the other side, Percy's mum lived alone with her son because something mysterious had caused her husband to leave the house in the middle of the night and never come back. She was prone to fits of hysterical crying and the dropping of china when left alone, or suddenly laughing in a high-pitched scream that sounded like someone trying to choke-start a Ford Cortina. Her name seemed to be Margaret Poor-Soul, because that's what everyone called her.

My mother came up with a solution to the guest short-age. She would invite Bill's parents down the hill to take tea with our family. It would be their first-ever visit. Mrs Fowler would finally see what a good wife Kath was, conversation would be made, the good teapot would come out, there would be angel cake, serviettes and doilies. The best crockery would get an airing and the rift would be healed.

My father was sent to negotiate, but it took several visits to reach an agreement. His parents would come down and see us at four o'clock on Sunday afternoon for

*A weekly periodical that preferred articles on crocheted jumpers to the discussion of orgasms, which weren't invented until 1985.

tea, then leave. It was like getting Jews and Arabs to the same table.

Kath opened her ancient, linen-covered Mrs Beeton* book and started baking. Like many English cooks of the era, she was wonderful when it came to pies, puddings, cakes and pastries, and appalling with meat and salads. All meat was either slow-roasted to shoe leather, or boiled until it resembled human flesh. Salads consisted of lettuce, hard-boiled eggs, tinned beetroot slices, cucumber and quartered tomatoes, with no dressing other than the vinegary bite of Heinz Salad Cream.

In honour of the occasion she baked fairy cakes, an iced fruit cake, angel cake, a Battenberg cake and marzipan slices with almonds. My father coated the cracked hide of the three-piece suite with something called Leather Nourishment and spent an hour blowing under sheets of newspaper to get the front-room fire started.

At twenty past four, my mother's calm demeanour started to crack. At half past, the doorbell finally rang. There they stood, William and Mrs Fowler, looking like Grant Wood's painting *American Gothic*, with the barn replaced by a Victorian terrace. My grandfather had put on the only shirt and tie he owned, and had been made to wash his hair. He looked like a cross between a scarecrow and a badly embalmed corpse. And there *she* stood, the terror of the neighbourhood, decked out in navy blue, the black wicker hat wedged down hard over her steel-grey hair, the heavy ebony walking stick supporting her thick legs. She waited to be invited across the threshold, like Mrs Dracula.

'We were expecting you at four,' said Kath.

---

*The only cookery book that existed in English households for about 150 years. Mrs Beeton died at the age of twenty-eight, surprisingly not from her own cooking.

'I was told half past four,' said Mrs Fowler, daring her to disagree. As she removed her coat she glanced at the cheap hall wallpaper and sniffed disapprovingly. Her husband looked as if his collar was slowly choking him to death.

Kath attempted to guide them into the front room, but lacked the force to pull it off. Mrs Fowler walked straight past the carefully prepared neutral territory and into the little kitchen parlour where we spent most of our time. It was the only place in the house that had not been tidied up. She looked about in unconcealed distaste, pulled a handkerchief from her sleeve and wiped the kitchen chair before seating herself. 'I thought you said you had a garden,' she said, pointing out of the window. 'That's a back yard.'

'Oh yes, we do overlook the yard here,' my mother anxiously agreed, 'but the garden is conveniently located around the corner.' Anyone would have thought she was showing the place to a prospective buyer.

Mrs Fowler lumbered to her feet and went to inspect the flowerbeds. What she saw was a thirty-foot-long rubbish dump containing a collapsing corrugated-iron shelter, the remains of two old motorbikes, various holes and piles of nettle-covered bricks, some diseased nasturtiums and one stem of a succulent plant that the narcoleptic tortoise had taken a few beakfuls out of. Just below the window, a dead bush shook as the cat strained inside it, extruding a pale poo that it could not be bothered to bury. A half-eaten sausage sandwich lay on the windowsill, left by Bill when he was working on his bike.

'I'm surprised next door hasn't complained to you about rats,' said Mrs Fowler, peering at the enforced proximity of the neighbours' washing. This would have to have been the day when Percy's mum's gigantic pants were all hung out. The annoying thing was that Mrs Fowler didn't have a garden at all, so she had no right to criticize.

Discomfited by formality, William was itching to get outside and attack something with a ring spanner. He was clearly suffering from shed withdrawal.

Mrs Fowler hated being in a house where she was not in charge. She reminded me of Peggy Mount in *Sailor Beware*, a film about a pinafored battleaxe who wrecks her daughter's wedding.

'What are you feeding him?' she asked, heading towards the scullery cupboards, but Kath managed to attach herself to the passing arm that held the stick and veer it around in a smart pivot, relaunching her in the opposite direction.

'We're having high tea in the front room,' she announced, glaring at her husband and eldest son. We looked back from the doorway like a pair of craven cowards, then reversed into the narrow corridor as an advance party.

After pausing to inspect the room, my grandmother entered and lowered herself on to the sofa. Beneath her, one of the leather cushions released a dreadful flatulent sigh. Her hands could not gain purchase on the arms of the suite because they were still slippery with Leather Nourishment, and she slowly slid over.

'Move up, old girl,' said William, making a joke of it. 'We won't be giving you pickled eggs again.' She fired poisoned lances at him.

My mother offered sandwiches. Mrs Fowler took one and lifted a corner, checking inside. 'Is this paste?'

'Shippam's,' Kath assured her. 'Salmon and shrimp.'*

---

*It was a known fact that you couldn't open a jar of fish paste without wanting to eat the whole thing. Perhaps it contained morphine.

'I don't eat things from jars, you never know where they've been.' She returned it to the plate with a sniff.

'I'll have one,' said William, but his hand was slapped away.

Kath was on safer ground with the cakes, and passed them around to general compliments, with a notable silence from Mrs Fowler that everyone took as a good sign.

William's thick ridged fingernails looked absurd when placed on either side of a fairy cake. 'Are there any gherkins?' he asked. His wife made it plain that if he was planning to let the side down every single time he opened his mouth, he might as well be somewhere else. 'Come on, Billy, show me this problem with your pressure gauge,' he said, rising and wiping his hands on his trousers.

Bill released an audible sigh of relief. 'Righto, it's a bit of a bugger, but if we can take it to bits . . .' He didn't dare catch my mother's eye as the pair of them scuttled from the room. The door closed. The clock ticked. Mrs Fowler coughed. The silent seconds stretched to a minute.

'My son likes a good hot meal when he gets home from work,' she announced, apropos of nothing at all. 'Thoroughly cooked right through, not half raw. Lamb chops.' A pause. 'Pork.' No reaction. 'An occasional steak.'

Kath wasn't rising to the bait.

'Peas.' Mrs Fowler left little pauses to give her words gravitas.

'Cabbage.' Pause.

'Onions.' She stared hard at the wallpaper above Kath's head, thinking.

'Sponge pudding.' Pause.

'Custard.' Pause.

'And a banana. My son—'

' – is also my husband,' said Kath hotly. 'He is always provided with a tasty, attractive and nutritious meal.' She now sounded like a post-war diet pamphlet.

' – loves strawberry jelly for his afters.' Mrs Fowler sniffed and looked around. 'Are you planning to have more children?'

Kath looked mortified. 'No,' she said quietly, glancing at me. Steven was asleep upstairs.

'I ask because the last one clearly wasn't planned. You should think about having a coil fitted. When there are unexpected mouths to feed, you must learn to cut your cloth according—'

'I don't think I need to be told how to have children!'

'Well, there's obviously not enough money to go around.'

'We manage perfectly well.'

'Then I wonder why he complains about the amount of mince you cook.'

'Bill doesn't believe in giving me housekeeping money. I have to take night jobs—'

'Unsuitable jobs for a homemaker, no wonder he has to come to me for his meals.' She was finally enjoying herself. There was nothing like a good row to create an atmosphere in which she could breathe more freely.

'He comes to you because you won't loosen your apron strings.'

'It's his choice. I have never told him what to do.'

'Of course not, you've made it amply clear what would happen if he didn't.'

Mrs Fowler's back straightened, like a hedgehog un-furling. 'What do you mean by that?'

'You haven't spoken to your daughter for ten years. You act as if she doesn't exist, and your son's not strong enough to stand up to you.'

'So this is what you really think of your husband, is it? You push him into a marriage he's not ready for—'

'We were engaged for *six years* before he found the courage to defy you and propose!'

' – and you're still not happy with your lot!'

I buried myself in the intricacies of my train set as the two women fought for control of my father. It seemed peculiar to me that a man as weedy and inconsequential as Bill should be the subject of so many arguments. He didn't seem much of a prize. I tuned back in as my grandmother was saying, 'I didn't come here to be insulted!'

'I wonder where you usually go,' Kath speculated.

'I will not stay in this house for another minute!'

'You had to be dragged here in the first place. I'm amazed you managed to last this long,' my mother volleyed back.

'William!' called my grandmother. 'We're going home *right now*.' Turning to pick up her wicker hat, she discovered that Wobbles had just finished stripping it to shreds. She slapped the cat so hard that it flew across the room, hackled and yowling, roused from deep slumber to a state of heightened terror. Rising to her full, imposing, navy-blue light-absorbing height, she swung around to her daughter-in-law. 'I knew it! I always knew you would be nothing but trouble.'

'Of course you did,' said my mother. 'I committed the unforgivable sin of marrying your son.'

My grandmother stumped towards the door as her husband caught up with her and turned to the family with a sheepish apology on his face. Kath was white and shaking, but held her ground on the front step until he had bundled the old woman out of sight.

'Well,' she said, slamming the door with satisfying

finality and marching back down the hall, 'I feel much better for that.'

What upset her most of all was not her mother-in-law's attitude, but the fact that Bill's loyalty remained firmly planted on the wrong side.

15

The Big Picture: Part One

'We're going to be late,' I yelled down the hall.

'No, we're not,' Bill yelled back. 'There's plenty of time yet. It'll only take us ten minutes to get to the Blackheath Roxy, five minutes to park and buy Mivvis, then you've got trailers before the first feature so we'll have a good ten minutes spare. And afterwards we can look in on Mrs Fowler and Granddad.'

'It's a double bill, *Carry On Cruising* and *The Cracksman*. We'll never make it in time for the beginning,' I insisted. We were going on the only one of my father's motorbikes that was running at the moment, and part of it was still in bits on the floor of the back room. Why did I want to see *The Cracksman*, starring squeaky-voiced, baby-faced, curly-headed comic Charlie Drake? Why would anyone? It seemed as if half of all the films that showed in our cinemas were British.

'It'll only take me a minute to put the silencer back on,' Bill yelled. 'Go and find the Swarfega, I'm covered in oil.'

The best way to get out of the House of Recriminations

was to start going to the pictures in the evenings, and after much begging, it was agreed that on my eleventh birthday I would be allowed to do so. The timing was right, as I had read virtually everything in the library deemed suitable for my age except *The Mechanics of Soil Erosion* in the reference section.

I had always been allowed to go to the flicks during the day, but that limited you to Disney films starring blue-eyed, perky, pigtailed talent-vacuum Hayley Mills, and Ray Harryhausen's piratical fantasies. Not that I had anything against Harryhausen; he had souped up Jules Verne stories to create movies like *Mysterious Island* and *First Men in the Moon*. His finest moment came with *Jason and the Argonauts*, as the gods showed signs of mortality and mortals displayed heroism close to godliness. The jerky stop-frame animations actually helped certain scenes, especially in the electrifying moment when the huge statue of Talos came creakingly to life and stepped down from his pedestal, complemented by a wonderful Bernard Hermann score that set the hairs rising behind my ears.

In *The Valley of Gwangi* Harryhausen pitted some rather camp cowboys against stop-framed blue-tinged dinosaurs. It never occurred to me that this was a strange subject for a film, since I had encountered it before, in a stinker called *The Beast of Hollow Mountain*. Sadly, there were only two cowboys-versus-dinosaurs* films for me to see, but the former was blessed with a stirring score and some genuinely peculiar moments involving a very tiny horse. Later, I also loved *One Million Years BC*, a historically dubious cavemen-versus-dinosaurs film that looked like the 'before' section of a hair-conditioner commercial,

*The only thing more exciting than this scenario would have been pirates versus aliens.

which had Raquel Welch posing in a chamois-leather bikini and little chamois bootees while giant prehistoric turtles lumbered sleepily across Gran Canaria.

Gradually I came to see how such films worked their magic. The classic Harryhausen signatures, I noted in my diary, were as follows:

A dinosaur tethered with a rope, simply to make kids ask, 'How did they do that?'

Mysteriously tousled fur, which indicated the problems of working with hairy animated models.

A climactic roaring fight between two mythical monsters, which ended with one biting the other's neck.

I tried re-creating these creatures in the form of plasticine models, but the more I re-used the modelling clay the more it merged into one colour, which was usually a sort of foul-smelling brownish purple.

There was other children's fare at the pictures, of course. *tom thumb* was a rare example of a successful English film that could stand beside *The Railway Children* and the horrible-but-indulgently-recalled-with-fondness *Chitty Chitty Bang Bang*. *tom thumb*'s creepy Yawning Man, with its resemblance to every child's weirdest old relative, and a lengthy dance piece involving Russ Tamblyn somersaulting around a cupboardful of animated toys, lingered on in my dreams for years.

Other films disturbed, creating ruffles in my subconscious that could not easily be smoothed away. Moments in the most innocuous Disney films bothered me, usually ones involving sudden upheavals in home life. Every child got upset when brave hillbilly pooch Old Yeller died, because everyone related to the loss of a pet, but I found the idea of uprooted kids setting off in search of relatives deeply disturbing. I was also bothered by the way in which handsome American heroes seemed comfortable strutting around without shirts on, not minding who looked at them. I always wore a vest, a shirt, a jumper and a raincoat, topping the ensemble with a cap and a scarf, like a Victorian child actor.

My mother had decided I was unusually sensitive after seeing me reduced to tears by the animated version of *One Hundred and One Dalmatians*, not because the dogs had been kidnapped by Cruella De Vil but because their loss had really upset the maid. Was this normal behaviour in a child, she wondered?

It also bothered me when characters met in a restaurant and left before finishing their meal, or, worse still, when one ordered, argued with the other and left before the food arrived. I also hated characters half-shaving before wiping the rest of the soap off with a towel, or getting out of the shower and wrapping a towel around themselves without drying their backs properly. I hated them getting out of taxis and thrusting a note at the driver without saying thank you, or not giving a full address or time on the phone but just saying something like 'Meet me at the station.'

Kath could see how this fastidiousness might derail more significant concerns, and wanted to keep me on track. She quietly decided it was time for me to leave behind kiddie fare. I would finally be allowed to see 'A' films.

The English attitude to film suffered from the weight of the nation's theatrical past. Our cinemas had grown out of converted variety houses and music halls. In 1921, *The Four Horsemen of the Apocalypse* had premiered at London's Palace Theatre with thirty members of staff creating live sound effects with coconut shells, as if it was still a stage play.

Variety acts and one-reelers shared the same bill right up to the Second World War, and many theatres kept projection equipment to fill in between acts. After the War, while Hollywood was sending John Wayne* across the Nevada horizon, the English were busy transcribing the delicate slights of *The Importance of Being Earnest* to celluloid.† Only a handful of English films had any sense of landscape, and those that did had but a fragmentary connection with the past, which, in a country with an urban society more than two thousand years old, was a little odd.

For the rest of my life, the act of going to the cinema would trigger deep-seated childhood memories in me; not just the tang of cheap snouts and Jeyes Fluid,‡ but the whole experience of communal emotion. For a child who was imaginative and a bit lonely, the cinema was a place where barely acknowledged feelings crystallized into something real and vivid. I grew up with strange loyalties to certain films – why else would I and all my friends have sat through so many identical incarnations of James Bond? Attitudes to class percolated through English comedies in order to condescend to the working man, sneer at the nouveau riche, vilify management and pillory the State, until it was hard to work out who on earth I was supposed to empathize with.

But I needed to see English films because Hollywood didn't reflect my world. I watched mystified as Californian kids went to school in sports cars, girls in eye make-up were branded 'bad', dads attended a weird ritual called Little League, people said, 'Try to get some sleep, you look terrible' when the person they were talking to looked fantastic, teenagers climbed into each other's bedrooms

---

*Real name Marion Morrison. You can't have a butch cowboy star with a name like a girl and a supermarket.
†The Americans were exploring wild new frontiers while we were working out how to say 'A *handbag*?'.
‡A disinfectant whose smell is inextricably bound up with the smell of sick.

via trellises, fathers called their daughters 'Pumpkin' and boys called their fathers 'Sir', black people didn't mix with white people, police handcuffed you face-down for doing nothing wrong, wives always died instead of getting a divorce, and everyone shrieked and bellowed at each other at the tops of their voices instead of having normal, quiet conversations.

What was it with the brown paper grocery bags that had no handles? How were you meant to carry them? And there were all those guns. To children raised on *Dixon of Dock Green*,* America seemed like the Wild West. Having been taught that displays of public emotion were a sign of innate vulgarity, the mix of violence and sentimentality I witnessed on the screen was thrilling and shameless.

All films were partly about recognition, so it mattered where they were set. It was great being able to recognize a local area when it appeared on screen, so films were also about geography. American movies often had a wonderful sense of location. Theirs was a lateral society, an open, sprawling, outdoor canvas upon which to paint colourful, exciting pictures. English films, by comparison, reflected an indoor sensibility. Where Americans rode and drove and waved and shouted and fired guns at the sky, the English sat and discussed and apologized and cupped their cigarettes inside their hands so as not to annoy the person next to them. This private indoor distinction, the careful attention to space and conversation, was one of the most noticeable traits in English films.

For me they acted as an alternative to the view from Hollywood, and even though many of them were truly

*'Evening all.' It wasn't much of a catchphrase, but after watching this TV series no child could pass a policeman without saying it.

dreadful, I was able to find fractured reflections of my life there, my language, my hopes and fears.

The gap that existed between British cinema and Hollywood became clear when I considered the word 'pilot'. In the context of American film, I got John Wayne killing Japs. In the British equivalent, I got Terence Alexander muttering 'Crikey' and fondling the ends of his handlebar moustache.

The British studios had been built on London's drab outskirts, and if their films reflected the past, they presented an image of a rapidly disappearing country: a world of chaps in sensible jumpers and strange hats, misty suburbs, empty roads and grimy canals, coffee-bar girls in pointy sweaters, spivs and dolly birds, jokes about pickled onions and wind, steam trains, bombsites, cheery constables armed with whistles, nurses in suspenders (often in drag), stationmasters, dowagers, vicars, workmen and bureaucrats. The received wisdom was that British films were constipated, class-ridden, conservative and vulgar, but I found them slightly magical, if only because I sensed they represented a world that was soon to vanish completely.

In the years that followed, my movie-going involved visiting cavernous damp auditoriums with names like Roxy, ABC, Forum, Bijou, Gaumont, Gaity, Victory, Eldorado, Tolmer, Essoldo, Embassy and Granada. Cinemas were everywhere. I came to revel in films that were populist, unfashionable, unfunny, forgotten, offbeat and very, very bad, because they were all concerned with telling English stories. Many of them had developed into series: the Hammers, the Carry Ons, the Cliff Richard films, the Doctor films, the Quatermass films, the Will Hays, the Arthur Askeys, the George Formbys, the Bonds, the horror anthologies, the Norman Wisdoms, the St Trinians and numerous other strands that wove themselves through the decades. All too often they scraped by on the goodwill of the entertainment-starved public and the barest of cinematographic credentials. Television could not compete; even *Carry On Nurse* was better than squinting at a picture through a ten-inch rectangle of thick glass. Little did I suspect that I would one day get the chance to watch it again on the two-inch screen of a mobile phone.

Of course at the age of eleven, glued to a horsehair chair, sucking a Jubbly in my school-regulation gabardine mac and interference-encouraging short trousers, I was hardly an image-saturated jade. Everything was new. When a movie character in a tense situation said, 'I've got a bad feeling about this', 'We should all try to get some sleep' or 'You search the basement, I'll take a look around outside', I did not think it was a cliché, I thought it was utterly original. When the soundtrack music boomed ominously and the heroine went off to wander about a basement full of dripping pipes, I, fragile, easily influenced and perched on my itchy seat as delicately as a piece of Dresden, was coated in a moist craquelure of fear, my attention dragged away from poking about in confectionery, my jaw slack with amazement.

I knew I had betrayed my beloved books, with their cracked spines and dusty pages, for their flashier, shinier cousins, but I didn't care. By its very nature, seduction requires a loss of reason.

16

The Big Picture: Part Two

I lost my innocence in the damp smoky stalls of the last great palaces, the ones with interiors the size of bus garages. There was a post-war reek about those rows of curve-backed seats with ashtrays, the peeling art-deco ceilings lined with partially fused stars, the handful of silhouetted patrons sprouting out of the stalls like tombstones. Cinematically speaking, I was a child of the sixties, but still spent my time in the picture houses of the forties.

I read books on the history of film, and discovered that it had long been a risky business. Prior to a back-spool being invented for projectors, the highly flammable nitrate stock unwound into a wicker basket that would periodically burst into flame. On 4 May 1897, at the Paris Charity Bazaar near the Champs-Elysées, wood and canvas booths had been constructed in the style of a sixteenth-century town, and a cinematograph caught fire. One hundred and forty distinguished guests were burned alive. The cinema industry had already been having trouble finding favour with the public, but this high-profile disaster set it back years.

The cinema projector remained a dangerous item long after the invention of the back-spool, because it depended on the burning of a magnesium-alloy stick which illuminated the footage as it passed. The stick had to be wound forward manually by the projectionist as it burned down, and if the film jammed it blistered and ignited in the heat. This system remained in place until well into the sixties, and in some cinemas until much later. It seemed bizarre to spend so much money developing sophisticated film techniques, only to print them on to a flammable strip that had to be clawed through a clanking mechanical device the size of a Victorian boiler.

One evening, on my way in to see *Pirates of Blood River*, I picked up a recruitment leaflet at the ABC that said 'Become a Cinema Manager!' Inside the folded A4 sheet was a picture of a man in a two-tone lime-green polyester suit and matching tie, looking very pleased with himself. This is what the copy beside it said:

Your Schedule as a Cinema Manager

Thursday – A chance to see your new film.

Friday – Check local advertising for misprints.

Saturday – Meet and greet visiting film stars on publicity tours. [Unlikely, seeing as this was in suburban Blackheath, not then known as a playground of the stars.]

Sunday – Check confectionery stand and re-order ice creams.

Monday – Pensioners' matinées will keep you on your toes!

Tuesday – Cinema washroom hygiene check and another chance to see your film.

Wednesday – Your day off, and a well-earned rest!

Hurrah, I shall become an ABC Cinema manager, I thought, *but first I'll get Mum and Dad to take me to the pictures regularly. They'll fall in love properly this time, holding hands in the dark sharing Kia-Ora* and Maltesers,[†] and everything will be fine.*

Except that didn't happen because Kath had to work, so my father and I started going by ourselves twice a week, on Mondays and Fridays (the programme changed on Thursdays). The ABC Blackheath and the Greenwich Granada were both within walking distance of Westerdale Road, but we always managed to miss the beginning of the support feature because Bill took ages locking up his motorbike or had to refix a nut that had become loose.

As a consequence, I saw hundreds of films minus the first twenty minutes, and so had to extemporize some sort of plot device that would place the characters in the situation I found them upon arrival. The one that confounded me most was *They Came to Rob Las Vegas*, because by the time we had seated ourselves, the cast were already stuck inside an armoured car that appeared to have sunk underneath the desert sand. I could not work out how these people had got themselves into such a situation. For years after, I remained at a loss to explain what an armoured car was doing underground.

I watched all sorts of popular rubbish, but often found reasons for liking films that others had overlooked. I was quick to notice that the music from many of the Carry On films was wittier and subtler than any of the scripts.

---

*A drink in a plastic tub you could slurp dry and then bang with your fists, scaring everyone.
[†]Purchased in boxes because they were sophisticated, until you dropped them all over the floor.

It turned out that the co-composer, Bruce Montgomery, also happened to be the brilliant crime novelist Edmund Crispin, who created one of fiction's greatest detectives, Gervase Fen. He and Eric Rogers quoted everything from Giuseppe Verdi to Percy Grainger in their slapstick sound-track scores. It was a tradition that continued for years. Much later, I noticed that the theme to *Carry On Matron* echoed part of *The Beggar's Opera*, presumably because one of the film's subtitles was *The Preggars Opera*.

Bill's taste ran to Elvis movies, of which there seemed to be several thousand, all exactly the same and all featuring a scene in which Elvis sang to a girl while driving along a back-lit road in a sports car the size of a carnival float, late-period Jerry Lewis movies when he was at his most shrill and imbecilic, and films shot in Cinerama to make up for the fact that they stank. On Sundays there were ancient double-bills, usually St Trinians, Norman Wisdom, horrible old cowboy films and threadbare medical comedies designed to test the faith of the most devout cinema-goer.

My mother had more genteel, if somewhat conflicting, tastes; the first two proper films she took me to see were *20,000 Leagues under the Sea* and George Bernard Shaw's *The Devil's Disciple*. We veered between *Hamlet* and *South Pacific*, *That Darn Cat!* and *Becket*, *Nicholas Nickleby* and *Monkeys Go Home*. She did not think that this was any odder than my father sitting through three-quarters of an Elvis movie before watching *El Cid*. Kath freely admitted that her ideal film would probably have starred Richard Burton and Mitzi Gaynor.

When it came to films, the family was profligate with its praise, in awe of Technicolor and hopelessly uncritical, although my mother had a lower threshold for comedies, most of which she regarded as unnecessarily silly. She couldn't handle slapstick at all. 'That's not acting,' she would say, tightening her cardigan in disapproval, 'that's just showing off.'

There was something quintessentially common-sensical about English films. The heroes wore woolly scarves. They strode upstairs with a purposeful air. They drank lots of tea and were polite to ladies. They said 'Oh . . . hello!' when greeting other members of the cast, as if bumping into old friends.* Even when they were married to their co-stars in real life, like Bill Travers and Virginia McKenna, they never indulged in granny-frightening sexual banter. They lived and worked in small English towns where no riff-raff was tolerated, and where policemen stopped single women in the street to ask what they were up to. I came to prefer the dubbed, squeezed and censored Italian films that ran as B-movies, and was able to see lurid *giallos* like Dario Argento's *Four Flies on Grey Velvet* and SF-tinged capers such as Mario Bava's *Danger: Diabolik*. Cut to bits, lackadaisically dubbed into Americanese and scratched to buggery, they always featured blonde Euro-starlets like Elsa Martinelli and Virna Lisi in heavy eye make-up and white kinky boots. English girls just weren't like that. They were more like Una Stubbs.†

The 'Pah pa-pa-pa, pa-pa pa-pa' of the white Pearl & Dean temple heralded the arrival of pinkly faded ads for restaurants whose stern middle-class voiceovers always began, 'Come to the restaurant where the service is friendly and the food excellent. Come to the restaurant in *this* high street,' cutting to a badly superimposed address over a generic shot of a hugely coiffured man in wide lapels and his miniskirted bird, eating orange spaghetti in front of radioactive wallpaper.

---

*In *Horror Express*, Peter Cushing greets Christopher Lee with a cry of 'Well, well, look who's here!' as if they had just bumped into each other in the studio canteen.
†Finest hour: squeaky girlfriend in *Summer Holiday*.

In post-war England, there was something apologetic and embarrassed about my film heroes. They wore pullovers and drove Morris Minors. They sounded like the Speaking Clock. They smoked pipes and told their wives, 'You're looking a bit peaky, darling.' It was a long way from John Wayne. I wanted to see more cowboys and dinosaurs, but instead got Rita Tushingham wandering around in black and white.

The problem was paradoxical: I related to English films, but was drawn to the dumb chromium-plated gorgeousness of Hollywood. American films had embraced the power of the image. England was still obsessed with words. *I* was obsessed with words.

Thinking about it, I realized that most English books for boys were filled with the adventures of explorers, sea captains, hunters, generals and brave, self-sacrificing men and women. They were never disreputable. The catalyst for most adventures, in fact, seemed to be an unforgivable breach of manners on behalf of the villain.

Before I was born, England had produced more than its fair share of costume dramas, both in literature and on screen. There had been a rush to translate the classics and the great historical stories on to film. Alexander Korda's *The Private Life of Henry VIII* had been followed by films about Nell Gwyn, Rembrandt, Queen Victoria, Florence Nightingale, Henry V, Caesar and Cleopatra, Nelson and Isadora Duncan. Between them were social comedies, morality plays, dramas, musicals, filmed versions of the great Dickens novels, the plays of Oscar Wilde and Noël Coward, work from Shakespeare, D. H. Lawrence, A. J. Cronin, Graham Greene, Terrence Rattigan, John Braine, H. G. Wells and Nigel Kneale. But by the time the sixties rolled around, the nation was reconnecting with a largely ignored underclass, and would soon become obsessed with soaps like *Coronation Street*.

I wondered why England lagged so far behind the rest of the world when it came to producing cinema, until I discovered a sobering fact. By the time the English authorities decided to tear down the doors of Newgate Prison, London's notorious seven-hundred-year-old lair of highwaymen and cut-throats, America was already showing its first motion pictures to delighted audiences. It was one of those peculiar historical overlaps that seemed impossible but true, like the idea of Oscar Wilde travelling by tube, or the fountain pen being invented after the telephone.

The country's venerable traditions held everyone back from entering such a technologically innovative field as cinema. A crippling war had shut down production, the limitations of Odeon and ABC exhibition reduced choice, the property boom hastened the end of large auditoriums, and English cinema was allowed to slink silently away. There was a paralysing stiffness in old English films that didn't really fade until the late fifties. I could see it in the actors and in my parents, who clearly aspired to be Celia Johnson and John Mills. The only difference was that my mother would never try to chuck herself under a train for unrequited love, any more than my father would attempt to trek across North Africa. If anything, they were more like Moira Lister and Sid James.

I knew the screen lied. As a child I saw two real-life celebrities in the flesh. At the Lord Mayor's Show, my mother held me up above the barrier to see Dick Van Dyke driving Chitty Chitty Bang Bang at the head of the parade. I was shocked to discover that the actor had a bright-orange face, and seemed to be wearing a brown wig made for someone with a smaller head.

Worse, Frankie Howerd had once stepped from a rather old, rented Rolls Royce to open our local fête. Curiously, he too had an orange face and a wig held on by clearly visible sections of tape. He was also extremely camp in a pleasant auntie-ish way, and as he was a film star everyone loved him. Had he tried not being famous for half an hour and merely walked to the shops for some fags, the locals would have kicked him unconscious.

Cinema retained its ability to grip. The defining features of being a very small boy in a very large auditorium were:

The sound, which boomed in an eerie lighthouse-in-the-fog fashion that could induce melancholia in the happiest scenes.

The bored ice-cream girl, whose sulky glossed lips and sleepy eyes made a Drink-On-A-Stick appear provocative.

A pleasingly musty smell that has now vanished from cinemas, possibly due to the invention of upholstery shampoo.

And of course, the possibility of being tampered with by a man in a gabardine raincoat.

Eventually, low-budget English films played in London cinemas that were far too grand to support movies with such low production values. This anomaly became apparent when I noticed that the curtains of the Odeon Woolwich were more luxurious than the film I was watching.

No matter. An education in the world of adult storytelling had been initiated. Now I could go home and tell Kath all about the films I'd seen, instead of her always telling me. I decided to fill my Letts Schoolboy Diary* with reviews of all the films I sat through, awarding them between one and four stars. If I couldn't illustrate the reviews with stills, I would do the next best thing:

---

*Listed important calendar dates like 'Public Holiday in Tonga'.

re-create the scenes with cardboard scenery and six-inch-high plasticine models, then take Polaroids of them. I would use black and white plasticine for the monochrome movies. It never occurred to me that adopting this hobby over, say, constructing an Airfix Messerschmitt would make me appear as mad as a bag of cats.

Just as I had predicted, it took my father longer than he thought to put the motorbike back together that night, and we ended up missing the first twenty minutes of *The Cracksman*. By the time we arrived, Charlie Drake was trapped in a sewer, but we had no idea why. Perhaps now, I thought, I would be allowed to go to the cinema alone. At least that would mean I would no longer have to spend my evenings in the kitchen watching my father taking the clock to bits before putting it back together again and finding he had three cogs left over. And I might even learn something about storytelling in the process.

It occurred to me that I was all set up for the rest of my childhood. I was happy enough at home, doing well at school, there were cinemas and bookshops near by, I could fill a thousand notebooks with drawings and stories, and my parents could carry on arguing into the next century as far as I was concerned, because I no longer wanted to be a cinema manager: I wanted to be a scriptwriter, and if no one could show me how to do it I would have to teach myself. I'd seen *The Parent Trap*. Good God, it couldn't be that difficult. All you had to do was remember to leave a gap where Hayley Mills could sing a song on a banjo.

The future looked great, provided everything stayed exactly as it was.

And then we were forced to move out of our home.

17

Running Away

On the balsa-wood model in the Perspex box at Greenwich Town Hall, the Council's planned six-lane motorway went straight through East Greenwich, splitting it in two. On either side of the grey band, smiling plastic figures in hats strolled past as if taking the air in Monte Carlo. In the middle of it was the spot where our house should have been, so it stood to reason that we would have to move.

Number 35, Westerdale Road was to be compulsorily purchased and knocked flat, along with the whole end of the street. This meant destroying the furniture shop, the bakery, the grocery, the newsagent and the launderette, and chopping the town into two halves, separated by a roaring, stinking channel that would be impossible to cross. It meant wiping a London village off the map and covering it with a very wide bit of Tarmac.

Incredibly, nobody complained. Not so much as a leaflet was produced arguing against the plan. There wasn't even a meeting held in Farmdale church hall entitled 'Town To Be Demolished For Six Lane Motorway – Good Or Bad Thing?' Did everyone hate living here that much?

Of course, at a time when everyone was smashing up every last bit of the past and either replacing it with hardboard or shovelling it through a letterbox on *It's A Knockout*, the motorway was perceived as progress. So what if it didn't lead anywhere and killed a community in a manner that everyone would be complaining about thirty years later? A rallying cry for the future had been raised: *What do we want? A road to nowhere! When do we want it? Just as soon as we can get out of the way of the bulldozers!*

The future was coming and the car was king. Beeching* had closed all the railway branch lines that merely served annoying little villages, supermarkets needed supplies and motorways were to be built everywhere, especially pseudo-American freeway-type roads on stilts that looked stylish when carved out of balsa wood, painted white and put in a Perspex box in the mayor's office, but which proved to be less ideal when they were constructed in concrete next to your bedroom window, and became covered with soot overnight from the exhaust of passing trucks delivering Vesta Chow Mein to the Co-op.

If you had asked any of the architects whether they thought kids might start stabbing each other or doing drugs in the ominous shadow of the underpasses, or whether lives would be destroyed in quieter, more desperate ways than ever before, they would have raised their eyebrows incredulously and waved you from their presence, reciting mantras of progress. Everyone wanted a car, didn't they? Everybody wanted fabric softener and tinned cocktail sausages? Well, there was a price to pay for status. Westerdale Road, Farmdale Road and Ormiston Crescent

---

*Dr Richard Beeching, hated politician, who pruned back a railway system that had existed since Edwardian times. Made a Baron, of course. (It has been suggested that Beeching was unfairly scapegoated by other, more culpable politicians.)

could boast just four cars between them, and one of those had been on blocks since the days of petrol rationing. Just imagine a world where everyone had a car!

The instruction to move came from the government in the form of a terse two-paragraph letter, so the residents of East Greenwich went into cap-doffing mode and did what they were told, assuming that those in charge knew better than they. A very thin man in a black astrakhan coat came around and peered into the rooms of Number 35, marking ticks and crosses in his book.

'Oh dear,' he said, peering gingerly into the garden. 'We really must get rid of these outdoor lavatories.'

'That's the only place where I get a bit of peace and quiet,' said Bill indignantly.

'How would you like a nice bath?' said the thin man from Greenwich Council.

'How would you like a punch in the mouth?' said Bill, who was usually never brave enough to say anything rude. Kath shot him an embarrassed look. 'Well, he's saying we're not clean.'

To smooth things over, the man from the Council went into the front room and admired it. 'Oh yes, very nice,' he complimented Kath. 'Do you collect art deco?'

'No,' Kath replied. 'This is our furniture.'

The man noted the cream-tiled fireplace with disapproval. 'You're in a smokeless zone now, you know.'

'Oh, we know,' said Kath. 'We don't use it. My husband just keeps brazil nuts in the coal scuttle.'

Just two weeks after he went away, we received another letter with an offer for the house, only it was not really an offer because my parents could not refuse it. Kath had a little cry in the kitchen. Bill stood in the rubbish-strewn garden, looking out towards the railway embankment as if taking his last sight of England's shores.

I sat on the end of the sofa, trying to console my mother.

'Look at it this way,' I offered, 'we can finally get away from Mrs Fowler. We can move further into London, the other side of Greenwich, the nice side. There'll be bookshops and cinemas and libraries and things for us to do. We can make new friends and start afresh in a nice brand-new house that doesn't need anything doing to it. Dad will enjoy himself so much that he won't feel the need to saw up sheets of asbestos in the kitchen while you're trying to lay the table.'

'Your father already has an idea about where he wants to move,' said Kath glumly. 'Further out, to a run-down place called Abbey Wood. He's seen a great big old house in the middle of nowhere, away from anyone. It still has gas lamps fitted on the top floor. I haven't seen it yet, but apparently it needs an awful lot of work. It's cheap because it's virtually falling down.'

If there had been a basement in our little house, my heart would have tumbled into it.

We were to be refugees. The Council was tying little tags on our raincoats and packing us off to the hinterland.

I had to say goodbye to Pauline.

She was sitting on the low wall at the end of the street, waiting for the express to pass by. Her summer eyes and bobbed hair made her look French, or what I imagined French girls to look like.

'Have you finished with the Ark?' I asked casually.

'Oh, I've outgrown that,' Pauline explained, tugging her dress over her knees. 'I've moved on to a Junior Miss Make-up Kit.'

'We're going away,' I said. 'I'll probably never see you again.'

'Yes, we're moving too, up to Derbyshire. They're knocking down our house as well. My mother says the Council is full of Philistines.'

Trust her to bring up the Bible at a time like this, I thought. *I'm better off without her.*

'Do you want me to kiss you goodbye?' I asked.

'It's a bit late now, isn't it?' she said, obviously mis-interpreting the concept of a goodbye kiss.

'Do you want my new address then?'

'I suppose so.' She didn't sound too bothered either way.

'Can I have yours?'

'I've no idea what it is. I'll write to you once I get it.'

I had already scrawled out my new address on the back of one of my mother's cigarette coupons. I handed it to her. 'You won't forget, will you?'

'I'll try not to, although I'll be making a lot of new friends soon. Girls reach puberty earlier than boys.'

I had no idea what she was talking about. My sex education had consisted of my father coming into the kitchen one day and asking, 'Do you know about the birds and the bees?' When I had nodded, Bill said, 'Thank God for that,' and went outside for a fag.

'I'm going to miss sitting here waiting for the five eleven to pass,' she said wistfully. 'Look, there are bluebells all the way up to the track.'

'I'm going to miss you,' I decided.

'Don't be soft,' she told me, heading off to pick flowers on the embankment. I watched Pauline in her yellow cotton summer dress, intently uprooting stalks as clouds of dandelion seeds drifted past her into blueness. On that afternoon she was the archetypal fifties little girl in white socks, sandals and plaits. Soon she would grow tall and become aware of herself and what she meant to others. But for this brief moment she was still a child, intent and dismissive. The sunlight was so strong that perhaps she would leave behind an after-image of herself at this spot, untroubled, self-absorbed, picking flowers forever against an infinite azure sky.

I knew that I would never see her again. Five years later, she wrote to tell me that her mother had died, but her letter had the stiff formality of a stranger's.

The next Saturday, we all went to take a look at the property. It was infinitely worse than my mother and I had feared, perched on a hill that managed to be in permanent shadow because it was surrounded by tall trees with dripping, sticky leaves. The house was vast, damp and rambling, half-buried beneath cobwebby undergrowth that would ensure it never saw light even in midsummer. It hadn't rained for a while, but everything was wet. The peeling red iron gate stood beneath leering, broken gargoyles. Broken chequered tiles tripped us up. Fat dark spiders sat in the dripping eaves, waiting to drop on our heads. Cracked, filthy windows peered blindly down. Furry green stuff had formed on most of the brickwork and the window frames nearest the woods were covered in cankerous toadstools. It was as if the house had died about twenty years ago and was slowly rotting away. I looked up at the attic window, half expecting to see Norman Bates peering down.

We knew that Bill would never be able to afford to renovate the place. My heart had flattened to a pancake. My father would try to do it all by himself – or worse still, would get me to help him, which spelled certain doom. He would do this by making me put away my notebooks and forcing me to hold things covered in Bostik and G-clamps, and the house would never be finished as long as we lived, and we would be wretchedly miserable and it would spell a long, slow, damp, creeping death for us all.

So I decided not to go there.

On the Saturday morning that the Bishops removal van*

*Venerable removal service. Motto (over picture of chessboard): 'It's Your Move!'

arrived, I packed a bag of books and some jam sandwiches, and ran away. In retrospect, I should probably have thought the whole thing through and picked somewhere less obvious to hide than in the Granada cinema, but the library was now off-limits. I watched a double bill of *The Bulldog Breed* and *Carry On Regardless* go around three times before the usherette grew suspicious and called the police. She knew that no one could survive such repetition unless they had an ulterior reason for doing so.

The new house was called Cyril Villa, which was about the most embarrassing name you could give to a human being, let alone a house. The woods at its edge were not beautiful, but filled with rotting ferns, reeking orange fungus, stinging stuff and dog shit. The other side was overlooked by an incredibly ugly council estate, where the residents kept bikes and laundry on their balconies, and shouted 'Oi, d'you wanna punch in the faghole?' if I caught their eye. The people who lived there instantly hated us because they thought we must be posh. Obviously, they had no idea who they were dealing with.

My mother made me stay away from the council-flat children as they swore and smoked and stared too hard at passers-by, as if thinking about robbing them. I imagined that as they too were broke and bored they couldn't be all that different from me, except that they never seemed to carry books about, not even comics, and I couldn't think of a way of talking to them that wouldn't make me sound like Prince Philip, visiting their estate on a fact-finding tour.

My brother loved the new house and its secret back door into nettle-swamped woodlands, into which he could toddle out and fall down, to be lost beneath tendrils of bindweed. There were millions of places for him to get trapped in, including a dangerous derelict building with a collapsing roof and penises drawn all over it. As a little boy, Steven was blonder, bluer-eyed and even more adorable than he had been as a baby, while I remained a knobbly, lumpy pile of bones arranged in a roughly upright stack.

The house was awful. Its aura of melancholy pervaded the very air, reducing my mother to tears. Bill failed to notice this as he set up his Black & Decker rotary saw and wondered if he could get Steven to hold a plank steady.

In order to protect the family in this remote spot, he bought a dog from a man at work which had supposedly been trained to attack burglars on sight, a hypertensive Dobermann pinscher with insane eyes and an uncontrollable drooling problem. It spent the whole time in the hall, staring at things that were either just out of sight or didn't exist, and would periodically explode into fits of apoplectic barking for no apparent reason, before over-exerting itself and passing out. Apparently something had gone wrong during its training, and it now suspected everyone.

The dog and the house hated me. Even the woods hated me. I half suspected that the trees might start throwing things at me, like the ones in *The Wizard of Oz*. At the first available opportunity, I caught the bus back to Westerdale Road, and to my horror arrived just as the workmen were smashing down the front wall of our house with bulldozers.

A small crowd had gathered to watch as the wrecking ball swung and our interiors came into view. There was our kitchen, and now our outside toilet was being revealed in all its utilitarian shame.

Mortified by the sight of the silky, wanton Japanese wallpaper in my parents' bedroom being exposed to the people on the street, I lowered my gaze and beetled off to the Roxy to fill my head with ludicrous stories.

18

Mother Makes a Friend

Reasons Why the Era of Swinging London Began in 1960

John F. Kennedy became President of the United States, a country England adored, despite the fact that their war reparations crippled the British economy for nearly six decades.

The UN called for the end of apartheid, which my mother said was A Good Thing.

National Service ended, giving rise to the phenomenon of the Hairy Good-for-Nothing Layabout, according to my father.

The Pill appeared, signalling the end of back-street abortionists and films set beside Black Country canals.

Lady Chatterley's Lover was published uncut and turned up on Bill's bedside table, the only time he ever tried to read a classic. Judging by the cracks on the spine, he got about a third of the way through.

Hitchcock's *Psycho* gave birth to the slasher movie. Sales of showers dropped off.

Just around the corner, temporally speaking, were sex and violence, Andy Warhol, James Bond, graffiti, the World on the Brink, the Berlin Wall, topless dresses, hippies, punks, skinheads, Vietnam, Crimplene, Carnaby Street, race riots, psychedelic drugs, Corfam,* colour TV, *Hair*, discotheques, Monty Python and everything else that heralded the beginning of the end of the civilized world, according to my father. Not that he was involved in any world movements, because by this time we had lost him to the wonderful world of DIY.

Now that we had the new house and Christmas was approaching, Bill announced that he would get some serious home improvement done. My mother did not greet this news with enthusiasm. Humming to himself, Bill fired up his blowlamp and set about destroying Cyril Villa.

Being now geographically removed from his parents (albeit only by about six miles), Bill could not simply ramble up the hill to see them every five minutes. He needed something else to do, and as the house we had moved into was virtually uninhabitable, the siren call of DIY beckoned. Other men had a passion for busty platinum blondes who worked in espresso bars. Bill was in love with hardboard.

He scraped off half the wallpaper in the lounge, then

---

*'The miracle leather replacement!' Except it didn't breathe and never softened. Bill had a pair of Corfam shoes and nearly crippled himself with them. He also owned an eight-track cartridge player that only had two tapes: Jim Reeves and Elvis.

sawed through several of the banisters. He demolished half the kitchen wall. He tore up carpets and some of the floorboards. He hacked a number of huge holes in the concrete side alley, just to see what was underneath. He fell through the ceiling in my brother's room, then glued a sheet of brown paper over the hole, which remained in place for the next eight years. He painted over the beautiful Victorian varnished wood of the staircase with magnolia undercoat, then repainted it an unnatural shade of faux-wood, dragging a comb through the garish paint to create artificial wood-grain. The overall effect was like looking at a cheap prop staircase from an unpopular period TV series. He glued several rolls of wiggly-line wallpaper that resembled television interference all along the landing. It could give my mother a headache just walking past the bedrooms.

We spent our first Christmas in Cyril Villa without any heat at all. My father had nearly blown us up by demolishing the gas mantles on the top floor without realizing that the pipes were still connected. He tore out the boiler and the fireplaces, but didn't get around to putting anything in their place. He laid thick olive-green nylon wall-to-wall carpet that electrocuted you if you walked across it in bare feet. Finally, he added more fake-wood panelling to the house, making it even gloomier and more depressing than it had been to start with, so that it eventually looked like a witches' forest inside as well as out.

For reasons known only to himself, he decided to hardboard the walls of the upstairs toilet and add mock-Tudor beams, which he painted gloss magnolia, a shade that was fast shaping up to be his favourite colour. Then he lowered the ceilings, covering up elaborate cornicing and ceiling roses with more hardboard, polystyrene and asbestos, all of which he sawed up in the kitchen. For months I watched my father chain-smoking un-filter-tipped Woodbines and hacksawing, surrounded by drifting white clouds of asbestos fibre.

Bill learned how to varnish from a magazine, mixed his own solution and covered every remaining surface with it – only he'd balanced the solution wrongly, so it had the consistency of a freshly made toffee apple and never fully dried. Five years later, Kath's cardigan sleeves would still stick to the dining-room table as though they had been Velcro'd in place. She only made the mistake of leaving table mats on the bare surface once – it had taken a chisel to get them off.

After the War, many of the houses that had been presumed to be sturdy survivors of the Blitz were revealed to have bomb damage. Sometimes mere hairline cracks had weakened walls so much that they simply fell down on random dates. As a small child, I had been taken to the doctor one morning with a chest complaint, and while my mother and I were out the lounge ceiling dropped down, smashing the furniture to pieces. For the next five years I had slept with a blanket over my face, in fear of my dream-weighted skies falling in and crushing me to death.

At least Cyril Villa wasn't going to collapse. It would probably still be standing in a million years' time, long after the rest of the country had been blown to Kingdom Come and the ants had taken over. Bill proudly pointed out that the walls were as thick as a church's, which was probably why it was so depressing inside and nobody could ever get warm. Sometimes you could see your breath in the lounge.

Because the house was surrounded by high trees, the only place that had any television reception was a spot seven feet off the ground in the corner of the rear attic, so nobody bothered watching TV. Anyway, Bill preferred to bash things to bits in the back room while Kath tried to read. Gigantic rhododendrons with flowers the colour of fag ash blocked the remaining light from the windows, and as Bill wasn't keen on putting the lights on, it was a wonder we didn't all go blind. The building creaked and groaned. The floorboards broke wind and a cold draught seemed to come up through the toilet.

As Steven clearly wasn't up to it, I helped my father by holding spanners, wrenches, socket sets, screws, nails, sticking plaster and bandages. And then, once I'd had enough of watching my mother tearfully eyeing yet another of Bill's destroy-it-yourself jobs, I would go off to the Woolwich Odeon, an altogether spivvier picture palace than the Greenwich Granada.

This left my mother at home with a large, run-down house, a small child and an insane Dobermann. Bill's determination that we should live inside a bubble, permitting no friendships or visits from neighbours, made life almost unbearable for her. Even though she took a series of unsuitable part-time jobs to get her out of the house, she was not allowed to have co-workers call, or be out later than six p.m.

But Kath wasn't entirely alone; on two separate occasions, disturbed mental patients from the local hospital found their way into the shadow-filled house and threatened her, one of them with a serrated carving knife. The Dobermann, which had been intended to protect us, seemed to side with these intruders, as if recognizing fellow travellers in the realm of the deranged. At these moments, Kath must have felt that she was living inside a double bill of particularly bad horror films.

However, my mother did make one friend who was not daunted by the house, the dog, her husband or even me. At half past eight one evening, Maureen Armstrong came to call. My father heard the bell ring and pulled a sour face. 'Who on earth can that be at this time of night?' he complained, trying to see through the drab riverscape painted on the stained glass of the front door.

The overweight woman on the step was a riot of colour: red hair, pink glasses, green top, orange slacks. 'Is Kathy in?' she asked loudly in a broad Lancashire accent, peering past Bill, who had opened the front door a crack and was blocking her view of the hall.

'She's clearing away dinner.' He tried his best to imply that it was a task which required privacy and great concentration, like tightrope-walking, but the visitor wasn't having any of it.

'I know she's in, because I saw her pass by the window as I was driving up.'

So, I could tell Bill was thinking, *she's not only watching the house but a woman driver.* 'She's very busy right now—'

'I'm here,' said Kath behind him. 'Hello, Maureen.'

'I'm one of your wife's ladies,' said Maureen, stepping into the hall uninvited as my father took an alarmed step backwards. 'I'm on her team. We do the top half of Woolwich together.' My mother was currently collecting forms from low-income families for a status poll company. 'Oooey, Kathy, he's a right little terrier, is your old man. Doesn't want to let me in! You want to keep him on a leash.' She turned and barked merrily in his face. 'Grrr! Woof! Woof!'

Bill had never been faced down by any woman other than his mother. He flattened himself against the wall as Maureen breezed into the house, trailing colour and energy like a dissolving rainbow.

'Don't mind me, love,' she said, giving my father's arm a good pinch as she passed. 'I speak as I find. I'll have a cup of tea, though, I'm ruddy gasping.'

'I'll put the kettle on,' said Kath.

'No, I want a chinwag with you. Can't your old man do it?' she asked cheerily. 'Husbands, they're basically useless but we need them for babies, don't we? If we could do it ourselves they'd be out of a job.' Bill looked as if he was thinking about stabbing her rather than putting the kettle on.

Maureen found her way into the lounge and took a sharp breath when she saw the eccentric decoration. 'Deary me, I see what you mean about your front room. Who did it up, Doctor Crippen? I bet you can't wait to get this lot ripped out and replaced with something flowery.'

'Bill's just finished it,' said Kath.

'What a shame. You can't leave it to a man to do. I've seen happier colours in a chapel of rest. And it's cold enough in here to bring your nipples up. He's not rationing the heat, is he? What are all those sheets of hardboard for? Bit of a DIY fan, are you, Billy?'

Dumbstruck, my father retreated to the back room, which he had turned into a workshop, although what he was working on was a mystery. He did not reappear until Maureen had bounced out of the house.

'I don't think we want *her* calling here,' he announced, checking to see that she had driven off.

'I can't stop her,' said Kath. 'We work together.'

In the days that followed, Bill tried to ban Maureen from the house, but she stood her ground and nothing he could say would put her off. He referred to her as 'that bloody laughing woman', and came to dread her coarse roars, and her unflinching gaze when he tried to blockade her. She knew exactly how to handle men like him. She could have eaten him up like a sardine, crunching his soft bones between her strong white teeth.

'I'm not stopping,' Maureen said when she called one evening. 'I'm just collecting your Kath for the pictures.

We're going to find ourselves a nice soppy love story and have a good cry. I always see weepies. If I wanted sex and violence I'd stay in with my old man.'

'I haven't had my tea,' said Bill, shocked.

'You're not in leg-irons, are you? You must remember what the kitchen looks like. It's down the end of the hall, where your missus lives. Come on, Kath, we'll miss the beginning.'

My mother was different when Maureen was around. Stronger, braver, more sure of herself. Maureen always took her side, blocking Bill out of the conversation, but doing so in a cheery manner that made it impossible for him to take offence.

Soon the women had become so pally that Kath invited Maureen to the seaside with us, thereby breaking a centuries-old rule that no one was allowed to join us on a family day out. Maureen screamed when she paddled in the sea, screamed when she had to walk over hot stones in bare feet, and screamed when she dropped tutti-frutti ice cream down the front of her polka-dot bathing suit. She bought Kath a large straw hat tied with red ribbons, and took her on the dodgems. After a while, my mother stopped worrying about what Bill might think, and started to enjoy herself.

In retaliation, my father went on a conversation strike, but nobody noticed because we were all having fun. He sulked, then huffed, then stormed off, only to creep sheepishly back.

On the way home, Maureen suggested we stop at a country pub, and even I put away my books to sit on a five-bar gate in the garden with a pint of lemonade and a packet of crisps.* Maureen's huge breasts quivered

*There were no flavours other than Plain in those days, but at least you could choose if you wanted to put the salt on.

when she laughed, and she laughed a lot. She bought rum and gin, but would not let Bill have any alcohol because he was driving. I wished she was a relative, because she seemed able to counteract in a single afternoon all the horrible times we'd had.

Maureen wasn't the sharpest knife in the drawer, but she understood the importance of enjoying life as it passed, and inspired others to do the same. When she stopped coming around, I was immediately suspicious. I assumed that my father had taken her to one side and said something unpleasant, scaring her away. But no, when she reappeared it was obvious that she had lost weight. Her once-rosy cheeks were yellow. She had come by to tell Kath that she would have to give up work for a while because she needed an operation. She'd had several operations before, and only took piece-work now because a regular job wouldn't allow her to take off so much recovery time.

Maureen went into St Alfege's Hospital, but the doctors were not able to do anything for her this time, and she died a few days later. Even Bill, who should have felt triumphant, knew better than to say anything mean.

19

Celluloid Relatives

I knew I was spending too much time at the pictures when
the cinema manager started to greet me by my first name.
I was so at home in the Odeon that I used to go out to the
foyer snack bar in my socks. The ice-cream girl would say
'Your usual, Chris?' as she poked about in her tray for a
Zoom! lolly.

Although I saw most of my relatives so rarely that I
would have had trouble recognizing them in the street,
I discovered through cinemas like the Odeon a group
of people far more familiar to me. These were not other
patrons, but the character actors who inhabited English
films in the Sunday double bills. Every comedy of the
fifties and sixties featured permutations of the same
stalwarts, and I loved them all, because I could rely on
them always to play the same parts.*

---

*American readers may wish to skip this part. I just felt the need to
name some unsung heroes.

These included:

Irene Handl (charlady)
Anna Quayle (posh woman)
Lance Percival (dim nerd)
Sid James and Sydney Tafler (spivs)
Arthur Mullard (common stupid bloke running tea
    stall)
Margaret Rutherford (tweedy academic)
Joan Sims (jolly den mother)
Richard Wattis, Eric Barker and Thorley Walters
    (men from the Ministry)
Dick Emery (bookie)
Sylvia Syms (indignant girl in coffee bar)
Terry-Thomas (cad)
Peggy Mount (battleaxe)
Raymond Huntley (corrupt official)
Sabrina (busty cheesecake)
Cecil Parker (shyster)
John Slater and Harry Fowler (cheeky barrow boys)
David Lodge (copper)
Reginald Beckwith (official)
Leslie Phillips (ladies' man)
Avis Bunnage and Hattie Jacques (matrons)
Miles Malleson (vicar)
Eleanor Summerfield (prim indignant lady)
Francis Matthews (wide-eyed innocent)
Felix Aylmer (wise priest)
Warren Mitchell (tailor)
Bernard Bresslaw (endearing thicko)
Joyce Grenfell (toothy hockey teacher)
Reg Varney (Brylcreemed oik)
Liz Fraser (indignant girl in tight sweater)
John Le Mesurier (bemused solicitor)
Alfie Bass (scruffy loafer)

Lionel Jeffries (prison warden)
Bernard Cribbins (removal man)
June Whitfield (shocked genteel lady)
Peter Jones (smarmy shop assistant)
Terence Alexander (wing commander)
Bernard Miles (bucolic fogie)
George Cole (endearingly inept crook)
Terence Longdon (posh airman)
Esma Cannon (dotty old dear)
Deryck Guyler (jobsworth)

A man called Michael Ripper played all the other parts that no one else wanted. In fact, he was such a ubiquitous character actor that I was able to buy a small book about him called *Michael Ripper: Unsung Hero*. Sample dialogue:

> *Interviewer*: 'What do you remember about
>   working on *Captain Clegg* with Peter Cushing?'
> *Ripper*: 'I can't remember much about it.'
> *Interviewer*: 'In 1957 you were in *The Steel
>   Bayonet*, do you remember? You kept coming
>   on with cups of tea saying, "Here's your tea,
>   sir."'
> *Ripper*: 'No, not really.'

Oddly, I didn't remember the stars, just the extras. They made the stories seem real. I had always felt that the library was my second home, but the regularly disinfected crimson foyer of the Woolwich Odeon now became my safest haven.

To enter a cinema was, I felt, to enter a contract between film and viewer. Something special was transmitted, and the oddest films and characters left a lasting mark. Only in England could someone have produced an entire book about the eccentric bit-player Charles Hawtrey.*

To me, this intensely personal obsession was the dark heart of English storytelling. The most marginal books and movies helped me form a mental library, a catalogue of touchstone images. Time found a way of rendering them special, turning them into secret memories.

Just as I had become fascinated by the wrong comics and the wrong stories, I fell in love with the wrong films. I knew what I was *supposed* to like – I was meant to be obsessed with James Bond, but I wasn't very much. Instead I loved the odd little English films no one else noticed. Besides, I thought grandly, James Bond was for reading, not watching – although the books were pretty dreadful because they merely exposed the awful snobbery of Ian Fleming,† who spent many, many pages wagging a finger at his proletarian readership and lecturing them on the correct hour to dine at private members' clubs and what not to wear on golf courses, as if they would ever need to know. It was easy, I realized, to appear well-bred if you only ever addressed the social classes beneath you.

But it was impossible to overestimate the effect that the James Bond films had on my schoolmates and their dads.

Here was the first English hero not wearing a sensible V-neck jumper; he didn't need one because he was in Jamaica, a place that could only be imagined by penniless post-war audiences. The series might have started with *Dr No*, but it was with *Goldfinger*‡ that 007 truly became an

---

*The weirdest (and saddest) of all the Carry On characters. The book is called *The Man Who Was Private Widdle*.
†His sister-in-law was Celia Johnson. She didn't get offered the part of Pussy Galore.
‡Villainous Auric Goldfinger was named after Erno Goldfinger, designer of the unloved Elephant and Castle development and London's Trellick Tower. He was very upset with Ian Fleming, apparently.

aspirational symbol for the times. Everyone remembered the gilded Shirley Eaton, Pussy Galore, Oddjob and the Fort Knox countdown (destined to be the first of many urgent bomb deadlines), but audiences conveniently ignored the fact that 007 was first spotted with a stuffed seagull attached to his head, or that he talked flippantly about heroin-soaked bananas before the opening credits rolled. In fact, after he had blown up a drugs empire filled with cartoonish barrels of nitro-glycerine, had a fag, snogged a pneumatic semi-naked lady and fried an attacker in his bath, it seemed highly appropriate that camp icon Shirley Bassey should start screaming out the title song.

I knew that Bond was never serious, only manpower pushed to the zillionth degree, which was why his women needed ludicrous identities and pumped-up sexuality to compete. It was a rule, of course, that no matter how old a legend became, he was still allowed the embrace of a hot young girl. This reached levels of horror in the late Roger Moore 007 films.

But to a rationed post-war nation for whom a roulette wheel represented exoticism and a cigarette case sophistication, Sean Connery could hardly fail to become a hero. He wore cufflinks. He travelled to places few English people had ever seen, and ordered cocktails at a time when Babycham* was the height of glamour. I could tell even Bill thought he was wonderful, because suddenly he was an expert on spies. He was an expert on a lot of subjects about which he knew absolutely nothing. '007 is a man's man,' he said admiringly. 'Mind you, you can tell he's never had to put a shelf up with those cuticles.'

*The only alcoholic drink it was impossible to get pissed on. Women were encouraged to say 'I'd love a Babycham' after the War, because they hadn't been in pubs for five years and had forgotten what to order.

This was now the era of the Swinging London movie, but as the family had moved further out of the city instead of further in, London – swinging, dangling or otherwise – was more distant than ever, and anyway I wasn't entirely sure what 'swinging' actually meant.

Middle-class England was still easily shocked by anything brightly coloured and fast-moving. It shushed everything above a whisper and had nearly dropped dead from fright over rock 'n' roll. It was even more mortified by a towel-draped Brigitte Bardot at a time when Londoners thought Al Fresco was an Italian chef. Only a handful of art teachers would actually see Bardot in a film, but everyone was disgusted by the idea of foreigners coming over here with their chianti bottles and nipples and seafood starters, corrupting the country with mucky continental values.

My family never ate out unless it was in a café, the kind of place that served two slices of bread and butter with battered cod. Kath fantasized about having a starter – not just the ones you saw on set-meal menus, which were always either half a grapefruit with a glacé cherry in the middle or a glass of tinned tomato juice, but a proper starter like prawns with avocado. It wasn't the taste she desired, but the ritual of folded linen and courses and wine. The most she got offered after the pictures was a saveloy. She wanted to go 'up west' to see a play – not a musical but something with substance. Once she took an evening off to see *Krapp's Last Tape* by Samuel Beckett, and loved it, but the experience could not be discussed because it had to remain a secret from Bill, and he was always listening out for warning signs of artistic conversation.

I knew that there was a world outside the Woolwich Odeon; I just couldn't access it. Britain did its best to keep out American excess, while its citizens secretly craved it. Marlon Brando's motorcycle gang film *The*

Wild One was banned in England for over a quarter of a century while the horrified tabloids predicted a teen-induced mass breakdown of social order. Although I did not know it at the time, London had a handful of dedicated independent cinemas: the beloved and much-missed Academy screens in Oxford Street, with their beatniky hand-made wood-cut posters; the Biograph in Victoria, which had become a useful pick-up joint for lonely bachelors; and railway-station cinemas that I got to visit with my mother whenever we were early for a train after going to Moorfields Eye Hospital. These places ran Warner Brothers cartoons and continuous Pathe newsreels that showed Princess Margaret opening smelting plants, the Dagenham Girl Pipers,* jets breaking the speed barrier and 'the cheerful people of Fiji'.

I loved tatty English films because I could relate to them. Nearly all of them took place indoors, and it was always raining. The sets were full of wavy wallpaper like the stuff in Cyril Villa, and the actors were like the relatives I wished we had. People used words which were soon to vanish from the English vocabulary:

Scarper
Clot
Barmy
Rozzer
Shiv
Blithering
Bint
Lolly
Twerp
Snout
Punch-up

*A female bagpipe marching band that formed the butt of a thousand sixties jokes. They're still going strong.

Of course, there was an upper echelon of respected performers that my parents held in high esteem. Peter O'Toole, Dirk Bogarde, David Niven, Stanley Baker, Michael Caine, Laurence Olivier, Albert Finney, Vanessa Redgrave and Julie Christie had, after all, been raised into the world pantheon of stars.

Male film heroes were cut from different cloth, tending towards the boy-next-door cheeriness of John Mills, the elegant sturdiness of Richardson and Gielgud, the daydreaming Tom Courtenay, the effete charm of Alec Guinness, the neurasthenic mannerisms of Peter Sellers. English performers had grown up handling the twice-nightlies and provincial tours. They eschewed method acting and considered their work a craft. During the filming of *Brief Encounter*, Celia Johnson apparently asked if David Lean could hurry up with the shooting of her big romantic scene because she had a train to catch.

Moira Shearer might have inspired a generation of hefty county girls to worship ballet in *The Red Shoes* but she didn't cut the mustard in Woolwich. Our family had a history of enjoying 'popular' English films: Michael Redgrave trying to silence his ventriloquist dummy in *Dead of Night*; Joyce Grenfell's gormless Miss Gossage ('Call me Sausage') in *The Happiest Days of Your Life*; Barbara Windsor's airborne bra in *Carry On Camping*; films in which Stanley Baker bared his dimple and blew things up.

None of us realized that this was the last gasp of old-style Great Britain. The Beatles were soon to spearhead a new musical movement that would switch our world from monochrome to colour. There would be an explosion in literature and art. Ken Russell would direct sixteen films in three years. The Union Jack minis that never broke red, white and blue file in *The Italian Job* were on their way. If it all seemed so much easier in the sixties, it was because suddenly people had the confidence to make themselves heard. The English films of the fifties had been about community spirit and the after-effects of the War, but the sixties charted a social upheaval that exploded into celebration, and almost as quickly collapsed into decadence. It would be like witnessing the rise and fall of an isolated civilization in a single decade.

Swinging London's psychedelic mindset lived in films and music, and I desperately wanted to be a part of something fresh. It was a hopeless dream, of course, because I had nothing to offer. Like today's celebrity wannabes, I could not understand why I would never be allowed in merely on the merit of my enthusiasm.

But it didn't stop me from reading or going to the cinema. I made no friends in Abbey Wood, a town that made Lagos look like St Tropez, and barely spoke to anyone at school. Even my teachers were learning to avoid me. I found it safer to keep my mouth shut and my eyes on the pavement when walking anywhere. The contract was between me, the page and the screen, and would not be broken by anything as boring, untidy or unpredictable as real life.

20

Still No News from Michael Winner

'Any news from Michael Winner yet, then?' asked my mother, on her hands and knees as she tackled the dog's hairs with her new 'Static Wonder Brush'. The house was freezing cold because Bill had accidentally put the end of a pickaxe through a boiler pipe.

'Nothing so far,' I told her, returning to my notebook critiques of movies. It was the end of term, and my English teacher had asked for an essay on any aspect of being English, a subject that was deemed very important at the time. My classmates were writing about a seaside weekend, a trip to the funfair, meeting a girl at the school sports day, a country holiday. I concluded a lengthy dissection of English fiction with:

> *I think there is something in our national*
> *character that makes us admire authors like Evelyn*
> *Waugh, whose heroes never get anywhere, always*
> *ending up back at the point where they started, or*

*far worse off. Our novels are peppered with weak
men who observe the action of their lives from a
distance. Our nature seems drawn to these types of
stories. We admire plucky losers and anti-heroes,
boffins in tatty jumpers, chaps on the sidelines,
headachy women who apologize about their nerves
while arranging daffodils, men who never loosen
their ties. As a race, we've completely dried up.
We're emotionally dead. I think this is very useful
to know, in order to be prepared for adult life. One
day I hope to travel and see if it is the same in other
countries.*

I headed the essay with a quote from Alfred, Lord
Tennyson:

Howe'er it be, it seems to me, 'tis only noble to be
    good;
Kind hearts are more than coronets, and simple
    faith than Norman blood.

The quote had been used for a famous Ealing comedy, but
the point was lost on Mr Piper, my teacher, who stamped
the page with the following note:

Marks: 2/10
English Teacher: Mr Piper
Comments: *Well, I really don't know what to make
of this, Christopher. You start with Tennyson and
end up with Evelyn Waugh, but you are discussing
low art. More worryingly, nowhere do I find any
sign of who you really are. I would say that you
are a chameleon, but I don't know what you are
supposed to be blending in with. There's no doubt
that you have strong opinions, but the peculiar*

disarray of your mind leaves me completely
flummoxed.

'What did your teacher think of the essay?' asked
Kath.

'He says I'm probably not a chameleon,' I said unhelpfully.

What did Mr Piper know? He was stuck in a minor
grammar school, teaching Anthony Trollope to kids who
preferred masturbation and Thunderbirds. I skipped his
final English lesson and went to the Woolwich Odeon
instead.

My introduction to sex was via Carry On films, matrices
of suggestive codewords layered over tissue-thin plots.
The most important words in any Carry On film were
'it' and 'one', as in 'She wants it' and 'Can you give
her one?' – the entire lexicon of sexual tomfoolery was
buried within such phrases. The director evidently thought
Barbara Windsor was sexy if she took tiny steps with her
arms held back, like a duckling learning to walk. But
if the girls were in need of a month on a Stairmaster
before donning unflatteringly tight pink hotpants and
white patent-leather boots, the middle-aged men who
lusted after them were quite astonishingly ugly, sporting
what was eventually to become the defining look of the
seventies: the beer-gutted, sideburned, bulbous-nosed,
queer-baiting, fashion-impaired, leering 'lady's man'. I
watched in amazement as a gallimaufry of Hogarthian
grotesques chased wobbly dolly birds across the screen.

The tragic and frequently grotesque clowns of the
Carry On films reflected sexual insecurity, shame and
embarrassment, just as *Brief Encounter* had done a
generation earlier. That film, after all, wasn't about love
at all, but about guilt, loss, repression and humiliation.

I tried to watch it every time it was on television. At one point Celia Johnson was treated like a common prostitute for daring to fall in love. Her emotions ranged from fruitless yearning to feeling cheap. Her attempts to define the sensation of falling in love were undercut by the men around her. Even her faithful husband couldn't think of the word 'romance' when filling in a crossword clue, and Trevor Howard's seduction technique involved describing the symptoms of black lung disease in a husky voice.

Between *Brief Encounter* and the Carry On films were the St Trinians films. Ronald Searle's wartime drawings of horned and horny schoolgirls inspired a series of family farces in which sexually aggressive pupils seduced older men. I could not help feeling that there was something very peculiar at work here. Cynicism at the inefficiency of bureaucratic England seeped through the series like damp. The men from the Ministry of Education sang 'The Red Flag' on election night, praying that Labour would win and abolish private schools because they themselves were too ineffectual to act, and had to be reminded by a passing charlady that, as civil servants, they were not expected to have political affiliations. Shiftless workmen repairing a hole in the Ministry floor became long-term fixtures accepted by everyone. Seduced civil servants hid in the school greenhouse for months on end rather than returning to work. Councillors took their lift-man (played by Michael Ripper, naturally) along on a European fact-finding mission. The English attitude to Europe was summed up in Naples by Ripper, who tapped the barometer and complained, 'If it gets any hotter, I shall have to take my pullover off.' This was the English character actor at work – mundane, earth-bound, dry, bemused. Ultimately, the school – financed on stolen money and immoral earnings – was seen as a more decent institution than the inert, corrupt and powerless state. A story was just a story, but was I also meant to read this as a reflection of my country? More importantly, was there some lesson to be learned here about the act of writing?

Norman Wisdom was even stranger. Strip away the sentiment and you arrived at the surreal, whether Norman was imagining his landlady with a horse's head, singing an eye-chart off-key, turning a police pursuit into a back-garden steeplechase, playing golf upside-down in the top of a tree, being induced with pneumonia or seduced in weirdly convincing drag. Male comedy stars spent so much of their time dressed as ladies that it seemed an entirely natural occurrence.

It took me years to work out why I enjoyed these films. I knew that admitting to my classmates that I liked Norman Wisdom would make them treat me even more like a leper, because in my year you were only allowed to like Steve McQueen. But they were missing the point. The shrill, inarticulate little comic had his roots in the class war. In *One Good Turn* he made straight for the first-class train carriage for no other reason than to disturb its occupants, and this was a trend that continued throughout his films until it became open anarchy. He destroyed posh buildings, wrecked institutions, smashed up expensive cars and gleefully encouraged others to be drawn into fights; this was a schoolboy's anarchist manifesto, a reaction against the ration-book restrictions of post-war England that consistently attacked authority figures, including mayors, corporate executives, government officials, police sergeants and politicians, and only caused destruction to status symbols – Rolls Royces, country mansions, gala dinners and State visits. I could see that – why couldn't they? And why did they run off to play football whenever I enthusiastically broached the subject?

I started taking my notebook to the pictures, and perfected the art of writing in the dark. I noticed that a large number of English films featured American actors whose careers were on the skids, and that *Get Carter* was the closest England got to producing anything cool, mainly because Michael Caine owned a coffee grinder.

I paid my money, watched them all and continued making crabbed, obsessive notes.

Many English comedies pitched a small, crankily run private business against a faceless modern conglomerate, and foolishly suggested that old-fashioned commerce with the personal touch would always defeat slick efficient enterprise. True to form, the English had nailed their colours to the wrong mast. These wish-fulfilment fantasies became increasingly harder to swallow as the nation was overtaken by huge supermarket chains. There was nowhere left for the self-effacing cardigan-clad hero to go. He was as out of date as Colonel Blimp, the old soldier left behind with his morals and charm intact, but without a pot to piss in. No wonder Bill spent so much of his time in a bad mood.

During my very many trips to the Odeon, I discovered one English director in a class of his own. To my highly critical mind, he was the worst English director of them all, and from 1960 to 1998 he silted up cinemas with some thirty-four films, most of which I found unwatchable. It seemed to me that Michael Winner, bon viveur, director, producer, writer, editor, actor and casting director, never knew when he was making a horrible mistake.

His casts seemed to be stuffed into the kind of clothes that could become collectable costumes for bad-taste parties. It was probably just the fashion of the times, but everyone was badly dressed. The men wore wide-lapel suits of the kind once found in Mister Byrite.* The women all looked like hookers, or rather how a man would imagine hookers should look, with tight blouses, shiny boots and big hair.

Most outrageous of all was *The Cool Mikado*, which united the terpsichorean talents of Stubby Kaye, DJ Pete Murray and lip-pursing comic Frankie Howerd. Although it only ran for just over eighty minutes, it felt like the longest film ever made. The production employed the John Barry Seven to re-work the songs of Gilbert & Sullivan, setting them against the dancing of Lionel Blair,† with eye-rolling, end-of-the-pier jokes from Mike and Bernie Winters and Tommy Cooper.

The Cool Mikado had the kind of cinematography associated with lower-end porn films: everything looked cheap and cramped, everyone looked sweaty, the crimson and green sets were emetic, the dialogue and dancing were worse than on a drunken stag night. Even to my untrained eye it looked technically inept, with bizarrely delivered dialogue lines, crossed camera lines, wrong angles, misfiring jokes, and everyone jostling for camera attention except the extras, who were chatting among themselves, waiting for direction or possibly nodding off. There appeared to be little trace of Gilbert's original plot, although it might have been there – it was hard to tell, because one scene had very little connection with the next. After a while the film became a Dadaist artefact with the power to hypnotize the hardest-hearted critic.

One day, I knew, this film would be recognized as a thrilling, visionary work of art.

---

*A super-cheap clothing store that seemed to have a permanent sale on elephant-cord flares and Budgie jackets.
†Twinkling, perma-tanned choreographer who defined variety-show camp.

I realized what I had to do. Rushing home, I dug out my notebooks and began storyboarding the entire screenplay from memory. It was time to use my imagination to produce something worthwhile and meaningful. Where better to start than by re-writing Gilbert & Sullivan via Michael Winner and Tommy Cooper? I could correct all the mistakes, right all the wrongs, and turn what I saw as a fat, smelly old sow's ear into a beautiful silk purse.

Over the next few weeks I worked feverishly on the script, often including my plasticine-model Polaroids of particular scenes. Then it was simply a matter of tracking down Mr Winner's swanky Holland Park address and mailing off my masterwork. I felt sure that the director would be thrilled to have all his continuity errors, poor characterization, weak plotting and tenth-rate overdubbing pointed out to him. Thrilled by my initiative, he would commission me to make a new version, putting everything right. Together we could save a masterpiece.

The only thing was, I hadn't thought to make a copy of the script before I asked my father to post it.

After waiting patiently for about a year, I realized there was a good chance that the director might never get in touch with me. The truth was that Bill had completely forgotten to mail the package and had left it in a motor-cycle repair shop somewhere.

21

Hard House

The move to Cyril Villa had coincided with me sitting the eleven-plus, an examination which took place in the gymnasium at school and featured what I considered to be a series of totally irrelevant problems.

A train with nine carriages takes 75 seconds to
pass through a station at 40 mph. How long is the
station platform?

Who knew? How on earth could I be expected to know about the design of the station from the mechanical efficiency of its rolling stock? And what about the people who were waiting to get on the train – would they now all be late for work?

What is a levee?

Something you waited on, surely? Didn't the Black and White Minstrels sing about this? Could be a trick question. It was the geography section, after all, not musical comedy.

> *What have been the reasons for the United Kingdom's balance-of-payments difficulties on both current and capital accounts over the last ten years?*

Hang on, I was eleven years old, not the Chancellor of the Exchequer, and besides, wasn't that a bit politically loaded? Talk about giving ammunition to the Shadow Cabinet. Pass on that one.

> *Who do you think was the 'Dark Lady' of William Shakespeare's sonnets?*

Now I knew it was all a wind-up. Scholars had been arguing about this for centuries and now they expected some spotty schoolboy to figure it out for them? A bunch of examiners were having a laugh somewhere. Better wing this by making up some fantastical travesty of my own.

> *A particle travels 2×10^8 centimetres per second in a straight line for 7×10^{-6} seconds. How many centimetres has it travelled?*

I'm sorry, I felt like writing, your call did not go through. Kindly replace the handset and dial again. The question appears to be broken, or you are speaking in French, or are quite possibly mad.

I put down my pen before anyone else. Was that a good thing or a bad thing?

Good, it transpired, because somehow, by some mysterious process, I appeared to have sailed through the exam. I could only think that there were bonus points awarded for surrealist answers.

My score qualified me to go to Colfe's Grammar School, the Royal Leathersellers College, one of London's oldest guild schools. There would be posh boys there. Parents with money would be dropping off their darlings in Rollers – the cars, not the hair-care equipment. In fact, there was a very good chance that I would be the poorest pupil in the entire school. When everyone else went off on the school skiing trip I'd be the one left at home. A whole new world of humiliation was about to open up before me.

I was reading *Gormenghast* at the time, and living in it, too. In my mind, the towering edifice in Peake's book became synonymous with Cyril Villa. The vast crumbling castle sinking under the weight of its history and traditions, a gloomy labyrinth of corridors and chambers so knuckle-scrapingly real that I felt trapped inside them, was a fractured mirror of England, frozen in time and smothered by centuries of conservatism, suffocating in meaningless rituals, doomed to disappear from the moment the youthful kitchen underling Steerpike climbed from a window to view his home from the outside. Death stalked those pages: the death of tradition and the end of all things, as well as human destruction. I carried the book everywhere I went, because it deserved to be revered, its heart-rending language and images remembered as long as there were books left to treasure. Plus, reading was more interesting than staring at the dark, damp-patched walls of our TV-less lounge, listening to my dad's rivet gun.

The house did have beautiful Edwardian mirrors over marble fireplaces with twisted pilasters and golden statues of chariot racers, but Bill ripped all of these out and replaced them with iridescent metallic log-flame-effect gas fireplaces, which he got cheap from his Elephant and Castle gas showroom.

Cyril Villa also had a view, down Knee Hill (why did we have to live in a part of the body? Why couldn't we have moved to a place with a normal address?) and out on to the misted grey marshlands that lay between the Woolwich armoury and Erith, where London's last wild horses had cantered. Bill would jingle the change in his pockets while he watched brown-sailed barges heading up and down the Thames. 'I should think that's probably carrying jute to Southend,' he would announce knowledgeably, as if anyone was going to argue with him.

But times were changing. Work had nearly finished on a new estate which the local paper held a competition to name. It was christened Thamesmead, and was going to be a cross between Metropolis and Shangri-La, but for the first decade of its life it became a watchword for shoddy British workmanship. Bill reckoned that some of the houses were starting to sink into the marshes because the land had not been properly drained, but the final nail in the coffin came when *A Clockwork Orange* was filmed on one completed section of the estate. Nobody wanted to live there after that, my father told me, not even displaced gypsies.

I found the film version of Anthony Burgess's novel too close for comfort, because when I walked home past gangs of kids behaving like Droogs, it felt as though fiction had crossed over into fact. Strewn with chip paper and fag cartons, Abbey Wood was designed for insolent loitering, the gateway to teen delinquency. The neighbourhood kids were neurotic, doped-up, walking scar tissue, groomed for early failure. Hanging out with them was not an option, so I stayed at home.

The house was getting my mother down. Friendless

once more, and resigned to a loveless marriage, she spent her days fighting the dirt that sifted like creeping death into the house from the surrounding woods. After Bill became disenchanted with the Dobermann's Quisling*-like ability to change sides in a crisis, he got rid of it and bought an Alsatian, an albino with pink eyes, strange-smelling breath and a permanently moulting dry coat – not the kind of dog you wanted with deep-green carpets – and Kath found she had a new enemy to oppose. Whenever anyone went near the beast it bared its teeth, even when it was being friendly.

It seemed impossible to imagine that my parents had ever found anything in common at all, but the thought that they might get a divorce seemed as likely to occur to them as the idea that *Homo sapiens* had evolved from wheelbarrows. In Bill's book, no divorcee should ever be allowed to walk around with her head held high, not unless the word SLUT was branded across it in poker-work.

Kath tried to make Cyril Villa more cheerful. She bought a rickety telephone table for the dingy hall, even though we had no telephone. She had paid for it with coupons collected from her packets of fags. Presumably it had not crossed her mind that having to smoke that much to get a telephone table would quite possibly prevent her from speaking in anything above a croak when she did finally get a telephone. After all, the lady who lived down the hill had chain-smoked Kensitas all through her pregnancy because she was collecting cigarette coupons for a pram.

*Norwegian fascist whose surname became an eponym for 'traitor'. Not to be confused with Kipling, who became the butt of a seaside postcard joke. 'Do you like Kipling, Miss?' 'I don't know, I've never Kippled.'

After Kath's pale, ethereal mother had evaporated entirely beyond the mortal coil, her sweet existence reduced to a faded sepia photograph on the beside table, my mother realized she was truly alone. She began to look permanently tired, as if she was preparing to go next. At least I had started my new school and was out from under her feet, so she could concentrate on looking after Steven and keeping the rising tide of drifting dog hair at bay.

I had unintentionally become the keeper of my mother's secrets. I was the only person to whom she could really talk. It was a burden I hadn't wished for, and one which Kath had not meant to bestow on me. Sometimes, when she sought me out for a talk, I hastily made myself invisible, heading off for a long walk without a destination in mind. I got just one chance to explore the area on my new bicycle before it was stolen, but it was obvious that there was nothing much to see. I did, however, discover Plumstead Public Library, which had a lending record section and a peculiar museum above it, which contained dusty cases of coins dug from the Thames, a length of hair from a medieval dog, and bits of grey wood from two-thousand-year-old boats. But age alone did not make the exhibits interesting, so the curator had extemporized unlikely handwritten stories for each find, carefully using phrases like 'this was thought to belong to . . .' and 'might well have been of the type used . . .' I could tell that the good people of Plumstead weren't too interested in local history, because whenever I visited the museum the curator had to come and turn the lights on.

The record section's most recent acquisition was an album by the Rolling Stones, purchased as a sop to those who complained that the library did not stock modern music. However, they did possess a complete set of Sir Malcolm Sargent's Gilbert & Sullivan LPs, which came with notes explaining the topsy-turvy world created by their composers.

I fell in love with their concept of paradox, which in *The Pirates of Penzance* dictated that because Frederic was born on 29 February in a leap year, he only had a birthday every four years and would therefore not be indentured as a pirate until he was in his eighties, on his twenty-first birthday. Similar rules explained why Nanki-Poo could marry Yum-Yum for one month on condition that he would then be beheaded in *The Mikado*, or why *Iolanthe*'s member of parliament Strephon was a fairy down to the waist and a human below that. Wherever Gilbert set his verse, he was always writing about the absurdity of England. He must have got right up Queen Victoria's nose.

The library was guarded by an eagle-eyed matron who held every LP up to the light and compared it to a chart, marking each new scratch. Every time she spotted some damage, she added two shillings to the bill that I knew I would never be able to pay. When I eventually peered over her shoulder and saw that I owed over seven pounds, I was forced to admit that I was broke.

'Don't worry about it,' said the collection's guardian with a conspiratorial smile. 'These record-ledgers are so complicated and confusing that no one in the Council will ever be able to work them out.'

'Then why do you put them down at all?' I asked.

'The by-laws only state that the fines have to be noted,' she explained. 'No one ever got around to setting a date for their collection, so I marked it down as a leap year.'

It was an explanation worthy of W. S. Gilbert himself.

22

Bad Influence

The school had been bombed during the War, and was still housed temporarily in a series of asbestos-riddled bungalows on a piece of waste ground in Lewisham while a new modern building was being constructed. I was eleven, a new boy in a class of hostile, suspicious pupils. I wanted to have a black friend because I only knew white kids, but the only black boy in the entire school was a geek called Jeremy who longed to be a Young Conservative. English children of the period knew no one other than those like themselves. It would have been exciting to make friends with kids from different cultures, just to vary the stultifying predictability of daily suburban life, but in Greenwich there was as much chance of sighting a Martian. From what we learned in books and films, dark-skinned races seemed less emotionally guarded than we were, less arrogantly convinced that they were born to govern the world, plus they ate exotic food, dishes that came seasoned with spices instead of being smothered in rubbery gravy. Mrs Harper, the woman in the fish shop, said she knew a Caribbean lady, but this friendship was so jealously guarded that no one ever got to meet her. We finally decided that Mrs Harper had invented her to sound more interesting.

On my first day, I was seated next to Simon, a pasty-faced boy with freckles, an insolently knotted tie and a silly haircut. The teacher warned me to stay away from Simon during break as he had an attitude problem, which in those days merely meant impertinence, whereas today it usually means carrying small firearms. When I looked in his eyes I could see something untameable and mad. It was the start of a lifelong friendship for both of us.

I had been born unfashionable, from my Oxford toe-caps to my short-back-and-sides haircut. Pens leaked in my shirt pockets. I always wore my cap. I was a classic hopeless case, and, worse still, I knew it.

School was a different planet. To get there, I had to pass through Blackheath, which was filled with dark antique shops and genteel tea rooms, and called itself a village. The residents would have liked to build a moat around the place to keep out the proles. Later it filled with crimson boutiques selling lime-green miniskirts, much to the horror of the retired colonels who lived there. But it was a better place to hang out in than Abbey Wood, not least because there was less chance of being murdered by someone from a rival school who had decided you'd looked at him the wrong way.

When you found yourself being bullied, I discovered, it was best to team up with someone frightening and unpredictable. United by the fact that our classmates went out of their way to avoid us, Simon and I proceeded to bring each other's most disruptive qualities to the fore. First, we reduced our maths teacher to tears of frustration, contributing to his decision to embark on a year-long sabbatical in Wales. Then we started on the English master.

Our friendship was a source of great mystification to all. When he was sixteen, Simon horrified the teachers by riding to school on a motorbike like the one in *Easy Rider*, and suggested that we should take the headmaster's car to pieces behind his back; we laid it out in the school car park as neatly as a stemmed Airfix kit. The art master was thrilled because in Simon he recognized a true rebel who, when asked to create a piece of art for the school corridor, produced a plate of ketchup-smothered fish and chips.

We began manufacturing a libellous magazine in Simon's bedroom, and recording sarcastic comedy radio programmes mocking everyone we knew. Our symbiotic partnership was deplored by all, as Simon was seen to be perverting me from the course of true devotion to learning, and I gave Simon a devious sense of credibility that encouraged teachers to grant him a stay of execution every time he glued the school cat to something or made prank calls around the neighbourhood masquerading as a telephone engineer, encouraging locals to whistle down the phone in order to test its acoustics.

Boys never tire of bad behaviour. Quite the reverse; we developed sophisticated new techniques for disturbing our elders and disgusting our classmates. Through years of fine education, through the principles of economics and the laws of physics, through the Wars of the Roses and the symbolism in Shakespeare's sonnets, we cut open golf balls and tied pupils up in elastic, carved rocket ships into desks, forged each other's signatures and translated jokes from Monty Python into pig-Latin. Drawing enormous pleasure from defacing the English classics, we targeted Anthony Trollope's novel *The Warden* for destruction, simply because it was the most unforgivably dull book ever written – and we got away with it, not because we were arrogant or privileged, but because we were bright and bored, and didn't even realize it.

Simon made me look cool. I made Simon look academic. Simon's mother wore a business suit and made transatlantic phone calls. My mother wore a Sainsbury's apron and made buns. Simon wanted to ride a Harley across America. I wanted to get through the day in one piece. Simon laughed. I worried.

In desperation, the careers officer asked us to provide him with clues to our futures. Simon said he would like to design cars. I said I wanted to write novels. With a barely suppressed smirk, the careers officer advised me to go into insurance, and suggested that Simon should enlist in the territorial army. As we left the room, we wondered what kind of loser would want to be a careers officer anyway.

By now, we had become obsessed with Monty Python, remaining fans even after John Cleese left, when a fourth series exhibited a devil-may-care attitude and featured some of the most surreal writing ever produced in the UK. Monty Python created a true generation divide. Without jokes to cling to, many audiences found themselves adrift, and an older generation used to punchlines involving black people, the Irish and mothers-in-law turned off in droves. Python was not the only bizarre comedy around. Charlie Drake's experimental TV series *The Worker* also reflected British playwrights' fascination with stripping back reality to surrealist arguments and set pieces. Incredibly, it ran for decades. Simon and I wanted to create feverish, disorienting fantasies, not kitchen-sink chatter. Dialogue, we knew, was not conversation. If we didn't bother to investigate our dreams we wouldn't catch glimpses of our souls, and without souls Simon said that we were mere ambulatory meat-sticks. True surrealism was ageless because its roots ran deeper than current fads. Plus, you didn't have to explain it to anyone.

BAD INFLUENCE

Simon said that the further West you went the more everything was explained to you, so that even death was shown to be not only safe and harmless but also tastefully decorated. In Eastern Europe, where death still maintained a strong link with the living, surrealism was alive and well. It survived in any books and films where dislocating events went unexplained. The critic Kenneth Tynan pointed out that you didn't need to know why two people fell in love, only that they did. So many irrational events were happening in the world, but it seemed that in England they were rarely put on paper. The English still liked their stories with neatly tied-up bittersweet endings.

Rebellion; it was all very annoying and predictable, my mother thought, but Bill was convinced that decency had departed the world when National Conscription ended. Kath merely endured her children's teenage years; Bill would have preferred us to have prison sentences, or at least classes in engine maintenance.

Puberty reared its ugly head in the form of spots, silly clothes and even worse haircuts. Simon bought a leather jacket. I opted for an orange nylon polo-neck shirt with Velcro fastenings, bought from one of the catalogues my mother worked for at the time.

Nobody in our class ever got a chance to speak to an actual real live girl, because it was an all-boys school where strapping chaps played lots of healthy contact sports in shorts. In due course I discovered that our head boy and the gym master were involved in these contact sports in the shower room after games. Years later, someone told me they were still running one of Blackheath's antique shops together.

Simon met a girl called Jane, although she only ever saw him from around thirty feet away. He worshipped her from afar, because ironically the school's toughest rebel had a secret – he was too shy to talk to her. I had to make the phone call, but as we still had no phone on the hall table at home, Simon and I had to go to the urine-reeking public callbox next to the campsite in the woods.

'Hello, Jane, you don't know me but I'm a friend of Simon . . . Yes, Psycho Simon, that's the one . . . Well, he wondered if you'd like to go out with him . . . No, why would I be joking?'

Simon was hopping around outside the callbox, desperate for an answer. 'Well? What did she say?'

'She says thank you very much, but could you continue to stay more than thirty feet away from her?'

Simon insisted I had misheard and made me call her back half a dozen times. There were no restraining orders in those days, otherwise we might both have gone to jail.

The only other way of meeting girls was to sign up for the annual operatic production arranged with our sister school, Prendergast.* Simon naturally baulked at this, but only after I had already foolishly joined, assuming that he would too. Consequently he got to hang around with girls backstage while I made nightly appearances as a dancing villager in a shrill, off-key production of *The Bartered Bride*.

We double-dated. Simon met a blue-eyed blonde called Erica, whose breasts were each bigger than her head. Erica had a look of sensual insolence that suggested she would introduce herself by sticking her hand down your pants. I got her best friend Dina, who had legs like a bentwood chair and a complexion like wood-chip wallpaper. She wore so much make-up that I couldn't touch her for fear of getting it all over my clothes, like fresh paint. Even in summer Dina usually had a vest on over her bra, then a

---

*Where did these names come from? It sounds like a passive verb describing the state of being horrified by the sight of suspenders.

shirt, then a jumper, and only allowed me to touch certain parts of that.

Simon played it cool at the school disco, refusing to dance to T Rex's 'Ride A White Swan', while I put my back out moving spastically to Led Zeppelin's 'Stairway To Heaven'.

Simon bought a purple E-type Jaguar before he was old enough to drive it, not because it attracted girls but because he really liked the engine capacity. I had a pushbike and a bus pass.

I hung around Simon's place so much that his mother must have thought I'd been recently orphaned.

We made lists of all the things we wanted to do. I said, 'I've always wanted to go to Paris. Frank Knight in Upper-4 B says I would make a total *branleur*.' I thought it sounded cool. I didn't know it meant wanker. And also 'I'm thinking of taking up pottery.'

Simon said, 'I've worked out how we could burn down the school without getting caught.'

Sometimes I wondered what on earth our intense friendship was based on. Then I realized: Simon stopped me from being beaten up. He gave me visibility, confidence and a kind of filtered-down charisma that reached me like the effects of secondary smoking. He stopped me from feeling that there was no one else in the world who would ever understand. And there he remained, in my mind and heart, comfortable and constant throughout the years, like Peter Pan's shadow, ready to be re-attached if ever I needed it.

When Simon came to my birthday party many years later, friends said, 'Are you sure this is your old rebel schoolfriend? He's got a grey moustache.' I had to assure them that this was indeed the same boy who had once circulated a press clipping of a former classmate convicted of being an axe murderer with the words THIS IS WHAT

A GRAMMAR SCHOOL EDUCATION CAN DO FOR YOU emblazoned across it.

But all that was a long way in the future.

Meanwhile, Simon and I decided to write and distribute a humorous magazine, and discovered how to press the Greek technique *stichomythia* into service. Short, sharp volleys of conversation had been used for comic effect by everyone from Oscar Wilde and Noël Coward to Saki, Joe Orton and Monty Python. We stole jokes, re-wrote old gems and stumbled across new ones, but the material remained stubbornly scatological, stolen, scurrilous, sophisticated yet childishly obscene. Anyway, Simon soon became more interested in engines and girls, in that order, and I returned to filling up exercise books alone.

In order to allow myself more time to concentrate on books I broke up with Dina, telling her that I didn't fancy her any more. This proved to be a case of poor judgement and even poorer timing, as no one had ever denied Dina anything before and she ended up hanging on to my ankles in the middle of Woolwich market, screaming, until a policeman apologetically trotted up to make sure that I wasn't a mugger.

23

A Nice Day Out

'I think we should have a nice day out.' Bill stared out of the window, jingling the change in his pockets. 'That looks like a barge full of wood heading for Dagenham.'

It hadn't stopped raining in over a week. The woods behind Cyril Villa had sprouted into a murky, dripping jungle. Somewhere far above us, water dripped steadily through the attic beams on to the floorboards below. Bill had spent the previous day hammering at the other end of the house until there was a dangerous-sounding crack followed by ominous silence and a sheepish retreat. When it came to DIY, his motto was 'There's no job that can't be started.'

He had also decided to start on the garden, which had clearly not been touched since the outbreak of World War Two. To assist him in this task he had purchased a chainsaw, a band-saw, a sledgehammer and a new pickaxe. My mother had been hoping for a few boxes of peonies and some crazy paving. Instead she got a huge pile of rubble removed from the concrete forecourt of the garage. Bill had decided to smash up the old surface and relay it, but the concrete appeared to be several feet deep, and he only succeeded in removing the top layer, creating a bomb crater that remained for years to come. Every time it rained, the hole filled with brackish water that attracted flying things from the woods with long legs and stingers.

Bill was bored, if truth be told, and was always looking for something to do. His life was slipping by in slivers of wasted time spent working on projects he was never enthusiastic enough to finish. He had recently decided that we were spending too much money on over-priced shop products like fizzy drinks and soap powder, and had passed a couple of fruitless months attempting to create his own versions more cheaply. He knew a lot about chemistry and physics, and broke down these items into their chemical components, coming home with five-gallon drums of an industrial-strength Teepol*-derivative, explaining that the solution was used as the basis for all washing-up liquids. He only stopped after Kath pointed out that he was giving me and Steven skin complaints.

To escape the noise of power-tools, my mother spent her time huddled in the kitchen trying to get warm. It was the only room that ever seemed to have any heat. I lay on the floor of the lounge, trying to concentrate on filling my notebooks in the fading light. Steven rolled in the saw-dust, playing with screwdrivers and nails, gurgling and laughing and smiling delightfully. It somehow escaped our attention that Kath had recently undergone a kind of nervous breakdown.† We all still expected our tea to be served on time.

Although I had been going to the cinema a lot lately,

*The longest-established detergent brand in the world.
†Little was known about these. People went funny for a while and were then all right again. The cumulative stress of providing for families in the post-war years must have been enormous.

I always came back to books. I knew that if I had to choose between a film and a book, I would always go for the latter. Films were better shared, and it took time to organize the right person to see them with. A book was a private transaction between reader and author. It would let you hide inside its covers. It would protect you and keep you safe. The volumes silted up my unfinished bedroom, covering the walls like lichen.

Bill finally bought a car, a rusty lemon-coloured Mini Minor into which the four of us barely fitted. In response to the sense of creeping misery induced by the house, he now insisted on Sunday trips to the coast, whatever the season, whatever the weather.

My father's ability to choose the most depressing seaside resorts in England was uncanny. We were driven to Sheerness, where the beach was covered in reeking green weed, and sat huddled in a wooden hut watching huge tattooed women eating whelks while their children dropped bricks on stranded jellyfish. We went to a place called Point Clear, which looked like the surface of the moon, only not as verdant and with more broken glass. We went to Herne Bay, where the elderly sat in shelters watching the sun go down on their lives. We went to Dymchurch, famed for the poor quality of its arcade trinkets, the insolence of its disaffected teen street population and its army shelling range, on to which doped-up youths occasionally blundered. We went to St Mary's Bay, where severely handicapped schoolchildren were arranged in wheelchairs on the brown mud like human groynes. We went to Dungeness, a wind-blasted stone beach dominated by the eerie glow of its humming power plant. There had to be more attractive places to visit.

The journeys were passed filling up deadly boring I-Spy books. There were about forty of these object-spotting volumes, with titles like *I-Spy Churches* or *I-Spy Something on the Pavement*. You had to tick off the appropriate box whenever you spotted an item on the list, and when the book was full you could post it off to Big Chief I-Spy in return for a merit badge. Big Chief I-Spy said he lived in a wigwam, but the address on the envelope was somewhere on the Edgware Road in central London. Still, it made the journey go faster and the sooner we got there, the sooner we could set off home. I gave up buying the books after Big Chief I-Spy expressed his disgust at what I had managed to find on the pavement.

It occurred to me that my father might be trying to bond us into a family unit. Faced with a choice between losing our parking change in penny arcades reeking of candy floss and sick, or hiding behind a windbreaker trying to spoon beetroot slices out of a jar, there was a danger that we might actually start talking to each other.

'Where do you fancy?' asked Bill. 'Dungeness, Sheerness, St Mary's Bay or Herne Bay?' It was like a restaurant with a very limited menu, where none of the dishes were any good. I wanted to stay in a hotel, but my father was scared of them. Hotels were for posh people who would find ways to belittle him because they knew about tipping and cutlery and cocktails. Besides, I was halfway through writing a new review and didn't want to have to stop in order to spend two hours in a fag-smoke-filled car to emerge in a town that stank of chip fat and hot seaside-rock-making equipment.

'Herne Bay, I think,' he said after much consideration. 'But don't think you're bringing those bloody books with you.' By now, he had transformed my obsession with filling notebooks into *the topic we never mention*. The topic was creativity. After the War, the English had developed a deep suspicion of anything artistic. To a nation founded on land ownership and keeping horses, a green and pleasant kingdom now dedicated to rebuilding itself, art was something kept in galleries that no one needed to visit. Art had stopped in 1890, and was certainly not to be produced at home. The Pre-Raphaelites had been reviled for weaving sentimental narratives with linear plotlines into their paintings; all art since had committed the sin of being inexplicable, and was therefore feared and ridiculed.

In the shires, art became grimly egalitarian; any retired person should have a go at it to get them out of doors. When we had occasion to visit coastal art fairs (usually on rain-swept days when there was absolutely nothing else to do) we found three subjects under the brush: rowing boats at low tide, seagulls in flight and church steeples at dusk. Anything abstract provoked Bill's comment that 'a child of six could do it'. Art was feminized as something that would soften and damage maleness and corrupt the viewer. For decades, books and films had told solid stories, with tableaux, speeches and much worthy declamation. They were conservative, sensible, right-thinking, and that was how people wanted their art to be as well.

I wanted my family to eat at a seaside restaurant, even if it was the kind that served a brown pot of tea with every meal, but my father didn't approve of paying three quid for a piece of haddock served on a paper tablecloth. Instead he dug out his raincoat, the windbreak, a mallet, a shovel, the paraffin stove, the picnic hamper and assorted roadmaps covering areas miles away from where we were going, while I carried on writing up my review.

In 1969 I saw Richard Attenborough's film version of *Oh! What a Lovely War* and loved it because it was so experimental. The anti-war show had been staged by Joan Littlewood using seaside pierrots, singers and dancers in white conical hats and matching romper suits with black pom-poms down the front, but such characters had vanished by the sixties, so the history of the First World War had been turned into a surreal screen epic based on statistics and factual quotations. The setting was Brighton Pier, a folly that stood as a symbol of the War itself, so families paid for funfair rides that killed them, the great battles of Verdun, Loos and Ypres were represented by 'What the Butler Saw' machines, English high command operated from the top of the helter-skelter, losses were totted up on cricket scoreboards, and red tape literally stretched across battlefields.

For me, that was when the seaside finally came into focus, as a symbol for all things absurdly English. Here were the oldest and youngest, the richest and poorest, the gaudiest and the most sublime things to be found in the country. In the film, Brighton – that phlegmatic coastal Albion* – became a sinister surrealist playground. If I could have found the key to such places earlier, I would have enjoyed myself on family days out.

Other films I marked in my notebook included *Dr Syn*, *Sinful Davey* and *Where's Jack?*, which were all about highwaymen, and a film about Buddhist monks that Bill disliked because it had no action in it. Hitting someone counted as adventure, and was suitable for all the family. Nancying about in saffron was Labour and a threat to everything for which we stood. Lately, my father had started buying the *Daily Express* and muttering darkly about foreigners. To be fair, he wasn't alone in doing this. Men who were old enough to remember living through the War were now being subjected to more changes than at any other time in history, and many of them simply retreated into revisionist memories of happier times.

I looked through my reviews, which now filled more

---

*No longer Albion, but a sea-suburb of London filled with drunk children and media burn-outs.

than a dozen notebooks. Nearly all of the English films represented cinema on its beam-ends, too dull to be cool, too bad to be cult. How had I ever managed to sit through such rubbish? With no one to share my enthusiasm, not even my best friend, I hung around the cinema on the off-chance, like a horny sailor cruising the docks.

I kept some of those notebooks far into adulthood. Looking back one day, I noticed that *Eye of the Cat*, a film in which the lead character played an ailurophobe attempting to steal a fortune from a house filled with felines, had been given a four-star rating for one sequence involving a steep hill and an old lady in a wheelchair without brakes; I had not been very discriminating as a child. One of the rare double bills I had reviewed was *The Strange Vengeance of Rosalie* and *To Kill a Clown*. In the former, psychotic Bonnie Bedelia lured a businessman to her shack for sex, then kept him tied up there. In the latter, Alan Alda and Blythe Danner were hippies in a beachfront shack belonging to a fascist militiaman armed with attack dogs. This was a rare 'nutters in sheds' double bill. Suddenly I could see how distributors' minds worked.

I hadn't liked to admit it, but *Easy Rider* made me very uneasy. My notes reported that I saw it four times with Simon, at his urging, and suggested that despite those iconic shots of Peter Fonda riding his long-forked hog, I was frightened by the film's wind-in-the-hair freedom and lack of restraint; proof that carrying a heavy leather briefcase to and from an all-boys school for eight years could leave lasting damage.

It was around this time that I became obsessed with one movie.

It's a Mad, Mad, Mad, Mad World had sweeping blue skies, men in hats, primary-coloured boxy saloon cars, cleavages, shouting and the kind of deafening wanton destruction that propelled me through a feverish adolescent crush on all things loud, bright and American. I fell in love with its sheer bellowing energy. When a hungover Jim Backus reacted to bright sunlight by somersaulting over a billiard table, I collapsed too. I followed the film from one flea-pit to the next, watching it over and over, mesmerized, until I knew all the usherettes.

I watched it until every line repeated in my head milliseconds before arriving on screen. The film became a series of set-pieces to be ticked off one by one. I wrote about it endlessly, and through this process, some input of my own began to emerge. Years later, I found myself driving through California, and accidentally ended up in Plaster City, the town from which a hysterical Mrs Marcus, played by Ethel Merman, calls her son, Sylvester. It was a special moment; you had to be there. I left the area trembling and strangely fulfilled.

What I did not know back then was that this extremely shrill, rowdy and fairly unfunny Cinerama 'comedy to end all comedies', where even Buster Keaton and Jack Benny were reduced to walk-on roles, had been heavily trimmed by director Stanley Kramer to increase the number of times it could be shown in a week. Many years later, Tania Rose, the film's co-author, put me in touch with a very nice man who had dedicated his entire life to finding the missing pieces of the film. He was deranged, of course, but in the same way as I had been – and one obsession validated the other; if more than one person was affected, it meant I wasn't mad. When the film's missing plotlines were finally located and restored, a darker, more cynical film emerged – I was glad they had cut it, at least for the sake of my childhood sanity.

Another good thing about *It's a Mad, Mad, Mad, Mad World* was that it was too long to run with a short feature. Long after films ceased to be shown in double bills, audiences still had to endure execrable shorts about showjumping, the porters of Covent Garden or Princess Margaret attending Ascot. *Twisted Nerve* was always shown with a fantastically bad musical short filmed in Belsize Park called *Les Bicyclettes de Belsize*, presumably because the director had seen *Les Parapluies de Cherbourg*, with which it had absolutely nothing in common. Slathered with naff pop songs and shot in such soft focus that the audience must have wondered if they were suffering from cataracts, I regularly caught it drifting about the outer reaches of the cinema circuit.

Bad films weren't worth reviewing in a straightforward fashion, so I started to extemporize, adding descriptions of new scenes and new endings that I felt improved them. When I reluctantly showed my mother the notebooks, she asked me what exactly I was reviewing the films for, especially when so many of them were devoid of any re-deeming features.

'This is all very well,' she said finally, 'but you need tales of your own, not other people's.'

'I don't know how to go about it.'

She put down her drying-up cloth and thought for a minute. 'All stories are about the gradual disclosure of information,' she said knowledgeably. 'Look at Dickens. But take your time. There's no rush. You have plenty of years in front of you.'

She was right. The reviews were patched re-hashes of other people's work. Without rigour or originality, they revealed nothing about me.

She turned to me and placed her hands on either side of my head, as if trying to look inside. 'You know what I see here, Chris? A great big blank page. I suppose I should be thankful that nobody has written anything good or bad across you yet. But at some point, you'll have to start colouring in your own emotions, or someone else will do it for you, and then you'll never find your own voice.'

I wasn't entirely sure that I understood what she meant.

Still, later that day I slid the notebooks away beneath my bed and opened a brand-new Letts Schoolboy Diary. I would find my own voice. What I needed was something to write about.

'Look at it out there, bloody chucking it down,' said Bill, jingling his change at the window. 'Stair-rods. Just our luck. I'm wondering . . .'

I perked up. Maybe we wouldn't have to go, after all.

'I'm wondering if we should pack the blowlamp in case the paraffin stove doesn't start.'

I finally noticed that my mother was not her usual self. She always seemed to be on the verge of tears, and had stopped baking. The most she could be encouraged to muster up for dinner was mince with carrots and peas. Apart from that, we were mainly eating out of cans. True to form, I liked Heinz Kidney Soup, the thick sepia gunge with bits of ground-up kidney in it that everyone else hated.

Kath spent all her time cleaning or shut in her bedroom reading, and I wasn't making matters any easier by avoiding everyone. Instead of wondering what was wrong and trying to help my parents sort things out once and for all, I immersed myself in a world of words and artificially forced colours. Ink on paper, images on celluloid: everything I felt was created by someone else. There seemed to be a clear protective layer between me and the world, just like the plastic the new supermarkets now used to wrap up their meat, not raw and bloody but safe and easy to handle. I was also silent, bad-tempered, sulky and solipsistic, as adolescence demanded in a truly dysfunctional family.

I turned back to the blank pages before me. I needed a story. I needed a hero, or a heroine. What did I know? What had I been taught?

There had been a time when every schoolchild could recite the kings and queens of England in order. Whether one regarded this exercise as pointless or not, it was a cornerstone of education, along with parroting multiplication tables and knowing what a gerund was.

If England was a nation suffering from its history, at least everyone had a working knowledge of certain historical events, which provided a unique set of reference points for de-coding the stories of English heroes. The radio shows our family listened to ran comedy skits on everything from Mafeking to the siege of Sidney Street, and everyone from Sherpa Tensing to Svengali, and even the lowliest comedies were prepared to structure jokes around Anne Boleyn, Nelson, Sir Isaac Newton, Dr Livingstone, Madame Pompadour, Julius Caesar, H. Rider Haggard, Sir Francis Drake and Dr Henry Jekyll, knowing that they would be understood by the masses.

This was the shared knowledge of a once-finite national identity, which filtered the rest of the world through set texts featuring the South Sea Bubble, the Spanish Armada, Oliver Cromwell, the India Mutiny, Florence Nightingale and Queen Victoria – texts so rigid and perversely opinionated that they could be parodied by Sellar and Yeatman in *1066 and All That*. Naval heroes, explorers, commanders, scientists and pilots captured the national imagination, filled children's comics and provided the basis for nicely bowdlerized biographies. War exploits were honoured in *The Dam Busters* and *The Battle of Britain*, while Douglas Bader was held up as one of the last templates for the courageous twentieth-century Englishman, as if getting your legs blown off was a covetable right of passage.

Even my father could sense that the dawn of a new age was upon us; the celebration of celebrity, and even non-celebrity, was starting to replace English mythology. Steve

McQueen, sweating in a torn vest, had become everyone's idea of a star, replacing heroes like Barnes Wallis* and Captain Scott – but he was tacitly understood to be stupid. Virility and intelligence were rare partners. The English no longer persisted in telling stories about bright-eyed POW officers who dug their way out of prison camps with teaspoons.

'Show me what you're writing,' said Kath, making one of her rare forays from the bedroom. She had lost weight and was pale. Her fingers were always folded over each other, as though she could not trust her untethered hands. Her eyes were darkly shaded crescents, as if the light hurt her.

'I'm not,' I said glumly. 'I can't think what to write. Other people have done all the best stories.'

She pursed her thin lips and looked out at the street, thinking. 'Fiction means you can make things up. Don't worry about embarrassing yourself. You don't have to write from experience, you know. You just have to believe in what you write.'

'But I don't know what I believe.'

'Then copy someone good,' she said, wearily seating herself beside me.

'What do you mean?'

'You admire the work of others so much – make that your starting point. Take their material. Re-work it, like you did with that terrible film script, only this time do it with something more manageable, and put some of your own experiences in it. Turn it into something that's yours.'

It was the opposite of the advice I had found in books

---

*Inventor of the bouncing bomb used to destroy dams in Operation Chastise (filmed as *The Dam Busters*). Why was he named after a London suburb?

on the subject, which extolled the virtues of only writing about what you knew or had personally experienced.

'Write a short story. Nobody expects you to produce *Bleak House* the first time you finish something. It doesn't matter if the result is dreadful, the first attempt is always going to be less than perfect. It's nothing to be ashamed of and at least it will get you started.'

'How do you know so much about it?' I asked suspiciously, screwing up one eye.

She sighed, glancing at the wall with a why-did-I-raise-a-stupid-son? look. 'What do you think I wanted to be when I was younger? A copy typist in a company that made pumps? A greyhound-stadium cashier? We all have dreams, you know. You're not unique.'

Of course. I had learned all of my grammar from her. She knew shorthand. She loved concision. She always said 'comprises' instead of 'consists of'. She knew what synecdoche* was. Best of all, she could describe things in a way that made me feel I was actually there. She had a facility with language I could only dream about. It was just that she had never had the confidence to use it in public.

'The only women who write are ones with lots of leisure time. It's a suitable career choice if you're a lady, but not if you're a working woman.' Kath pointed to the notebook. 'Stick that up your jumper, but bring it with you. You can sit in the back of the Mini and write on the way to Herne Bay. And all the way back. I'll never look at what you've written and your father won't even notice.'

Kath's attitude didn't entirely make sense, but it was welcome. She owned a chipped black enamel Remington typewriter that appeared to date back to the time of William Caxton, but she let me take it to my room. It was heavy and made of cast iron, and looked like the Enigma

---

*When part of something is used to refer to the whole thing.

Machine. You had to hit the keys so hard to leave an impression on the page that it hurt your fingers to write more than a couple of sentences, and sometimes the bit inside the O fell out. Changing a ribbon was about as much trouble as changing a tyre on a lorry, only you got your hands dirtier. I started to use the typewriter, although I had to stop before my father got home because you could hear it throughout the house. It came in a metal case, and I kept the whole thing under my bed because I wasn't strong enough to lift it on to the top of the wardrobe.

I threaded in a fresh sheet of paper and typed my name, then the title of the story I was going to write. Loosely based on a dozen similar stories I had read, it was called *The Long Dark Corridor*. It would be about a lunatic who stalked his unsuspecting victims and when he caught them – well, I would think about that when I got there.

The more I wrote, the more puzzled and excited I became by the unexpected effect of words. I soon learned that:

Writing in the first person didn't necessarily mean you had to tell the truth. In fact, it was a lot more fun if you lied through your teeth.

Sitting in cafés filling up the margins of notebooks with spidery writing made people think you were either a flower-child, or you had polio and were marking time until you died.

If the lock slipped on your keyboard and you suddenly started typing capital letters, the effect was LIKE SHOUTING and could actually make you jump.

Tippex was a boy's best friend.

There was something comforting about the smell of a well-used eraser. And soft pencils, preferably a 2B. And the way a worn golden fountain-pen nib glided across a very smooth white piece of paper.

But a typewriter was best of all. Writing was more fun

than shivering on a rock-frozen rugby pitch, squinting at the sky lost in thought as a leather ball bounced right by your feet and everyone shouted at you for failing to do something with it.

In fact, the only downside I could see was that writers earned less than tar-spreaders or toilet-cleaners. And they probably ended up *going funny*, which in writers' terms meant suffering endless fits of melancholy, having violent affairs, committing murder, going blind or mad, and dying of cirrhosis of the liver.

How cool was that?

Appeased, I agreed to go to Herne Bay.

There's a melancholy sense of things lost in the shabbier British seaside towns; of comfortable failure and better times long gone. I always came home feeling depressed after a Sunday spent in Hastings or Folkestone. On one of these miserable days out we drove from town to town, stopping for tea in overlit glass cafés where pensioners sat picking at orange pieces of battered fish. We paced pebble-strewn promenades watching seagulls fighting the air currents, and sat in shelters with our eyes scrunched against the fierce sea light, until even Bill was bored.

'We could go up there,' I suggested, pointing to the downs at the back of the town.

'Nowhere to park,' said Bill, but I could see him eyeing the great green wall that rose steeply behind the houses.

'We could climb straight up. There's nothing to stop us.' The words came out of my mouth before the thought of what I had said hit home.

'No, it's far too dangerous. We wouldn't be able to get more than a few feet.'

I had no idea if I was afraid of heights. Being afraid of everything else, the answer was probably yes. I found myself running towards the start of the slope and taking the lower incline easily. Bill was right behind me, then climbing alongside in surprise.

As the gradient grew sharper I had to grab tussocks of grass to keep from falling backwards, but I kept going. Kath could be heard down below, shouting words of warning. After a few minutes I heard Bill call and point back. 'We should stop.'

I turned around and was amazed to see the sea far below, glittering distantly. I could suddenly hear the wind in my ears.

'You're scared!' I laughed, which spurred him on.

Scrambling like monkeys, we rose above the town. Exhilarated, I realized I had no fear of heights at all – finally, something to be unafraid of! I looked across at Bill, who was about thirty feet away, knowing that he was taking his cue from me.

'Do we keep going up?' he called. He was turning blue with cold.

'We keep going,' I shouted back. By now I knew we were clinging to a sheer cliff by nothing much more than the will to keep climbing together. I forced myself to focus on the green wall.

We were alone in a ragged bright world, emerald and azure and white. Back on the ground, my mother and Steven were barely discernible dots. The pier looked miniature. With one hand over the other we pulled ourselves up, nearing the top. I saw Bill from the corner of my eye, watching me with amazement and pride.

I never wanted to reach the crest, but suddenly the cliff flattened out into a disappointingly mundane vista with mown grass walkways and a caravan park. The world was spinning. I flopped on to the grass, out of breath, laughing, and my father collapsed beside me.

The joy of that moment lasted for the rest of my childhood.

24

Caravan Nights

'You'll thank me for this,' said Bill one day. 'I've bought us a holiday home.'

I was almost thirteen when in a fresh attempt to bond the family, and inspired by lack of money due to various half-finished projects around the house, my father blew what savings he had on a caravan. In my mind, the painted caravans that belonged to Arabs or gypsies were exotic and appealing, whereas a powder-blue tin box set into an oblong of concrete surrounded by fishing gnomes was only acceptable if you were a photographer producing a book on English eccentrics.

And a pikey caravan that was about ten feet long, like a home for circus midgets, balanced on two wheels and made of rotting painted hardboard, with a rusty tin flue, was not a holiday destination but an exercise in ritual humiliation.

Set on an acre of methane-filled marsh near Dymchurch, Kent, the site boasted an icy cinder-brick washhouse full of daddy-long-legs, a handful of bedraggled, stupid sheep notable only for the immense weight of clinkers hanging from their nether hair, and a grim little bar full of fishing nets, knots and floats which touted itself as a clubhouse, although it was hard to imagine the kind of prospective member they might turn away.

I pressed Bill's hand on the linen of the upper bunk. 'The bed's wet, Dad,' I complained.

'Good country air will do that,' he explained proudly, as if he knew anything about it. 'You need toughening up. People around here have damp sheets all the time.'

'Then why on earth don't they move somewhere nicer?' I tried lying down on the bed, and found that the gas mantle was frighteningly close to my head. I knew there was a hotel near by, full of varnished teak, soft yellow lighting and brass ship's fittings, where the landlady was serving prawn cocktails in little metal cups. I also knew that Bill did not consider hotels to be for the likes of him, and wouldn't dream of staying in one.

Many years later, Steven had to drive around the West Country on business, and insisted on taking Bill with him. The weather was foul when they arrived in Torquay, and Steven was running late for a meeting. Dropping our father on the steps of the nearest hotel, he told him to head for the bar, where he would pick him up in an hour's time. When he returned after the meeting, he found Bill standing forlornly on the steps where he had been deposited, soaked to the bone. He had been too embarrassed to enter the foyer.

I did not understand this, because here was a man who always looked immaculate in his grey suit, white shirt, grey silk tie and polished black Oxford toecaps, who did not own jeans or plimsolls, who even wore his suit on the beach. The idea of him coming on holiday to sit smartly upright behind the folding table of the world's smallest, cheapest caravan in the ugliest part of the British Isles outside of Canvey Island (another regular holiday destination) made no sense at all. Many men of Bill's age regarded a smart suit as a sign of respect and class, but even if he had been born fifty years later he would not have considered three-quarter-length camouflage trousers, trainers and a sleeveless top to be suitable apparel for a father.

I was angry with him for two reasons: his unthinking cruelties to my mother, and his determination to transform me into some kind of motor mechanic by having me climb underneath cars, bikes and now the caravan to hold a bolt in place or 'press hard on that until there's nothing leaking out', because I always did the wrong thing and got oil everywhere. I knew I was meant to be thinking about grommets and differentials, but instead I'd be worrying whether Dickens had got the train signals wrong in *Our Mutual Friend*. My lack of concentration on the job at hand would lead to a yell from above, a shower of petrol/oil/unidentified green liquid and a thump round the back of the head, along with an exhortation to 'Go away and read something, for God's sake, you're bloody useless.'

One miserable Sunday, I spent the entire afternoon holding up one end of the caravan so my father could make a wooden chock to fit beneath the wheels. When my attention slipped and I allowed the end to slide from my grasp, everything inside tilted over and smashed. Bill screamed blue murder, because his hand had become trapped in the process.

'Where's your strength?' he yelled, clutching his hand. 'You can't do anything. Flesh and blood? You're as dry as those bloody books you're always reading. You're just made of paper. I'm amazed you don't curl up and bloody blow away.'

There was a small plywood shelf in the caravan, and I quickly filled it with so many paperbacks that it came away from the wall. Reading prevented me from participation; for the rest of the family it must have been like having to lug an embalmed corpse around on holiday, from the miniature railway to the pier to the beach. The only time I remember speaking in anything approaching a connected sentence was to ask a question about Yosarian in Heller's *Catch-22*, forgetting that no one was remotely interested.

Recently, I read that children's brains hardwire themselves differently the moment they hit their teen years. The physical structure and layout changes, making teenagers more reflective and self-aware, but it also stops them from interpreting the facial emotions of others, creating a cognitive gap between them and adults. I had always selfishly thought that my parents were unresponsive to my needs, but it turns out they were being perfectly normal.

Even without this knowledge I resolved to be nicer, to help repair the leaking caravan, motorbike and car, to do chores around the house, stop reading, stop imagining, start being a better son. In brief, it was time to put away childish things and become a man.

But Kath hated the caravan as much as I did, and a fresh fault-line was developing through the family that sided Steven (practical, mechanical) with our father, and I (dreamy, vague) with our mother. Kath handled the ban on imagination by reading and going to see movies on the sly, but she was not allowed out alone unless she was working, so various subterfuges were used. She would 'take Chris to visit a sick friend' if she wanted to get to the cinema, or develop a headache that required her to spend the evening in her bedroom, where she would read. Even then, Bill couldn't resist looking in from time to time, so she had to be careful. He followed her everywhere, issuing warnings, unable to see how much he needed her.

Meanwhile, I was illicitly sliding the typewriter from

beneath my bed when no one was looking and tapping out stories in faint print, so that I would not have to make a noise with the keys. I could not have been more furtive if I had been bottling my own gin from a homemade still.

The pair of us were behaving like spies, mother and son, tangling ourselves in such complex webs of deceit that Bill must have thought his wife was having an affair. He was now the enemy of freedom, the head of the thought police, and as I was reading Orwell's *1984* at the time, I became Winston Smith, quickly learning how to hide my rebellious traits in case I awoke one morning to hear my father intoning 'You are the dead' out of the caravan's gas mantle.

The lies just kept on compounding themselves, until I could not be trusted to catch my mother's eye over the dinner table, in case I accidentally gave something away. We looked out for each other, stepping on unguarded conversations, creating alibis and cover stories, always ready to jump in with a dozen barely plausible excuses. Sometimes neighbours were roped into this complicity, and even the dog was enlisted on a couple of occasions with false visits to the PDSA and some protracted explanation involving distemper, the only animal illness Kath had been able to recall.

There was one good thing about being stranded in a caravan in a filthy field, and that was the farmer's house, because the old man let us watch his television. This was where I first came across re-runs of *The Quatermass Experiment*, whose hero was a grumpy, unlikeable professor attached to the government in some capacity as a space scientist. The stories showed a great mistrust of being instructed from above, as government yes-men told Quatermass that they knew what they were doing, creating artificial foodstuffs (probably Fanny Cradock's boiled-egg colouring) when in fact the entire country was being flogged off to alien forces. It was science fiction, but the series actually seemed to foresee the Thatcher era. Professor Quatermass remained a great English anti-hero, not just because he was shabby and unstarlike, but because he displayed a consistent suspicion of authoritarianism when most male icons were themselves authoritarians.

I outstayed my welcome in the farmer's house, and was eventually banned from the telly room for getting overexcited. I took my revenge by flying a kite threaded with pieces of silver paper from Bill's fag packets over the farmer's roof, in order to muck up the old man's television reception.

There wasn't much else to do near the caravan site except bring down sparrows with the aid of a thick elastic band and a box of mothballs. Bill owned an old Bolex cine-camera, but it was kept locked in a box underneath packets of silica, and was never used in case it got damaged. Valuable, attractive or interesting items were never used in the Fowler household; they remained in their original boxes where no harm could befall them. I would have liked to make an action film that involved tying my brother to the tracks of the miniature railway. Steven was happy to do it, and was trusting enough to assume that he would be untied before the train got there.

Around this time, my mother did something extraordinarily weird. Faced with the prospect of yet another week staring at the rain-darkened ceiling of the caravan from her damp single bunk, Kath vanished.

No one knew where she had gone. One minute she was there, and the next she wasn't. Her little suitcase was missing. It was the first and only time she ever did such a thing in half a century of marriage. She disappeared for precisely one week, and, like Agatha Christie before her, refused to talk about where she had been when she returned.

While she was away, the rest of us were obliged to pretend that there was nothing wrong. Bill never mentioned the subject, and quietly set about getting his own tea. It was as if Kath had been abducted by Quartermass's aliens and they had wiped her memory from our brains.

When she came back the following Sunday, she headed to her room to unpack her case, then came downstairs to prepare tea (sponge cake, banana trifle), acting as if nothing untoward had occurred.

In theory, given that Bill had been unable to acknowledge her absence, we could simply have picked up where we had left off and gone on as before. Bill refused to speak to her, however, and went to his mother's house, where he stayed for several weeks. Steven and I assumed that our mother had gone to stay in Brighton, where horrible 'Aunt' Mary, our maternal grandmother's paid companion, still had a flat. The thought that she might have nipped off somewhere exotic for a mad fling never crossed our minds.

Some while after Kath returned, an investigative rootle through her jewellery box provided me with a clue to where she had been. Beneath her fake pearls I found a small red enamel pin – the symbol of the Russian communist party. It transpired that she had fulfilled a childhood dream to visit the Hermitage in St Petersburg, staying alone in a government hotel on a non-existent budget. Eventually excitement got the better of her, and she came to speak of the wonders she had seen there, but only quietly, when my father was out of the room. She had pawned her mother's ring to pay for the flight.

Shortly after she returned, Bill got the message and sold the caravan.

25

Certificate X

The family had lined up on either side of the trench, with Bill and Mrs Fowler firing shots from one side, Kath and I sending up flares from the other, Steven slowly being annexed by my father, and Grandfather William operating as Switzerland, somewhere in the middle where we could both go and hide. My valiant effort to lie on my back holding a monkey wrench without thinking of Winston Smith's betrayal of Julia in *1984* had failed miserably, and I was forced to concede that the problem of growing up with imagination in a relentlessly sensible household would not go away.

Although we hardly ever had cross words, I could see that Steven was very different to me. Easy-going and naturally practical, he hid his anxieties so well that for many years I failed to realize he had braved a nightmarish time at school.

Sensing that I was being increasingly annoying, I decided that I needed to involve Bill, to make him see my point of view. My father freely admitted to having no interest in books, little taste in films and actively detesting the theatre, but the door had been left ajar in one area. Apparently, like my mother, he enjoyed horror stories.

It turned out that the book of *The Fifty Strangest Stories Ever Told* had belonged to him, not to Kath. I had never seen a proper horror film and was underage to do so (the 'X' certificate at the time being for over-sixteens), but I now worked on getting Bill to smuggle me into the cinema, which appealed to him because it was illegal and therefore somehow a manly thing to do. And if I could get my mother to come along too, we would all have something to talk about.

Close, it turned out, but no cigar. My father would concede to the horror double bill, but not if it involved bringing Kath along; he was still punishing her for the St Petersburg jaunt, and thought it was 'unladylike' for a woman to enjoy being scared, although by now he had scared her quite a few times himself.

We went through the local paper and I chose the most lurid Hammer double bill I could find. The first horror film I shared with my father created a bond that was certainly never there before.

'You probably want to get rid of your school cap for the evening,' he said, 'and put on some long trousers, for God's sake. If anyone asks, you're sixteen but you've been sick. I don't want you showing me up.'

Luckily I was gangly and already taller than my father. I just needed to find clothes that didn't make me look twelve years old, so the standard-issue grey and yellow school jumper was out. As I clumped up the steps of the cinema, I couldn't have felt more self-conscious if I had been balancing on someone's shoulders inside a double-height raincoat. But it was worth the effort to finally see a film bearing the forbidden, mysterious 'X' certificate.

Horror has always been seen as an adolescent roadhouse

on the way to more sophisticated forms of entertainment because the genre appeals at an early age. The young suffer few intimations of mortality, and children are morbidly fascinated by death and the supernatural. Each time I read or saw something that I liked, I drove another fence-post into the topography of my imagination, gradually mapping its outlines.

Horror regained respectability through the sumptuous period pieces that were Hammer films. English horror had extended from a civilized background, the world of Benson, James and Saki,* of ghost stories told over after-dinner port. Ghost and horror stories could be found in household collections all over the country because the literary tradition was respectable.

Because I was such a politely spoken goody-two-shoes at school, I felt riddled with guilt crossing the plush crimson Dettol-reeking carpet of the Woolwich Odeon to stand in front of the cashier while my father lied about my age. Luckily, the cinema had employed a new member of staff who did not recognize me. It would have been mortifying to be identified as the strange child who spent his afternoons wandering around the foyer in his socks.

Seven years had passed since the first definitive Hammer Dracula had appeared on screen. With no video and no MTV, youthful minds were less saturated with violence than they are today. Images retained the power to shock. Fast cutting had hardly been invented. All horror films appeared in double bills (the thinking seemed to be that two horror films equalled one normal film), so I knew I

*'Saki' was H. H. Munro, master of the poisonous short story. In his rarest tale, 'The East Wing', two men die in a fire to save a painting that, unbeknownst to them, has been sent away to be cleaned. He's very funny and unsentimental, and was probably a closet case.

would already be tensed up by the B-feature before we even got as far as Dracula.

On that very first occasion, the first movie was *Plague of the Zombies*, an elegantly photographed appetizer for the main event. It was not especially gory (only one beheading), but something about the class-warfare country-squire-using-undead-workforce plot held resonance, and those white-eyed zombies dressed in flour bags lingered in the mind. There was a doom-laden recklessness here, signified by the upending of a coffin that exposed a plague-corpse in broad daylight. I felt as if I was on unsafe ground. This was the first image I saw upon entering the darkened auditorium, because as usual we had missed the beginning of the film.

At the start of the main movie I was teased with the end of the first Hammer Dracula film, which I'd been too young to see. Dracula had shrivelled in sunlight, so I knew that the count was dead.

With tension creeping up my arms and legs, I waited for him to reappear. And waited. (This was a number of years before Hammer lazily allowed bats to vomit blood on to Dracula's ashes to revive him.) The next forty-five minutes represented, for me, one of the purest sequences in horror history, as the camera prowled the gloomy corridors and I thought, *He's been bloody cremated, so how the hell can they bring him back?*

When the servant Klove slipped his sacrificial victim's feet into a noose I was even more puzzled, so that the up-side-down throat-slashing over Dracula's ashes came as an astounding shock.

The scene was originally to have featured a beheading, which would have been much less effective. Luckily the censors had rejected that idea in favour of a blade across the jugular, proof (if any were needed) that they hadn't the faintest clue what they were doing. Nothing could ever recapture the peculiarly effortless sensuality that made the film work so well in the cinema. Those silent-movie reactions to crucifixes – the ridiculous throwing up of hands – soon came to appear stilted, so what made this minor horror film so special, beyond the fact that it was the first one to bury itself deep within my brain?

The film grew more perfunctory after its bravura opening, but for a while it was perfect. It played like a stripped-down version of the traditional legend. The coach-driver refused to look up at the impossibly baroque castle; prim, pent-up Barbara Shelley was transformed into a sensual (and somewhat middle-aged) hellcat; Dracula was invited in by a feeble-minded lunatic; crucifixes seared; fangs were bared with a hiss; James Bernard's sinfully lush score was backed by the ever-present moaning wind; and a dim-witted man of the cloth made a nuisance of himself. The only real romance on display was an unhealthy love of all things dead, and even the happy ending reeked of melancholia.

How could this not have been the start of a lifelong love affair with horror and fantasy?

Films were no longer enough; they were topped up with more Pan Books of Horror, and the New English Library of fantastic literature. A horror film, I later came to realize, was like sex: the first time might not be the best, but you would always remember it.

English horror revealed the apathy at the heart of a particularly cruel type of English personality. The films succeeded because they were made in a morally hypocritical country. This new sensuality of the supernatural seemed linked to the growing freedom of the times; Hammer films appeared with a fully fledged worldview of their own, surprising everyone with their paradoxically low-key, high-style acting and graphic gore scenes, but then they were created in a country still riven by class problems, and they captured the casually callous attitude of the English upper classes in a way that no one else managed to. Count Dracula could have been a member of the House of Lords. It was a subtext that only occasionally protruded far enough to be noticeable, but it was always there.

After this long night of fear I began to see all period horror films, even the tatty 'murderous she-moth' flick *The Blood Beast Terror.* The mystique of Hammer remained because their grand sets and full-blooded performances distanced them from surrounding shockers. In the same way that gentlemanly Kenneth Horne could make smutty jokes on *Round the Horne* over the Sunday roast beef and get away with it, the Hammer regulars could star in bloody set-pieces without appearing to be slumming because Peter Cushing and Christopher Lee were smart and mature, and I felt comfortable placing trust in them. They wore ties and spoke nicely. They were like my father.

All the other parts were played by a gallery of Dickensian character actors, including Thorley Walters, Francis Matthews and, yes, Michael Ripper, who lent gravitas to the duffest dialogue lines. Ripper was usually cast as a Transylvanian inn-keeper, and bizarrely chose a West Country accent to deliver his lines, crying, 'You'm bain't be goin' up to Carstle Draaakler tonoight!' And this was the point. Hammer films weren't set in Bavaria or Liechtenstein or Transylvania, they were set in England and they were about the English, only nobody could see it at the time. It was an England that was soon to fade from view.

The early Hammer femmes fatales were sexy maternal types who wore nightgowns apparently made of heavy sailcloth. One of them, Jenny Hanley, was a presenter of the children's TV show *Magpie*, so I figured it was probably illegal to have carnal thoughts about her. Hammer soon lost the courage of its convictions and presented risible versions of 'young people' on the screen, of whom blond-locked, caterpillar-eyebrowed Shane Bryant was the most appalling. The company's decline was perhaps the result of a growing disillusionment among young people, who were beginning to choose more morally ambiguous, cynical ideas over straight battles between good and evil. Eventually, when compared to the feral punks of the King's Road, Dracula came to appear positively benign.

Bill didn't stay the course with this new obsession. Like everything else that took his fancy, his interest waned before any real demand was made on his attention. Besides, his motorbike was playing up and we went from missing the first twenty minutes of every film to missing an entire hour. So, having gained confidence, I asked if I could now go to see adult films on my own.

The oddest of my discoveries was *The Wicker Man*, which starred Christopher Lee and featured Ingrid Pitt, but was the antithesis of a traditional Hammer horror. Filled with folk tunes, sunshine and light, flowers, earth myths and mysticism, it presented pagan worshippers as level-headed and attractive people, while Edward Woodward's painfully upright Christian copper was a humourless and prescriptive killjoy. The island of Summerisle's determination to worship the old gods seemed desirable and even sensible, throwing Woodward into relief as an emotionally frozen God-botherer who got a well-deserved come-uppance. The skewed, wrong-headed values of the Summerisle family also, if I had dared but to admit it, reminded me of my parents.

In many ways it was an English comedy, and English comedies were best when they were black, or at least cruel. The entire Fowler family – with the exception of the endlessly good-natured Steven – frequently found humour in human weakness, spite, sexuality, death and embarrassment. Post-war black comedy was a healthy acknowledgement of the absurdities of life that frequently blurred the distinctions between love and hate, between having plenty and having to go without. The idea that communities might exist in a debilitating, satanic war with their own natures, with a disregard for life, morals and decent feelings, could, it seemed, prove positively life-affirming.

This, I learned, was where English stories won on account of their unpredictability and sheer bad manners. Black comedy felt like a fantastical sidestep from the politeness of everyday life, more closely allied to the horror genre by its preoccupation with the power of fate and the ultimate selfishness of humanity. I watched *The Man in the White Suit* on television with the sound turned off and noticed that it suddenly looked like a horror film, not a comedy at all.

The English films of my childhood were now noticeably different from Hollywood films. Instead of sex bombs we had porky Diana Dors, although she gave her all and wasn't afraid to take common parts. Jenny Agutter brightened many schoolboy nights because she happily took her knickers off in *The Railway Children* just to let a train know about a landslide. Generally speaking, though, English women went from buttoned-down frigidity to being treated with a mixture of fear and schoolboy sniggering. The women rarely exhibited the frontier emancipation of American heroines.

I could see that the writers I most admired excelled in absurd dark comedy, horror, and sometimes in serious drama that mixed elements of both. *The Whisperers, Séance on a Wet Afternoon, A Day in the Death of Joe*

Egg,* *The Ladykillers, Morgan – a Suitable Case for Treatment* and *The National Health* were preferable to the social-conscience huffings of Lindsay Anderson, whose film *If* seemed like the sulky revenge of a disgruntled public schoolboy.

After my first double horror bill, I felt as if I'd just lost my innocence in the intimate embrace of the dark. I felt like smoking a cigarette. We didn't talk much on the way home. I wanted to go to sleep, because the experience had left me feeling exhausted.

As he parked the motorbike, Bill turned to me and asked, 'Did you enjoy that, then?'

'It was amazing,' I told him truthfully. 'I think I want to do it again tomorrow night, maybe with somebody else.'

---

*This and *The National Health* were written by the wonderfully acerbic playwright Peter Nichols, whose memoirs are entitled *Feeling You're Behind*.

26

Mummy's Boys

Books had connected me to the world. Now the cinema connected me to my father.

Although the horror fad didn't last long, the pair of us still went to double bills so frequently that I sensed I was being used as a weapon to fight my mother. When Kath complained that Bill was never around, my father could point at me and say we were going out together. But at the end of every ABC or Odeon night, there was a price to pay: a visit to Mrs Fowler, during which I was made to sit in the kitchen with a mug of thick brown tea or Bovril* while the old woman dug needles of doubt and suspicion beneath my father's thin skin. He had made a bad marriage; Kath was needy and grasping, a bad housewife and an unfit mother; her children were poorly behaved, weak-willed 'mummy's boys' who would never amount to anything unless they were shown more discipline. And he was a pathetically poor excuse for a husband. If he had

*During the Crimean War they tried to make a similar thick paste from horses called Chevril. It didn't catch on.

any spine he would have left her by now. In her day, a man knew how to keep a woman in her place. A man knew how to show he was the boss.

Quite what this said about the state of her own marriage was a mystery. How did William sit beside her in his easy chair and listen to so much implied criticism of himself without wanting to smack her in the mouth and prove her wrong?

After these trips, Bill was always more surly and curt with my mother. I no longer hated him, but my disappointment felt infinite. Why was he so easily swayed by his mother's venom? Surely he could see beyond the words to her real intentions? Either he loved Kath and should stand up for her, or he didn't, and should set her free. It was obvious to me that they were both made miserable by the gruesome roundelay of recrimination that occurred after each visit Bill made to his mother's house.

During the most recent visit, Mrs Fowler had surpassed even her own exacting standards, putting in a performance worthy of Iago by implying that Kath sought to be unfaithful to her husband whenever she was left alone. Since the main reason for my mother's loneliness was Bill's allegiance to his own mother, the idea required quite a feat of double-think to hold it together.

On yet another Saturday morning spent wedged beneath an oily motorbike, desperately hanging on to one end of a brake cable while my father swore and huffed with a spanner, I momentarily lost concentration and felt the greasy line slipping through my fingers. It whipped back, lashing me around the face hard enough to cause an instant welt.

My scream of alarm only served to anger Bill more than ever. I jumped up, clutching my cheek, the cable loosening as the bike toppled over on to a can of oil, tipping it across the hall carpet and splashing it up the walls.

My father's hand came down harder still across my forehead. He had forgotten he was wearing a ring. A gash appeared across my eyebrow, releasing a curtain of blood into my right eye. The injury looked worse than it was, but it made me howl loudly enough to bring Kath out from the kitchen, and to be honest, I was prepared to turn it into a full-blown drama.

'What the hell have you done to him?' my mother cried furiously.

Bill was never at his best when forced to defend himself. 'Your son's a useless little nancy, he needs some sense knocked into him.'

'He's not good at doing the things you make him do.'

'We all have to do things we don't like doing, even him.'

'So you thump him? And he's just *my* son when he's done something wrong?'

'I don't know who he is. I don't know what he is. There's nothing in him I recognize.'

'I suggest you take a good look at yourself. If he turns out to be like you, he's in for a bloody miserable life. *He* knows who he is.' Sometimes, Kath championed me at her own expense.

'Leave him alone, for God's sake. You're always pulling him about, he's not a baby.' Bill ran oily fingers through his thinning hair, frustrated. 'I just don't understand. He gets good results at school. He behaves himself. He's always well turned out. He knows right from wrong. It all looks good on paper, but when you turn it into flesh and blood something's just not there.'

'Here, let me see that cut. Goodness, you can stop making such a noise, it's not that bad.' I knew my mother would deal with the wound first, then the carpet and finally the walls. Her aim, as always, was to restore everything to how it was. No sign of upheaval would ever be allowed to remain.

This time, coming to my aid was the worst thing Kath could have done. It only served to widen the crevasse that ran through the middle of the family. The sides moved further apart, with both parents using their respective children as aides, and a few cinema trips were no longer enough to create a lasting truce.

Steven had no idea that his loyalty was being manipulated, so he and I were able to remain steadfast allies. But seated in the garden with a book on my knees, away from the house where no normal conversation could be held, I wondered about myself and my father. Perhaps we could never be friends, not because we were too different, but because, in some mysterious way that I had yet to understand, we were too alike.

Overhead the mouldering plane trees were rustling with fresh rain, and in the council flats opposite someone was screaming blue murder. Kath came out to join me with a red plastic first-aid kit in her hand. She sat beside me on a dead stump – all that remained of a once thriving tree my father had over-pruned – and put a quick stitch into my eyebrow. Thanks to her post-Victorian upbringing, she had always been handy with a darning needle.

'He loves you in his own way,' she told me sadly. 'But he'll always be his mother's son.'

So will I, I thought.

'This is going to sting,' she warned me, wiping the wound with disinfectant. 'Think of something else. Tell me something. Can you remember the first time you enjoyed reading?'

The memory was always quick to return. My first school, Invicta Mixed Infants, had a cherished square of grass behind its playground, just a small emerald patch of calm that caught the lunchtime sun, and you were allowed to venture on to it only if you were going to read a book; even comics were not allowed. I had taken an American novel from the library, *Two Years before the Mast* by Richard Henry Dana Jr, and lying on my stomach, began to read.

Soon the dust of the suburban street, the drowsy warmth of the sun on my back, the distant susurration of bumblebees and the faint dampness that could always be felt through English grass all faded away, to be replaced by the snap of ocean spray, the creak and sway of the clipper, the bitter mess of salt beef and hardtack, the coarseness of sail and rope on my hands.

Finally sensing the unnatural quiet surrounding me, I looked up and realized that I had missed the break bell, and the first twenty minutes of my afternoon class.

I wanted to try and explain my feelings to my mother, but found the words drying in my mouth. I could hear them in my head, but was not able to explain aloud.

Kath sat back, detachedly admiring her handiwork, and something broke. Her face refused to maintain its immobility. Her eyes shimmered as she tipped back her head. 'God, look at us. What a state we're in. We should all be rejoicing the fact that God has given us life, but instead we waste every single thing we have. And you're just as bad as he is – you couldn't be more selfish if you tried. Why can't you give something back, just for once? At least give him a reason to respect you.'

'Why? I don't respect him.' It was the wrong thing to say, but I could not help myself.

'Then we'll just go on the way we are. Not much to look forward to, is it?' She snapped the lid of the first-aid kit shut and rose, furious with me.

27

A Private Thing

Long before the sexually permissive sixties boiled down into the shabby, leering seventies, Bill began to notice that he was missing out. He re-read his elderly *Playboy** magazines and sent off for the odd bit of Dutch porn (clinical, scary, overlit and more instructive than arousing – second drawer down in the wardrobe behind the socks), and after seeing *Bob & Carol & Ted & Alice* fancied trying a bit of wife-swapping. But the only wife apart from his own that he even knew to nod to was his boiler-fitter mate Ron's missus, and she was a boiler. He'd never bothered to make friends with anyone, and was starting to see how small his world had become.

Sex was in the air, but everything conspired against Bill getting any. Kath had by now undergone a grotesque, painful hysterectomy that had involved a doctor waking her up to announce that her womb 'and the parts

*Playboy ran cutting-edge fiction in its pages and was a good friend to upcoming authors. It recently published an article on pubic hair-styling, so obviously the tradition continues.

governing your sexual feelings, which you don't need'
had been removed while she was unconscious, without
her consent.

Everything was changing around them. As a conces-
sion to modernity Kath finally purchased a cream plastic
trimphone, which was so light that it flew up into the air
whenever she lifted the receiver. She didn't have anyone
to call, but it had been embarrassing having a telephone
table without a telephone on it. Bill solved the problem of
the flyaway phone by supergluing it down. Kath would
stare at it longingly, half willing it to ring, half fearful of
what to do if it did.

And to make matters worse, 'Aunt' Mary came to live
with us. She'd had a stroke, and reminded me of a scary
old tree. Her smile involved a baring of the teeth that
frightened even the dog.

It seemed that the old lady could not do anything
for herself, except when she thought no one else was
watching, when she moved like The Flash and returned
to her position in front of the fire before you could
register what had happened. Every time she outstretched
a clawful of year-old toffees in my brother's direction,
Steven ran screaming from the room. She smelled of
old cupboards, damp and death, and the room seemed
brighter and more cheery whenever she left it. She was
also subject to narcoleptic fits, and after drooling for a
couple of minutes with a faraway look in her rheumy eyes,
would periodically fall sideways and drop off her chair,
once bludgeoning herself into a trance on the fireplace
surround. Somehow, these little moments of downtime
never seemed to faze her, and she would spring straight
back up with a croak of 'Well, what are you looking at?
Don't you have anything better to do?'

And there she stayed in the middle of the lounge at
Cyril Villa, sucking up the light, a silent, yellow-skinned,

joy-draining, tartan-covered obelisk who simply would not die, seated between parents and children, stifling any possibility of spontaneity, joy or conversation above a whisper. She was there before we got up and long after we went to bed, and she hardly ever spoke to anyone. I suspected that, having denied herself a life of her own, she now took great pleasure from crushing all communication that might lead, no matter how circuitously, to some form of happiness.

First, we made any excuse we could think of to leave the room. Then, when it seemed that she could levitate from one area to the next behind our backs, we made any excuse to leave the house. I took to walking the dog six times a day. Bill went off to dig up some rose bushes that had been doing quite well without his help. Kath took her copy of *Bleak House* to the bathroom for hours at a time. Steven played happily in the garden, because he was still innocent and adorable.

Finally, something wonderful happened to 'Aunt' Mary. She died. During the reading of her will, we discovered that she had left fifteen thousand pounds to a cat shelter, money that Kath insisted she had siphoned away from her mother. But at least we were free. It was only for a few weeks, though, because sadly my grandfather's lungs, thickly coated with tar from his old job on the roads and a lifetime of chain-smoking Senior Service, gave out and he too died, leaving Mrs Fowler with nowhere to stay.

I found my mother sitting in her partially wallpapered bedroom, crying. 'What can we do but take her in?' Kath said. 'Carrie can't do it, she's got her hands full with her nerves, and no one else will even talk to her. Bill wants her to come and live here, with us. She's not like Aunt Mary. She's strong. She's going to live for ever. She'll outlive all of us. She's like those tins of fruit that never go off, the ones that are still fresh after years and years.'

It seemed as though our family was cursed. That dark and rainy night, immediately after the funeral, Mrs Fowler appeared at the front door in her wicker hat and navy-blue coat, clutching her ebony stick like a character in a particularly dreadful Victorian children's novel. But now she also had a battered brown leather suitcase with her.

'Well,' she sniffed disapprovingly at the hall wallpaper, 'it would appear I'm to live here. My son has specifically asked for me. Am I to be invited in or what?'

I knew that once the invitation had been issued and she had crossed over the threshold, nothing would get her out until everyone in the house had been sucked dry of blood.

My mother held the door open and got out of the way as her arch-nemesis trundled forward like a gunboat entering a harbour. Having badgered her husband into a submissive decline, Mrs Fowler now had the little house in Reynold's Place to herself, but conveniently glossed over the subject when Kath asked her about it, moving swiftly on to the arrangements of the household.

Kath wrung her hands inside her apron, a stress-relieving habit she had developed along with pressing the back of her wrist against her chin. 'Would you like me to take you upstairs and show you your room?' she asked.

'Show me the kitchen,' said Mrs Fowler. 'My son needs a decent meal inside him.'

The tiny galley-like kitchen was Kath's sanctum sanctorum, the only place she could call her own. Now, it seemed, she was to share it.

After a good night's sleep, Mrs Fowler rose early and began the rehabilitation of her son's diet by restoring lots of peculiar old products to the kitchen: lard, dripping, treacle, suet, dried prunes, turnips, syrup of figs, castor oil, molasses, pickled eggs, gherkins, some kind of sepia cabbage in a jar. If she could have laid her hands on some whale meat or snoek she would have done so. In clouds of flour she bashed and rolled and thumped pastry about until it was grey. Filled with inchoate vexation, she inched across the workspace so that Kath was slowly driven back against the boiler, before being impatiently asked to move out of the way. My mother retreated to the door, hovering uncertainly while her rival boiled mutton to extinction.

Next, Mrs Fowler started on the lounge, dangling crocheted antimacassars from the backs of the armchairs and placing yellowed doilies under anything in the room that didn't move. Chalk and china knick-knacks began to appear: poodles, windmills, fishing boats, a giant fly made of brass that held pins. I realized what she was doing: she was turning our house into her house. Already crepuscular, the gloomy rooms sank into senescence. Once she was satisfied, she would march from the room with a mutter of 'That's *much* better.'

There are men who will do anything to avoid an argument with women. Bill meekly ate what was set before him, refusing to be drawn into the complex question of his preferences. I dug out my old notebooks, or retreated to the cinema. My mother chewed her nails, sensing defeat. Even the dog hid in the back room, developing a zoo-cage mentality that would eventually drive it to compulsive pacing, insanity and an early death.

There had to be some way out. Our family had never been close, but now it was quickly falling to bits. Like stress fractures appearing in the sixties concrete motorway that cut through East Greenwich, something had to crack. Eventually it did.

Kath put up with being relegated to an ever-smaller corner of the kitchen for three weeks, then fled to my room, where she sat biting her nails and peering from the window in abject misery.

'I don't know what to do,' she confided. 'Your father hates me more each day. You're the only one who understands that I'm not the villain in this, and you're just a child.'

I wasn't thrilled to be considered a child. I had started thinking of myself as an adult at the age of twelve. 'You're always telling me to act on what I feel,' I told her. 'Why don't *you* do it? Go in to the kitchen and throw her out. Chuck her into the street, and her suitcase after her.'

'She's his mother,' Kath said in awe.

'She's not just his mother,' I told her. 'She's a rude word.'

'You're right,' Kath agreed, the truth dawning. 'She's a horrible old bitch.' Shocked, she threw her hand over her mouth. 'Goodness.'

'And you have to throw her out.'

'I can't do that.'

'Then she'll continue to act like she's Dad's wife instead of his mother, and turn you into her daughter, and make this family into something really, really strange.'

'Oh dear.'

'Go on,' I goaded. 'Go down there. Put your foot down. Let her know who's boss.'

But she didn't. Kath went back to the kitchen and waited patiently while her mother-in-law took over the sink, the draining board, the counter. Finally, when Mrs Fowler realized that Kath was not going to move any further, she snatched a saucepan away from her. 'For God's sake,' she shouted, 'don't you know anything about the preparation of decent food?'

There was a small silence, then an explosion of pots, pans and crockery as my mother threw my grandmother out of the kitchen. Mrs Fowler burst forth, her navy-blue coat covered in flour and eggs. 'That's it!' she wailed. 'I won't stay in this house for another second, not if you paid me! I'll not remain in a house where all my goodwill and hard work is ignored and thrown back in my face!'

She stumped upstairs, packed her leather suitcase and returned to stand dramatically in the hall doorway. 'You can be sure that I'll let my son know it was you who drove me out on to the street!' She raised a hand, pointing a forefinger to the sky, preparing to issue a proper Victorian curse. 'And I swear that if I should die this very night,' she intoned solemnly, 'my death will be on your conscience until the day you die. Probably longer.'

And with that, the front door slammed, the wind dropped, the house fell silent and she was gone. After an hour the dog came out from behind the couch.

My mother should have been jubilant, but she wasn't. She felt she had committed a terrible sin, when all she had done was stand up for herself. She wondered what on earth she could tell Bill when he returned home from work. He would be furious, he would blame her for everything, he would not talk to her for months, years, possibly the rest of his life.

That night, Mrs Fowler went to her sister Carrie's to stay. After setting down her leather suitcase and asking for a nice cup of hot, strong tea, she sat down on the sofa, closed her eyes and died.

Kath took the phone call and listened with growing numbness. She had only just mastered the art of answering the phone, and now she was about to be put off it for life. By the time she replaced the receiver, she was distraught.

'What am I going to do when Bill finds out?' she asked. 'This is worse than before. I threw her out, and she cursed me. She willed herself to die, just to spite me. She's turned me into a cold-blooded killer. He's going to blame me for murdering his mother.'

But oddly, Bill didn't. He let himself in quietly and

stood at the window, watching the boats make their serene passage down to the wide silver reaches of the Thames. A thin pink mist had settled on the lowlands by the riverbank. The last remaining tatters of cloud disappeared, as if fleeing over the edge of the world. He stood there until the street lights came on and the sky to the North had turned a clear navy blue. Even then he did not move.

Bill remained quiet and thoughtful in the days that led up to the funeral. Mrs Fowler was placed in an urn beside her husband, where she could continue to have a go at him. Quite a few of the neighbours from Reynold's Place turned up and stayed timidly in the background, like Munchkins making sure the witch was dead.

Neither I nor my mother could understand Bill's mood. After a while, his taciturn demeanour slowly lifted and he became almost chatty. He seemed strangely free, happy even. And as the old woman's shadow slowly faded, he finally started to notice his wife. It was as if he had found something that had been there all along, waiting patiently for discovery, only it had been too small and quiet to see.

'Can I ask you something?' I said to Kath. My mother and I had taken the dog for a walk. The Alsatian was trying to claw its way ahead, spraying spittle and making strangled retching noises on its lead. 'When we were in Westerdale Road, I saw him hit you. Why didn't you just leave?'

'Oh you did, did you? I wondered if you had.' She fell silent. We walked on. The dog sounded as if it was choking to death, its pink tongue protruding obscenely from its mouth. She slipped it from its lead and it shot off into the woods to take a dump and chase a rabbit.

'Well, he only hit me a couple of times,' said Kath finally. 'You're talking about that evening you saw us through the banisters. He came at me again and I fell backwards.'

'But—'

'Then he hit himself. Over and over again. I sat there watching him while he did it. You can't imagine how I felt. I wanted to reach out and hold him, but he just wouldn't let me. He wanted to hurt himself. Well, you're the only other person who knows about it. It has to be our secret.'

'But I still don't understand. Were you ever in love with him?'

'No. Nor with anyone else, before you ask. It would have been nice, and I thought it might happen, but that wasn't the way things turned out. There are different kinds of love; I had you and Steven.'

'Then why have you stayed with him all this time?'

'Oh, there are things you don't know about your father. He grew up in that tiny dark house listening to his mother destroy the reputations of everyone around her. I try not to believe that there are bad people, but she really tested my patience. I suppose she was a product of her time, and the time before that, when a strong woman could rule the street she had been born in. He finally got away from her by taking a job in the city. But he'd picked up her habit of saying terrible, untruthful things about people behind their backs, and one day it got him fired from his job.'

I remembered the whispered mystery of my father's lost job.

'He was out of work, but stayed up at his mother's house so often that you probably thought he was still going to the office. After a long time he eventually landed a new job and his career finally took off. He started doing well – he's smarter than he seems, your father – and he rose quickly through the ranks. He worked very hard and was heading for the top of his profession, but the company decided to relocate to Toronto, and it broke his heart not to go with them.'

'Why didn't he go?' I asked. 'Why would he choose to end up in a horrible run-down gas showroom in the Elephant and Castle instead?'

'Why didn't he go?' She stopped and studied me, as if amazed that I could be so stupid. 'You know the answer to that, Christopher. He stayed because of you. He could see that you were clever. He didn't want to take you out of your school. You were so happy there. He gave it all up for you.'

I felt deeply ashamed. In my heart I had always known the answer, but I had given my father nothing back. Secret emotions, hidden feelings, pretending everything was fine: this was what we were best at. Why did adults have to bury everything? Our family problems, Bill had always told us, were a private thing. And he was determined to keep them that way, even if it sent us all mad in the process.

28

Rebel Rebel

The popular music of my mid to late teenage years was truly
terrible: Marc Bolan* whining about golden-haired fairies
and stardust, Groundhogs and Iron Butterfly sounding like
someone panicking in a roomful of dustbin lids, Jethro
Tull playing the flute while hopping about on one leg like
Worzel Gummidge. The only bands I could bear to listen to
were Mott the Hoople and Led Zeppelin, although, if truth
be told, I preferred *Die Fledermaus*. 'Whole Lotta Love'
received some major suburban-bedroom turntable time,
and was an antidote to the local disco, where everyone
sat in the corners of the room, nodding their heads and
grooving along with little spastic hand gestures. The girls
wore maroon floor-length crushed-velour dresses and had
long kinked hair tied back with ribbons, Pre-Raphaelite
virgins on cider and joints. Their idea of a good time was
getting smashed while listening to the screaming bit from
Pink Floyd's 'Careful With That Axe, Eugene'.

---

*The perfect parody of a tie-dyed art student. He hit a tree on Barnes
Common and went off to live in Fairyland.

For the weaker members of the school pack, it's always a strange, cocooned existence on the sidelines of the action. I enviously watched the other kids as they honed their social skills, getting their hands into drunk girls' shirts while they danced to 'Ride A White Swan'. The other geeks and I were still making Aurora model kits of mummies and werewolves. None of us were rebels.

The school had a good name. The head and his staff, stiff and imperious in their chalk-stained black gowns, flapped through the corridors like adrenalin-charged vampires. They were grudgingly respected because they did not try to be our friends, but kept their distance and occasionally maimed us when we went too far. We saw the movie *If*, in which Malcolm McDowell machine-gunned his teachers, and it simply wasn't us.

That was before our relief art teacher Mike Branch arrived. He was about thirty years younger than any other member of staff, and came for the summer term. Everyone fell in love with him. He was handsome and funny and a bit mad. He let you smoke in the kiln room, his long blond hair hung over his collar, and he *wore jeans*. To boys who were actually expected to wear school regulation underpants, this was amazing. He asked us to call him Mike, and explained that his classes would be very different from what we were used to.

The first time I saw him, he was lounging with his brown suede boots on the desktop, reaching an arm up to the blackboard to wipe away the masters of the Florentine renaissance. 'Forget the heavy stuff,' he told us. 'We'll be studying the Dadaist* movement, OK?' Then he wrote REBELLION IN ART in red and threw the chalk out of the window.

---

*We loved the Dadaist movement because you could look like a rebel just by nailing a Brussels sprout to a tree.

Suddenly art became the hot class to take.

Mike's lessons were unpredictable, and actually interesting. We created anti-meat art and self-destructing art and death-to-the-ruling-class art. The other teachers tolerated our displays because technically speaking they weren't very good, which made them less of a threat. Besides, as pupils we were Showing An Interest, thus achieving a prime educational directive. The fact that we would have donated our kidneys for transplant if Mike had asked us hadn't escaped their notice, either. The more ignored and hopeless teachers realized they could learn something from watching the art class.

One day Mike placed a single on the turntable of his record player. I was fist-deep in a gore-sprayed papier-mâché duck when 'Paint It Black' by the Rolling Stones came on. I had never liked the dirge-like song, but it transpired that Mike had a purpose for playing it.

'For the climax to our season of anti-art,' he said, strolling between my paint-spattered classmates, 'we are going to paint it black.'

'Paint what black, sir?'

'Everything. It will be a day of artistic anarchy. We'll take all the work you have produced this summer and paint it all black. Then we're going to glue it all together with the record player at the centre, along with anything else that you feel belongs in the sculpture, and stand it in the middle of the school quadrangle as a statement about ourselves.'

It seemed a bit stupid, but nobody argued.

'What if somebody tells us to take it down, sir?' said Doggart, a pudding-basin-haircutted weed who was born to say 'sir' a lot in his life.

'You don't take it down. You don't obey anyone's orders until the stroke of noon. Then I'll appear and we'll play "Paint It Black" from the centre of the sculpture. The art will last for the duration of the song, and then we'll destroy it.

'How, sir?'

'We'll set fire to it.'

'But this is a smokeless zone, sir.'

'Don't worry, I'll forewarn the other masters.'

So, preparations were made, the date was set for the last day of term, and we painted everything we could lay our hands on before adding it to the pile. Clocks. Chairs. Tyres. Lampshades. Toys. Tailors' dummies. Car exhausts. A washing machine. And all the time, the damned record played on and on until it wore out and had to be replaced with a new copy.

Mike Branch strolled around the art room, shifting from table to table, stopping to watch as Ashley Turpin, a fat kid with almost geological facial acne, attempted to get black paint to stick to a brass candelabra.

'Extremely groovy, Turpin,' he pronounced, running his thumb across his chin. Turpin, who had previously shown no promise in any area of scholastic endeavour beyond O-level Body Odour, was pitifully grateful.

Identified to other classes by our laminated badges (black, circular, blank – oh, the *nihilism*), we suddenly found ourselves treated as a creative élite. I and the other despised and shunned creeps had finally found our cause.

We began to be bad – bad as in modern bad, good bad. Soon we were discovering the non-artistic applications of Paint It Black. Minor-league anarchy: having pizzas with disgusting toppings delivered to the masters, cash on delivery; gluing their wipers to their car windscreens. Brian 'Third Degree' Burns upped the stakes by removing the back wheel from the French teacher's moped, painting it black and adding it to the sculpture. We made crank calls to masters' wives from the caretaker's phone. We started wearing black shirts to go with our black ties, and became threatening towards weaker classmates. Anyone who whined that it was wrong was ditched from the group and had his badge revoked. If we had paid attention during History, we might have learned something about Mussolini.

By now there was an all-or-nothing atmosphere among members of the group. On the last day of term, Mike had arranged a double art period for his band of angry young rebels. All of the black-painted sections of the sculpture were arranged around the room. The Rolling Stones record played at top volume. The art room was rechristened the Rock Shop, so you could say, 'Hey, if anyone wants me during the study period, I'm at the Rock Shop.'

We began to assemble the sculpture. Forming a chain, we passed the sections out into the school quadrangle. Table legs, television sets and dolls' arms poked out from the twisted black heap, which grew and grew. The record player was wired up but we were going to be late for our noon deadline, mainly because we were so strung out by now that we were repeating each other's tasks.

The big moment arrived and we were still building the sculpture. Most of the school had turned out to watch. The record player was started and the song began to play. Everyone knew that something special was about to happen. All kinds of rumours were flying around, most of them far more imaginative than what was actually planned. The headmaster appeared to see what all the fuss was about. He stood at the front of the crowd with his bony arms folded behind his back, like the Duke of Edinburgh watching native dancing, a look of attenuated tolerance upon his face.

All eyes were on us. We were the rebels and we had something to say.

Except that we didn't.

We looked around for Mike. Our Mike, the leader of the black. But there was no sign of him anywhere.

'If you're looking for Mr Branch,' said the headmaster in a clear Scottish Presbyterian voice that rang across the quadrangle, 'you will not find him here. He left the school premises last night with no intention whatsoever of returning today.' He carefully pronounced the 'H' in 'whatsoever'.

Our headmaster turned on his heel and led the other teachers back to the common room. And the record stuck. It stuck on the word 'black'. The repeated syllable taunted, and the derision began. Everyone drifted away, snorting to each other, too bored to even come and beat us up. The natural order had been restored, and we were back at the bottom.

I wondered if Mike Branch had ever intended to stay for the final act of rebellion, and what he might have done. Some years later, a friend told me that he had been spotted working as an estate agent in Kensington. I found myself wondering if he realized the effect he had had on all of us. He had given us pride and faith in ourselves, but also arrogance and ill-will. Then he snatched it all away.

It was incredible that we had put all our trust in someone who wore a purple turtleneck sweater and yellow beads beneath a brown patch-suede jacket. But I owned a mauve two-tone shirt with a huge round collar and canary hipster bell-bottoms, so what did I know?

29

The Safety of Scientists

Knowing that my father had sacrificed his career for me should have been the turning point you reach in films and novels, when bridges are mended amid welling tears, and a profound and lasting sense of respect is established between the protagonists as the son views his father with fresh eyes.

Unfortunately, this revelation came just when I had become an art rebel, so I carried on ignoring him. I was too busy dyeing all my clothes black and being moody. I had discovered *Hamlet* and studied it obsessively, searching for parallels with my own life. My father was not an adulterous murderer, but I was quite convinced that I shared qualities with the Dane, including prevarication, incoherent anger, impoliteness, a tendency to mope and an attraction to shoulder-pads. The phase was short-lived, though, and vanished with the non-appearance of the cowardly class warrior Mike Branch on our last day of term. I was quite relieved to be able to return to normal; being a rebel didn't suit someone who preferred Offenbach to Iron Maiden.

THE SAFETY OF SCIENTISTS

Things were a little easier after that, but being with my father was rarely a picnic. As Bill coped with the loss of his mother and re-discovered the existence of his wife, he came to depend more on Kath than he ever had done on Mrs Fowler, following her from room to room, hardly ever letting her out of his sight. He would sit beside the sink smoking as she washed the dishes, and would traipse from room to room behind her as she vacuumed the carpets. He curtailed her freedom in a thousand unthinking ways, but whenever she turned to talk to him he could find nothing to say. Perhaps too many years of silence had passed between them to allow conversation to return.

It seemed impossible, but the family circle had shrunk still smaller. Without 'Aunt' Mary or Mrs Fowler around to drive us mad, a torpor descended upon the house, slowing our days and flattening all emotions. It was as if we had all been tranquillized. Elsewhere in the world there were wonderful adventures to be had and great loves to be celebrated, but life in South London had flat-lined. When Kath had first laid eyes upon my father, I wondered if it had it been like Cressida's sighting of Troilus as he passed beneath her window in gleaming armour, then decided that as Bill looked more like Arthur Askey* than a Trojan prince, the answer was probably not.

Within a month my father and I were constantly arguing once more, so Bill refocused his affections on Steven, who shared his love of everything mechanical.

The time of waiting seemed to last for ever. I crept off to horror films as though paying furtive visits to a forbidden lover. It was a way of experiencing all the things I could not yet feel, or be allowed to feel. If it wasn't exactly improving my mind, it was better than digging out

*The archetypal music-hall-comic-turned film star, he now comes over as deeply annoying and rather sinister.

bottles of rum from the sideboard and getting pissed in the middle of the afternoon, or hanging around in bus shelters, casting weaselly glances at adults while planning gang wars over disputed territories. There wasn't a wide range of activities to choose from in Abbey Wood if you had no money.

I returned to writing longhand. The Remington had tangled its keys once too often. I had tried to straighten them with a pair of needle-nosed pliers, but now they defied any attempt at realignment. After each visit to the Odeon I headed home to fill up more exercise books with stories, notes, and ideas filched from everything I saw, but sometimes the sheer effort of being so self-absorbed got to me. By now my secondhand writing was suffering from the law of diminishing returns.

Girls take an interest, but boys become obsessed. In the past I had been obsessed with Thunderbirds, *Mad* magazine, Hammer films, *The Avengers* (Diana Rigg series only), *Monty Python's Flying Circus*, *The Prisoner*, *Hancock's Half-Hour* (radio series only), Superman, *Playboy* and Dracula.

Oh, to see a film in which Superman fought Dracula for Diana Rigg on a space station. Sadly, there was as yet no internet to provide solace for one's more exacting obsessions. I looked back at the dismally predictable list and felt very ordinary indeed. I re-read the short stories written out in my diary and the feeling of ordinariness grew. I was the same as every other child in the neighbourhood, probably the whole of London, England, the Earth, the Universe. I probably even had the same fantasies, which included:

Being the last teenager left alive on Earth and
    having the keys to every building in London.
Running my own television station, Fowlervision.

Owning a cinema and being the manager, so I
    could put on whatever I liked, as many times as I
    wanted.
Something vaguely to do with naked ladies, or
    possibly naked men, which was very different to
    being interfered with.
Owning every single issue of *Superman*, especially
    the one in which he dies: not a hoax, not a
    dream, But REAL!

I slammed my notebook shut when I realized that Kath
was reading over my shoulder. 'I think we need to have a
little talk,' she said, indicating the diary. 'Bring that with
you.'

We usually headed into the overgrown garden filled with
rusting motorbike parts whenever we wanted to be alone,
so as to keep our conversations hidden from my father.
Bill had lately taken to chopping chunks out of trees in
the adjacent woods, spreading his knack for destruction
into the natural world, so Kath made herself comfortable
on a sawn log and took the book from me. She read in
silence for what felt like ages, then closed it gently and
looked at me.
    'Well, they're not terribly good, are they?' It hurt me
that she could be so honest. Her green eyes gazed steadily
into mine, demanding that I reply with equal frankness.
    'No,' I admitted. 'They're rubbish.'
    'No, not exactly rubbish. But they're not really yours.
They're someone else's ideas, re-worked, which is fine if you
want to get a job in advertising. Instead of writing about
mad scientists, can't you write about people you know?'
    It was horrible advice, as nearly all the people I knew
were demented or damaged in incomprehensible yet
mundane ways. Not one of them behaved in the fashion

I was led to believe was correct and laudable. I preferred the safety of scientists. They only had killer plants and space viruses and evil mutants to deal with, not decade-long arguments, mammoth sulks, buried resentments and secret struggles for control. You always knew where you were with scientists because they gripped pipes between clenched teeth and strutted about thinking aloud with one hand in the pocket of their lab coats. I liked them because they were just like robots, not real at all. *Oh . . .*

Her point began to dawn on me.

'Will you write me a story about us?' she asked.

'I don't know. I don't think you'd like it very much.'

'Then write about your favourite singer. Do you like . . .' She searched for some form of modern music with which she was familiar. 'Cliff Richard?'

'No, I like Noël Coward.'*

'Oh.' She thought for a moment. 'Do you know what you want to be when you grow up?'

'A film critic.'

'Anything else?'

'A lyricist.'

'Why not become a proper writer?'

'They're poor and have no friends, and have to live in a garret. A writer spends years perfecting his first novel, which is usually a failure, and then spends more years trying to recapture the magic of his first novel because the critics now all say he's not as good as he used to be, or else he kills himself because he can't find a publisher for his first novel, and dies a lonely miserable death, upon which his first novel becomes a great success, partly because the public knows he killed himself. Whereas a sizeable number of lyricists own yachts.'

---

*Coward once said, 'Television is for appearing on, not for looking at.' You've got to love him for that.

'I can see you've thought this through.' She rubbed her eyes wearily, trying to imagine what should be done. 'It's probably best not to tell your father about your career plans. And I think your opinion of writers is not entirely accurate. I think we should start with what's actually on the page, don't you? Perhaps you need to find some new heroes.'

I could have told her I wanted to become a shepherd and she would have sought a positive solution. Drawing out a pen, she balanced the diary on her knee and made a new list on the last page. 'Go back to the old library in Greenwich and try taking out a few of these.'

I looked at the list. 'What are they?'

'Things I read and loved. I never owned them, although I wish I had.'

I returned to East Greenwich Public Library, but when I got there I found its shelves emptier, its parquet floor dustier than I remembered. Its rooms were almost devoid of life.

The seat where my old friend the librarian always sat had now been taken by a young woman with elaborately arranged blonde hair. She was eating a Mars Bar and reading a copy of *NME*. 'Oh, the Council retired Mrs Clarke, and she died a few weeks later,' she told me casually when I asked. She took my mother's list from me and studied it. 'We don't have many of these. We had a bit of a clear-out, gone more modern an' that. Spy thrillers, hospital romances. There's no call for the highbrow stuff any more. You wanna try a bookshop.'

Highbrow? I had never thought of my mother like that. I looked back at the list:

Scoop by Evelyn Waugh
Orlando by Virginia Woolf

The Best of Saki by H. H. Munro
Labyrinths by Jorge Luis Borges
Howard's End by E. M. Forster
The Bridge of San Luis Rey by Thornton Wilder
Brighton Rock by Graham Greene
Hangover Square by Patrick Hamilton
The Good Soldier by Ford Maddox Ford
Thérèse Raquin by Emile Zola
Twelfth Night by William Shakespeare
Elizabeth and Essex by Lytton Strachey
The Short Stories of W. Somerset Maugham
Diary of a Provincial Lady by E. M. Delafield
Music for Chameleons by Truman Capote
Madame Bovary by Gustave Flaubert
Childhood's End by Arthur C. Clarke

Were these highbrow? Some thrillers, some dramas, some comedies, some true stories, a lot of exciting plots, most written in easily comprehensible English. Were these books that people honestly found too daunting to read now?

There were perhaps another thirty novels and collections on the list, many of which I had not heard of and could not find in suburban Greenwich, although I managed to turn up more in the sleazy Popular Book Centre than in the library. My favourite purchase was a paperback that sported a racy cover showing a pair of swaggering, melon-breasted strumpets with their hands on their hips. Above the title was a strapline that read: 'He knew the truth about the city's sauciest sexpots!' It was a 1950s copy of Boswell's Journals.

Over my teenage years I located the rest of them, one volume at a time, and stacked them carefully beneath my bed. As each book I read provided me with illumination, it also withered and destroyed any hope of ever achieving an easy familiarity with words. Such grace and erudition was so far beyond my scope that it was pointless to try creating even the palest imitation.

Shortly after reading Virginia Woolf's *Orlando*, I dragged out a pile of my exercise books, filled with their witless, derivative stories, and burned them at the end of the garden, just as my father had burned my books in Westerdale Road.

As I watched the smoke curl in a thin blue trail over the treeline of the grey-green woods behind the house, I decided that my mother had done me a favour in revealing the gap between my own abilities and those of a real writer.

In that moment, my future was decided. The answer was so obvious that I wondered why on earth I had been struggling against it for so long. I would get a job in an office, where I at least stood a chance of being successful in a mediocre world. I would keep my head down, work hard, fade into comfortable invisibility and be content with that, like any other normal human being.

30

Being Normal

Having decided that I would live like the robotically predictable scientists I had written about, with none of the emotional upheaval experienced by my parents, the first thing I needed to do was stop hanging around with Simon, whom the rest of the school considered to be a cross between Peter Fonda and the Antichrist. Clearly, he was a bad influence and was preventing my rehabilitation. It was Simon's fault that I committed my only crime. Without him, I would never have stolen the gun.

Well, it wasn't a real one, but it was made of heavy black metal and was very realistic. We had gone into London's West End, to Berman & Nathan, the theatrical costumiers, and had presented them with a forged letter purporting to be from our headmaster, saying that the school was staging a musical version of *Bonnie and Clyde* for Parents' Day and we needed a gun. Incredibly they had given it to us, in a brown leather holster that fitted under a school jacket. I had no idea what we were expected to do with it. I assumed – rightly, as it transpired

– that Simon was less intent on holding up a post office than swanning about in his bedroom and striking poses in front of his mirror.

The argument over the gun made it easier for me to stop seeing him. I concentrated on being as normal as possible, so normal that I began to creep people out. Instead of sticking to my throwback short-back-and-sides haircut, I grew my hair over my ears like everyone else of my age and tried a gormless centre parting. I bought flared jeans like everyone else (I had been living in black flannel trousers). I experimented with bead necklaces. I even tried watching television, because everyone seemed to like *Rowan and Martin's Laugh-In** and quoted the catchphrases to each other at school, but the only way we could get BBC2 reception, albeit in a snowstormy, shimmering fashion, was still by holding the aerial in the corner of the attic ceiling, and staring so hard at the screen while standing on tiptoe made me feel as if I was experiencing some form of brain damage.

I went to the local pub with schoolfriends and tried drinking cider, but got so drunk that the dog didn't recognize my walk when I came home and bit me on the face when I tried to crawl upstairs.

I bought a Rolling Stones album, but hated it so much that I quickly reverted to secretly taking *Die Fledermaus* out of Plumstead Public Library.

I stopped trying to build all the characters and sets from *Barbarella* in plasticine, and bought a stamp album instead, only I never got beyond the triangular one from Fiji.

I made an Airfix aircraft carrier with my father, and a balsa-wood glider, but got into trouble for cutting out

---

*Innovative comedy show that even the US president, Richard Nixon, appeared on.

stencils on the dining-room table that left imprints of the wings in the still-sticky varnish, like the ghosts of lost pilots.

I bought some aftershave, even though I was clearly years from growing a whisker. It was called Aqua Manda and smelled of rotten oranges. I got through a whole bottle in a single week before someone explained you were only supposed to use it on your chin.

I went to a club with some disreputable boys from the local comprehensive, but it was before the days of disco, and the music was Blind Faith and Colin Blunstone. After drinking lots of cough syrup, everyone just sat on the floor with their eyes half closed, nodding and pretending to be stoned.

I tried to show an interest in the local girls, but they were going through a feminist phase that involved patchouli oil and joss sticks and wearing wooden sandals with floor-length maroon-and-yellow tie-dye dresses, and not washing their long frizzy hair, so they all looked like Cornish lady tramps. Plus, they tended to shout 'Stop objectifying me!' if you tried to talk to them.

I solemnly smoked a joint purchased from Frank Knight, whose older brother was a customs officer who brought home tons of drugs. I managed to get through half of it before falling face-down into a bonfire, losing my credibility, my sideburns and one eyebrow in the process. When I came home that night, the dog bit me again because it could only smell smoke.

I tried to remember what made my schoolfriends laugh and go 'Phwoar!', and laughed more loudly than anyone else, which just made me weird and to be avoided. On one occasion I laughed so loudly that the conductor threw me off a number 75 bus because I was frightening the passengers.

Being 'normal' was supposed to make you popular, but

it had the opposite effect. The only friend it attracted was a small troll-like boy in my class who kept asking me if I could come round to his house while his parents were out and wrestle with him naked.

I started writing again, tentatively, carefully. This time I would not do it just for myself, as I had with the densely narrated comics and volumes of film criticism, but would search out a proper audience.

As my parents had never given me much pocket-money, I needed to find a way of making some cash. Instead of taking a route as a paperboy, I studied the letters pages of local newspapers and noted that each week's star letter could earn its writer five pounds. It was a simple matter of studying the form of each paper and understanding what they were looking for.

I had always been a good mimic, and could finally put the skill to use. I wrote dozens of letters to magazines up and down the country, from *Knitwear Monthly* to *Yachts and Yachting*. Soon I was earning myself a schoolboy salary, while learning about everything from needlepoint to spinnakers. I did it guiltily, worrying that I might be robbing an old lady of the coveted position of star letter, but it was enough to give me renewed confidence. I wrote in masquerade as a college professor, a district nurse, a retired colonel, a dinner lady, a Chelsea Pensioner, a juvenile delinquent, a prisoner, a naval officer. I realized that I had spent so many years being quiet and watching people that I had picked up all kinds of useless information. It was time to wring out the sponge.

I began to quantify my personal feelings by making a list of all the things that made me happy, and when this proved far too bland and embarrassing (it included things like sunlight on wet streets and the smell of cut lemons) I made another list of all the things that made me fearful.

As this list threatened to run to several dozen pages,

I began to understand the nature of my problem. I was scared of being alive, just like my father.

It was odd that, despite having read hundreds of examples of what could be considered blueprints for good writing, when I sat down at a table to write I could not recall any of the lessons I had absorbed. I wondered if it was because my life bore so little relationship to Captain Ahab's or those of the five aristocratic families in *War and Peace*. After all, I was never likely to set to sea (unless you counted crossing the Thames on the Woolwich Ferry) or become embroiled in another Napoleonic invasion of Russia.

The answer lay in the idea that you planted little seeds of yourself and the people you knew in different plots. I did not know how my family would react to news that the world was about to end, for example, but I could take a pretty good guess. My mother would lay down stocks of tinned peaches and make sure that the house was tidy, as if preparing for guests. My father would attempt to build a bomb-proof bunker at the bottom of the garden, but would only get as far as finishing two plywood walls and an undercoated door before the apocalypse struck. Mrs Fowler, were she back from the grave, would blame Kath for being the underlying cause of the apocalypse. My brother would come up with the only practical and useful arrangements for the cataclysm. And me, I would probably pick up my notebook and start passively recording details without ever quite grasping the true importance of the event, just as I always did.

But what was the alternative? You didn't need to fight a bull in order to write about fighting a bull. I had read enough of Ernest Hemingway's prose to decide that writing was not the ideal tool for proving one's manhood. English authors were never daunted by the invention of passive heroes. Dickens's characters had plenty of strong personality traits but were pulled from shore to shore by the tidal forces of their turbulent times.

What about locations? If you wanted to set a story in Paris, did you have to go there? The furthest we had ever ventured was Broadstairs. We hadn't even been to Cornwall because, as my father was fond of pointing out, 'It's further away than France, for God's sake.' What about a story set on Mars? Where did you even begin to start with other planets? What would an alien look like if it lived on a planet with a million times more gravity than that of the Earth? How would he pick things up if his arms bent the other way?

And what about drama? If nothing more dramatic than a small bin fire had ever occurred in your life, could you still describe the collapse of empires? Were there perhaps laws against doing so, like the list of strange nouns governing language rules that I had discovered in the East Greenwich Public Library?

'This obsession with plots, well, it's not a bad thing,' said my mother, reading over my shoulder. She had lately begun making regular checks on me. 'But at some point you have to start using them to understand people. People shape the events of a story, not the other way round.'

'That's not true. Wars change people.'

'Yes, but whether they are brave or weak in terrible circumstances is decided by their character. And people's characters are very complicated and contradictory – far more so than you'd ever imagine.'

'Are you saying the stories aren't important?'

'No, I'm saying they're the part you can make up. But you can't make up emotions. They have to be real.'

'Then what do you do about stories?'

'Oh, those can come out of your head. If you're convincing in what you make up, it will feel real to the reader. You always liked *Hancock's Half-Hour*, didn't you?'

'Yes.' The Hancock radio shows drew vast audiences. The streets had always been emptier when he was on the air. Hancock was effectively playing himself, an embittered former vaudeville artist on the downslide from fame, yet he could barely improvise a single word. He relied on two scriptwriters whom he would eventually come to resent, Ray Galton and Alan Simpson, but without whom he was doomed. The pair had changed the face of radio comedy by making it sound naturalistic, even when the shows were absurd flights of fancy. There were pauses and coughs, sighs and – most feared of all on radio – passages of total silence. One episode, *A Sunday Afternoon at Home*, nailed the absolute deadliness of the English post-lunch Sunday: 'Nowhere to go, nothing to do, just sitting here waiting for the next lot of grub to come up.'* Galton and Simpson even acknowledged their debt to Harold Pinter in one of the show's episodes. 'This isn't a Pinter play,' they made Hancock announce, 'where you can say whatever you like so long as you put enough gaps in it.'

'When you listen to those shows,' said my mother, 'do they tell you what Tony Hancock is like?'

'Of course. He's rude and pompous and insecure, and everything annoys him.'

'So if the writers decide to put him in hospital or let him win the pools, you already know how he will react. And you think about how *you* would react in the same situation. And the gap between the two makes the comedy. To me, that's what being a writer is really about. Words can inspire a sense of recognition, but how much more exciting to provide a revelation!'

---

*Hancock continued: 'I thought my mother was a bad cook but at least her gravy used to move about.' Some of his finest shows were wiped by the BBC and remain lost.

'I haven't had any revelations.'

'Never confuse the writer with what he writes – they're two different things. Make up the circumstances, pour out the emotions and don't care what anyone else thinks of you.' She dried her hands absently on her apron. 'I grew up in a time that disapproved of anyone doing anything that might mark them out as different. No wonder writers and artists were always looked upon as outsiders by people of my generation.'

'I am a bit of an outsider,' I admitted. 'I'm always the last one to get picked in games except Griffiths, and he doesn't have all his toes.'

'Good can come out of not being included. Well, that's all I have to say. You'll have to work the rest out for yourself. Now come and help me lay the table.'

After that conversation, I abandoned my efforts to behave more normally than anyone else in the country, and went back to being my normal abnormal self.

31

The Naming of Fears

I looked down my list of fears and realized that fearfulness came as naturally to me as breathing.

It seemed a more real state than being happy. I had not experienced anything directly tragic. The heavens had not fallen in on my life. Yet so much passed unspoken that there was a danger we might all drift along from birth to death in a state of suspended animation, never waking up and noticing the powerful undercurrents that swept us along. More and more, I understood why writers like Waugh and Woolf and Dickens and Forster treated their characters like feathers floating in fast-running gutters. Perhaps there was nothing you could do until you gathered speed and were swept down the drain.

If I could not write about being an active part of the world, I could at least write about my fear of it.

Uncapping my handsome Waterman fountain pen, a purchase made with my Star Letter gains, I began a story about a power cut, and being stranded alone in the silent darkness, only to discover that there was something else in the room with me, some great darker-than-dark object that could not be named without terrible consequences.

The bloody thing leaked everywhere, spreading great stains of navy-blue Quink ink. I switched to a Biro.

I tried to put a name to my fears. Then I tried to sell the story. Oddly enough, nobody at *Yachts and Yachting* wanted to publish a gloomy odyssey into a schoolboy's dark recesses of the soul.

More oddly still, my father really seemed to hate me now. It was as though he thought I had adopted this latest persona – pretending to be a regular son – for the sole purpose of embarrassing him. I couldn't understand why trying to be normal had made me look so weird. Surely I was just doing what everyone did in our house? After all, Bill was pretending to be a well-balanced father and husband, despite the fact that he had once again stopped speaking to Kath and went out of his way to avoid me and everyone else, even hiding behind the door when a neighbour came to call. Kath pretended to be a doting wife and mother, even though she had suffered a nervous breakdown that no one was allowed to mention, and had fled to Russia without telling anyone. We were so determined to be normal that when we came home one evening to find that the dog had gone mad, spraying blood and vomit around the walls before dropping dead in the lounge, Bill had merely dragged its carcass outside and buried it in the garden without a word. When my beloved cat Wobbles had died, he had made me carry its corpse outside in order to toughen me up. These days, I'd get trauma counselling.

Kath needed to get out of the stifling, thick-walled house that kept so much out and let nothing in. Her experience of different types of work was ten times greater than her husband's, to the point where she had now run the entire gamut of legal employment. Her latest job involved deploying teams of housewives to deliver free samples of fabric softener, but they hadn't managed to reach their targets, so the entire house was stacked with thousands of gelatinous envelopes of softener and everything reeked of sickly-sweet chemicals, a scientist's approximation of the scent of roses. As the sachets grew warm and burst, they seeped into the wallpaper and carpets, staining everything cobalt blue.

Bill concentrated on grooming Steven to become a professional spanner-holder, and it worked because his youngest son was so gentle and well behaved that he did it with unquestioning loyalty. Steven clearly had his own anxieties, but his uncomplaining nature meant that he lost out in the battle for attention. His dyslexia and shyness went unnoticed until they were ingrained in his personality like the streaks in the faux-wood hall staircase. Even so, it would have been obvious to anyone, had they looked, that he was the only member of the family to approximate normality without consciously having to take a run at it.

Bill knew I conspired with Kath against him – he had seen the pair of us creeping down to the end of the garden together from his observation post at the window. He badly needed an ally of his own, but with no mechanism for creating one via the usual parental channels of emotional blackmail, he went spectacularly overboard on the presents. By buying Steven his own motorbike years before the poor kid could drive, we could all start considering the possibility of grotesque road accidents at the earliest available opportunity.

Bill seemed angry that I should be indulged by my mother, and especially that I might be allowed to choose my own path in life. After all, he came from a long line of men who had been set upon a track of minimal education and backbreaking work until the day their clothes were put in a box and given to the Salvation Army. I didn't understand it – surely my father should have been rejoicing that times were changing enough to allow a break in tradition. He didn't, though, because the changes were coming too late for him.

Through the passing years, Bill remained an enigma. Each time I thought we had finally reached a state of truce, the dream of an alliance slipped away once more, the warmth dissipated and my father retreated more deeply into inarticulate isolation, until there could be no more hope of a reconciliation.

When Steven met his first girlfriend and fell in love with her, the pattern was finally altered. Rather than bringing her back to spend time with the family, my brother shot from Cyril Villa to her house like a scalded cat, and was wise enough to stay there. Her parents were normal. They liked each other, and doted on their children. They didn't pass the years locked in arcane wars of attrition. I think it came as a bit of a shock for Steven to discover that our family did not set the standard for normality.

It didn't take Bill long to see how alone he would soon become, but he did not know how to make amends. Instead, he took out his growing anger on me. Every time I entered the room, he got himself into a state of barely suppressed fury, spoiling for a fight.

I passed my exams with good results. One day I was given a piece of advice from a retiring teacher. 'Boys are terribly single-minded, they only do well in the subjects they care about,' said the old man, who was permanently covered in chalk dust and whose name, appropriately enough, was Mr Scholar. 'What subjects don't you like?'

'Maths, physics, chemistry,' I told him.

'And what are your favourites?'

'English, art, history, economics.'

'Then stop revising the former at once and put all your efforts into the latter. The teachers won't care when they've realized that you've given up the ghost, I promise you. They only notice the ones who keep trying.' As he headed off, Mr Scholar paused to hitch his raggedy gown up to his shoulders like a tired night-club hostess. 'Remember what I said,' he called back. 'Nobody gets points for being a nice person. Nice makes you invisible. There's another lot coming up behind you. To us, you're already last year's class. You don't have to care about what we think.'

I followed Mr Scholar's instructions. I intensified the focus of my studies, vanishing within the house to become a pallid, slender ghost who occasionally emerged from my bedroom to eat or wash.

Friendless and determined to be unloved, my father remained stranded at the window as if keeping an eye out for enemy battleships. He glowered at me each time I passed with a stack of books cradled in my arms. He warned me there would be no money to go to university, and told me not to even think about the idea. He took to muttering insults under his breath.

'I think you need to look for a flat before your father ends up killing you,' said my mother one day.

'He's killing *you*,' I countered. 'Look at yourself, all the weight you've lost. When was the last time you did anything just for yourself? He won't let you out of the house unless he comes with you. You can't cope with the job and this place and him. I could stay for a while longer . . .'

'And what good would that do? You know what will happen. It will drag you down as well. Better that one of us gets away. Go and find yourself, fall in love, have some adventures, get hurt a few times. I should have taken the chance when I had it, but now . . .' She twisted the thin gold band that had grown loose on her finger. 'Some days

I wonder what would have happened if I had gone away and stayed away.'

'You could have gone off and had an affair. Instead you went to a Russian museum.'

'Who would have wanted me, the wrong side of thirty-five and unable to have children? I'm not one of those dolly birds up in London. Besides, if I'd had an affair I might have got a taste for it and not come back. And I couldn't do that, because who would have looked after you? You are my greatest hope for the future, but you must leave before he hurts you so badly that you become like him.'

A few days later, I rented a minuscule room above a shoe shop in Belsize Park, and moved out. I felt uncomfortable leaving my mother and brother behind, but as I seemed to be the cause of so much ill feeling, it was the only solution.

I found myself saddled with a pair of flatmates in the rooms on either side of mine. Kevin was a red-eyed corduroy-clad spectre who read Sartre aloud by night and sold advertising space by day, and was torn apart by the compromises he had to make in order to earn a wage. Sarah was a plum-voiced county girl who wore cheesecloth smocks, and passed her mornings sitting on the stairs in tears, refusing to go to her office because she felt too fat. They were messy and messed up, but I loved them because they were in a different kind of mess than the ones I was used to. None of us knew each other's pasts, nor did we need to know. We accepted, and were accepted in turn, for the help and comfort we could give each other, without sulks, strops, threats or year-long silences.

I continued to read voraciously, drifting into literature's byways – although to even class many such books as 'literature' would have turned critics apoplectic at the time. Amongst the modern authors, playwrights and lyricists who became alternative gods were B. S. Johnson, Hunter S. Thompson, Stephen Sondheim, David Nobbs, Kander and Ebb, Peter Tinniswood, J. G. Ballard, Alan Sillitoe, Charles Wood, Keith Waterhouse, Michael Moorcock, Peter Nichols and a million others. Best of all, I could discuss them with my new flatmates, who were also – whisper the word – readers.

I left school on a wet Thursday afternoon, and started my first job on the following Monday as a courier for an advertising agency. I spent my evenings in the smoky sepia-walled Railway Tavern in Belsize Park, writing short stories, killing the ones that rang false. When I was less than entirely dissatisfied with something I had written, I would post it home to my mother for criticism. Kath found herself adopting my former role as a reviewer, the difference being that she was clear-eyed and merciless. Still, nothing I wrote really seemed to work. I started to think about stopping, and then one day I simply stopped.

Instead, I concentrated on doing my job well, and tried not to think about what might have been.

32

White Paper

I would never have tried again if it hadn't been for the golfball.

The Selectric golfball typewriter* had been thrown out of the room laughingly referred to as my 'office' when a department updated its equipment. I repaired it, scavenged a desk that had last had its drawers emptied before the Festival of Britain, and borrowed a kitchen chair. The extra furniture meant that it was impossible to shut the door of my rented room.

I wasn't due at work for two hours yet – time for one last try. I seated myself, threaded a fresh white page beneath the bar of the typewriter and waited, my fingers hovering over the keyboard. I lined up a bottle of Snopake whitening fluid and a packet of Tippex sheets on top of the ream of paper that I hoped I might be inspired to use up.

---

*Fast and efficient, but also incredibly noisy. An entire office of them was louder than a busy shipyard.

There was nothing, in theory, to stop me from producing a masterpiece.

The clock in the hall ticked. I stared at the page. The seat wasn't very comfortable. I waited and stared. My throat was dry, so I rose and made a cup of tea. I drank it, returned to my seat. The bare page was making me snowblind. I tried to think of an opening sentence, like those tortured artists in movies who furrow their brows for thirty seconds before being hit with the inspiration to write something like 'The 1812 Overture'.

The white page drew me in. White, white. As white as a lab coat.

The scientist, grizzled, defeated, far into his middle years, had almost lost hope of ever finding a cure for the ageing process.

He raised his wire-rimmed glasses and rubbed at his tired eyes. Nine days without sleep or food was too much for anyone, even a Nobel-prize-winning genius with a loving, devoted, busty wife who had given up her career as a former Miss Sweden for her brainy husband. Pacing the length of the laboratory, he returned to his test charts and the electronic machine that showed a squiggly green line measuring something . . . don't know what, work that bit out later . . . and hoped against hope that this one last test would prove successful. He checked his – what do you call them? – Petri dishes, and saw that the culture in Experiment 857B had changed colour in the last few minutes. Placing the test tube in a centrifuge, he spun it until – what did cultures do, separate like bad milk? And what would that show? It was no good, I couldn't do this, I had failed science at O level. With a shrug of disappointment at not becoming a household name, the scientist dissolved into random atoms.

Back to the page. White, white. As white as snow.

Lance Quest, the renowned explorer, was ploughing

knee-deep through an arctic blizzard, his beard smothered in stalactites of ice. His toes were frostbitten; two of them were loose inside his right boot, the one that had been gnawed by the enraged polar bear. Lance could not find his tent. Had it been ripped away in the storm, or could it have fallen into the crevasse caused by the landing jets of the alien space ship? No, that was *The Thing* . . . Desperately the explorer searched the hostile landscape . . . he searched . . . the explorer was lost in a haze of snow . . . lost . . . but there was the red nylon tent just ahead of him, in fluttering, battered tatters. His supplies had all been blown away across the inhospitable tundra. He would have to eat the last of the dogs. What, raw? Or was he seriously going to stumble across a lighter and some kindling sticks, maybe a rotisserie? Sod it. Snow covered everything completely until the white page came back.

White, white. As white as stardust.

Stella Thrust was the kind of Space welder you'd surrender your last tank of oxygen for. In the velvet cosmos, she clung to the hull of the ship just as her silver spacesuit clung to the curves of her voluptuous body. She was repairing the airlocks as if she had been born to ride the unmanned intergalactic big-rig to Riga. The company had been lucky to get her; no one else wanted to work on such a volatile load, especially as their journey would take them within the gravitational pull of the sun – check to see if the sun has a gravitational pull – but then Stella – too obvious a name? – Stella was determined to take the assignment, because the only man she had ever loved was chained up in the ship's freezing loading bay, and only she could save him from certain death. Wait a minute – unmanned? Who was flying the damned thing? Autopilot, that was it. Then what was her lover doing chained in the hold? Too complicated, I was getting painted into a corner . . . Stella was tapping her gloved fingers on the hull, waiting. She had work to do and I was holding her up. Go on then, I dared, do it without me. Stella waved two fingers at me and shattered into a smattering of sparkling stardust, against the flaring of the sun.

Desert Sun.

The fierce white desert sun . . . was hammering down on another figure, Lavinia Buncle, a beautiful, sexy red-haired heiress whose jeep had broken down in the Australian desert. She had driven here to escape the . . . er . . . Australian Constabulary, or whatever the local police force was called, after the daring robbery she had conducted just to annoy her father in Melbourne. Or Perth. If either of them was near a desert. Sweat trickled down Lavinia's tanned cleavage. Red earth clung to her khaki boots, as if the ground itself was trying to keep her here, dragging her back into the parched, dead aboriginal land. Her lips were cracked and peeling. She needed to find water soon. And moisturizer. If she could just find a – some kind of cactus, wasn't it, and you stuck a knife in the side and could drink the sap or something? And it had Aloe Vera in it as well? I probably had its name in a book somewhere.

Clambering over the bed, I began pulling out old travel manuals I had been collecting, but could not find one on Australia. The books I had removed created a gap in my bookcase that I noticed was filled with dust and bits of fluff. It couldn't have been vacuumed in ages.

I went and borrowed the Hoover, and spent the next hour cleaning the room, before realizing that I was late for work.

The whole grisly, tortured process went on like this for days, then weeks, then months. Finally I grew tired of dusting the Selectric, drew the plastic cover over it and returned it to the top of the wardrobe, where it sat with all the half-formed arctic explorers, sexy bank robbers, frustrated scientists and thwarted lovers, until they faded and greyed with dust, crumbling away to nothing.

At first I was disappointed that I would probably never achieve my dream, but the feeling faded to a dull, distant ache, something only felt on cold, wet mornings. Then it even became difficult to recall what the dream had been. When I tried to summon up my ambitions, there was only a blank stillness where the obsessive enthusiasms had once lived. I guessed I had become an adult, because adults always shielded their feelings, and rarely showed what they really felt. It was a system that protected you while simultaneously robbing you of something essential, but I had seen what could happen to adults without it; they exposed themselves too much and got damaged, like plants left in fierce sunshine. Perhaps that was why such people were often described as 'burned out'.

I buckled down to my office job, made new friends, moved flats, went out.* I wrote copy for adverts. Kenning Car Hire had taken an ad in a charity sailing brochure: 'YACHTS OF LUCK FROM KENNING!' Potterton Boilers had brought out a model with a new flue: 'DON'T GET STEAMED UP ABOUT YOUR BOILER!' A rather dim monkey could have produced work with more originality.

One day towards the end of the summer, when the corners out of sunlight were growing noticeably colder and scarves had started reappearing on the streets, my mother called me to explain that Bill was having some tests in Canterbury Hospital, and it might be a good idea

---

*E. M. Forster once said he would have written more if he hadn't gone out so much. Samuel Beckett, asked what he had given up for his art, replied: 'I have fairly often not gone to parties.'

to look in on him. So I borrowed a friend's car and went to visit my father.

Illness had knocked some of the fight from him. Propped up in an enormous white bed, he seemed smaller and more jaundiced. The lines on his cheeks were deeper than ever, and his hair had thinned into wisps of grey. I thought, *This isn't a few tests, there's something very wrong with him.* Naturally, he pretended that everything was fine, as usual. We discussed the new lane system on the M2 motorway, digital watches and Potterton central-heating systems.

I had parked the car underneath the hospital, in a vast low-ceilinged concrete cavern with faulty, buzzing neon panels. I stayed for an hour in the hospital ward, but when I returned to the car and tried to leave I must have taken a wrong turn somewhere, for although the exit arrows continued to point around to the left, I kept spiralling downwards instead of driving back up towards the surface.

As I went deeper, keeping the wheel at a steady angle, the surrounding cars grew dustier and older; some of them looked as if they had not been moved in years. I realized that I had not been concentrating because I had been worrying about my dad and whether he might be dying, and suddenly I was lost. I had simply ventured into the long-term parking area, but it felt like a descent into hell.

I tried to find a place to turn around, but was now in a series of tunnels too narrow to manoeuvre my car. I passed a sign reading 'Car park closes at 8 p.m.' and realized that it would shut in less than five minutes. When I scraped the nearside rear bumper against the wall, my oldest fears surfaced and I began to panic. Forced to travel on in one direction, my sense of claustrophobia grew. My breathing became laboured. I had suffered several serious bouts of pneumonia and pleurisy as a child, and had been left with damaged lungs. I opened a window and was sure I could smell leaking petrol.

It was getting more difficult to catch my breath. I imagined the car becoming wedged in the ever-narrowing tunnels, imprisoning me inside it as petrol dripped and pooled underneath the wheels, the fumes rising to fill the dark interior.

I finally found a place to turn, of course, and corrected the simple mistake I had made, returning easily to the surface. I was crying and felt ridiculous, ashamed of not dealing well with something my father would not have thought twice about. Bill had once burst a tyre on a motorway one night during a terrible storm, and had hopped out with his jack to fix it in a jiffy. He had replaced the tyre in howling rain and darkness while facing three lanes of oncoming traffic, and the idea of being nervous about doing so had not even crossed his mind.

When I returned to my room, I climbed on the bed and heaved the Selectric from its hiding place. Threading in a new sheet of paper, I began to type up the story of my panic attack, expanding and exaggerating it, colouring it with heightened emotions. I created a protagonist who had come to the building above the car park in order to serve a writ. The man was cocky and confident, but as the peculiarity of the car park's layout made itself known he found himself trapped, his arrogance stripped away by something as simple as a 'Keep Left' sign.

It took me less than three hours to finish the first draft of the story. I didn't just put down the memory of being stuck in the car park. Everything I had forgotten about writing came thundering back.

After that, each time something happened, whether it was sad or frightening or a cause for small happiness, I placed the feelings into the framework of another story.

Gradually the pages mounted up in the corner of my room. At the end of the year I collated the stack of paper, and realized that I had finished ten stories.

I never sold a single one. Instead, almost by accident, I managed to sell the entire collection. The tales were fantasies, fables, adventures in lands I had never visited, but inside each one was a grain of unpalatable truth, something that I believed to my core.

The acceptance letter from the editor at Sphere Books was a pleasant and slightly distant single page, but it meant more to me than all the pages I had read in my life. The editor had not mentioned money, when the book would be published or how many would be printed, but it didn't matter. I wanted to run all the way across London to tell my mother that it had all been worthwhile, but she had always told me that bragging was common.

It appeared that I had done it without the help of swinging London, without the sexual revolution, without the hip young things who invented the first era of what later became cringingly known as Cool Britannia, without any of the much-publicized creative efflorescence of the period. Instead, I had been shepherded by a self-effacing middle-aged mother, a genteel, disappointed librarian and a couple of dry English teachers who I can now only faintly remember. Perhaps I did not want to run across London after all. Achievement, it turned out, was a quiet thing. I wanted to clutch some books to my chest and walk them back through the rain to the little library that lived under the Blackheath flyover. I wanted to see Ethel Clarke sitting behind the counter, and show her the letter. I wanted to see the slow warm smile of satisfaction spread across her face.

The book was published as a (to me, at least) handsome paperback, and I even managed to find it on a shelf in an Oxford Street bookstore, albeit at the very back of the shop, near the stockroom. At the last minute I had remembered to put a dedication to my mother.

Out of politeness, I added my father's name.

Short stories are one thing, a novel is another, and the first of these took a lot longer to gestate. The narratives I developed split up into thrillers, supernatural tales, social comedies, satire, science fiction, horror, humour, crime and mystery.

I did not attempt the Great British Novel. I was not fêted as the Hot New Talent. I did not become a Smash Bestselling Author. Despite hitting a few top-ten sales lists and garnering generally kind and thoughtful reviews, I joined the brigade of British mid-list writers, that groundswell of solid, reliable and often surprising authors who keep bookshops afloat once the public has sated itself with the latest overnight sensation.

It was more than I had ever dared to dream of.

One day, I hoped to add myself to the ever-expanding list of twentieth- and twenty-first-century writers I had so long admired, which now also included:

Alan Garner
Peter Van Greenaway
Edmund Crispin
Peter Barnes
Joyce Carol Oates
David Pownall
Michael Frayn
Hilary Mantel
Paul Bowles
Brian Moore
Christopher Priest

and a hundred other authors who deserved to be more famous and read more widely than any TV presenter or glamour model who had been paid a fortune to grace the cover of the latest ghost-written stocking-filler to provide, at best, an alternative to buying someone socks at Christmas.

It was something to aim for, at the very least. And now the door was ajar, letting in a thin sliver of sunlight and opportunity. Unlike the brother's cousin of the man who painted Shirley Bassey's bathroom, there was a chance that I might one day become known for something more than going to the same school as Daniel Day-Lewis.*

*Three years below me so I didn't know him, sadly. How cool could that have been?

33

A Brush with History

Bill emerged from hospital subtly altered, like one of the pod people in *Invasion of the Body Snatchers*, only in reverse, so that he was suddenly warmer and more human. On subsequent visits home, I found him becoming tentatively friendly, like an old holiday companion carefully renewing an acquaintance. On the rare occasions when Bill returned the visit, he would always enter my room in the middle of a complaint about the journey.

'You wouldn't believe the traffic on the A2. The last two junctions were coned off and we had to cut up through Kidbrooke, which meant we couldn't take the turn-off at the Blackheath roundabout.'

He had always been more comfortable discussing traffic systems than almost any other subject, probably because he was more familiar with the workings of the internal combustion engine than the human heart. We had reached a point where we could talk easily about boats and cars and sliproads and bridge construction, and I was careful never to mention anything as tricky as love, death or relationships. Bill came from the wrong generation for that sort of soft talk.

I could see that my father was ageing fast. Lines of regret had etched themselves deeply into his face, until he looked as old as his father before him. He had taken early retirement, but with nothing to do and no friends to see, he had simply remained at his post before the lounge window, watching the world bustle by.

When I discovered that Bill was dying of lung cancer, the result of a lifetime spent smoking unfiltered Woodbines, just as his father had smoked Capstan Full Strength all his life and died from them in similar circumstances, I went home and sat beside him in a spot where we could both face the view, such as it was.

My parents had moved from Cyril Villa to a neat, faintly nautical bungalow by the sea in Whitstable, but there was nothing much to see from the lounge. Typically, Bill had chosen a house set one road back from the water, facing the rear brick wall of the house that actually had the view of the sea. Apart from a single green thread of crimson roses on an orange brick wall, the garden had been denuded and manicured until its most noticeable feature was its barrenness. It was as though some retired people had punished their garden for being too small and leaving them with too much time on their hands.

'I think we need to get some air,' I said, passing my father an overcoat. Bill was still wearing his smart grey suit and tie, even though it was years since he had been to an office. The collar of his crisp white shirt had always been too tight, but now it looked two sizes too big.

We still struggled with conversation. I had never once discussed my success as a writer with him, and now it no longer seemed an appropriate subject.

'That's better. A bit of a breeze through the head.' We

rounded the crest of the road and stared down at the grey, wind-pocked channel below.

I sat down on a bench beside my father. He looked blankly out at the sparkling sea, the walkers, sunbathers, children, yachts, water-skiers, the rest of the world, as if trying to make sense of so much activity. It was as though he was spending his final days observing distant action from an obstructed seat at the back of a cinema. Whatever he did now, he would not be able to interact with what was happening before him. Somewhere a radio was playing Acker Bilk's mournful 'Stranger On The Shore', his favourite song. I tried to think of something nice to say.

'What was it like when you were a scientist?' I asked, remembering the monochrome photograph I had seen of him in a white coat, standing outside the laboratory that looked like a garden shed. I had been trying to write about a scientist recently, but a real one this time. Why on earth had it not occurred to me to ask my father before now?

'Those were exciting days,' he said, brightening up a little. 'The best days of my life. We were all so young and untested. It seemed as if anything was possible back then.'

'Why did it feel so different? Because you were young?'

'Not just that. The government put a lot of faith in us, even though we were all in our early twenties. They wouldn't do that now. Nobody trusts the young now. But there was a war on, and people like us were in short supply. We worked incredibly long hours, and the pay was terrible. We weren't sure what they were expecting from us. We were trying to understand the structure of strengthened glass, trying to make it and then find a way of applying it to some use. The brief was very broad.'

'Did you succeed?'

'Oh yes, we used it to seal wiring inside, you know, to hold the wires in place. Valves and wiring, they were all so clumsy, and took experts to connect. The idea was to seal the bare wires, or a conductor in molten form, inside glass tablets and lock them together. You could make the connections much smaller that way. We knew that some other boffins were trying to build the first computer. I kept thinking how much better it would be if we could pour conductive metal straight into channels cut in silica.'

'You mean like a silicon chip?'

'Yes, but of course it was impossible to do back then. Our tools weren't fine enough to cut the channels. As soon as they invented the laser, I realized it would become a reality.'

I remembered a moment of rare enthusiasm; my father coming into the garden to read aloud an article about the development of the industrial laser. I had paid him little attention.

I felt disgusted with myself. All this time, my father had been silently harbouring his own enthusiasm, and had brushed against one of the greatest scientific revolutions in history. In a slightly different time frame, under slightly different circumstances, he could have achieved something quite extraordinary. He could have helped to take Alan Turing's work on into the modern computer age. He might have been successful, even famous. He would certainly have been happier.

Who would you have been, I wondered, *what might you have done, without your mother to contain you? Two mothers, working in opposite directions – no wonder they never got on.*

'But there's no use complaining about what might have been,' said Bill, sinking back and looking out at the darkening sea. 'Come on, let's go home.'

'I'm sorry, Dad,' I said.

'What for?' Bill seemed mystified. As we walked back in silence, it struck me that it was perhaps the first time we had ever been truly comfortable in one another's presence.

'Look at you, you need a haircut,' I told Bill, noting the straggling white hair that curled behind his huge ears.

'I can't get there any more,' he admitted. 'My legs aren't working properly. Remember Morris's in the Old Dover Road, where I always took you for your haircuts?'

How could I have forgotten? The barber was about ninety and blind as a bat. Every time I went there I got my neck nicked with a cut-throat razor, so that I ended up dreading haircuts more than trips to the dentist. By way of compensation the barber would give me a red rubber mould of Robin Hood and a bag of plaster. He nicked me so often that I ended up with all of the Merrie Men and half of Sherwood Forest.

'Is he still there, old Morris?' my father asked.

'Oh, I imagine so,' I said, knowing that not only was Morris gone, but so was the Old Dover Road, along with an entire way of life. 'Let me cut it for you.'

'No, you don't have to do that. That's not your job.'

'I want to.'

When we got home, Bill sat very still with his back to me, rigid and upright on his stool, a towel tied around his scrawny neck, and remained very quiet while I trimmed his thin hair with the kitchen scissors. It seemed wrong to watch him behaving so compliantly.

My fingertips could feel the warmth of his neck. His creased, bloodless skin was much softer than I had expected it to be. It had always looked like roughly hewn granite. As I finished snipping the last pale strand, I lowered my hand so that my fingers brushed his bare wrist. It was the only time in my life that I ever remember touching my father.

Two days later, Bill Fowler died.

34

The Last Star in the Sky

'It's not a very nice job for you, dear, but I just don't feel up to it,' said my mother, pointing to the wardrobes. 'A few old grey suits, it's hardly worth calling the Salvation Army. Even they must have standards.' She had delayed clearing out Bill's clothes until I could get down to Kent and do it for her.

I looked at the cupboards. After years of being hard up and filling their little house in Westerdale Road with utility furniture, I was surprised to find that she still bought cheap, wobbly wood-veneered wardrobes. Material things had never meant much to Kath. She treasured books more than household items. She wasn't one for nostalgia. Finally left alone, she seemed quite content now, although there must have been regrets.

'Maybe we'll find something exciting tucked away. Evidence of a double life,' I teased her.

'Oh no, dear, we were far too ordinary for anything like that. Your father didn't bother to tell anyone we were moving from Cyril Villa, and not one person even tried to get in touch with us. Nobody really knew we were ever there. Sometimes I wonder whether we existed at all. The English can be such chimerical creatures when they choose to be.'

'I know what you mean,' I said. 'Nice use of "chimerical", by the way.' My mother laughed.

After Steven and I had both left home, our parents had sold the rambling old house where no repair had ever been completed, and the building had become an old people's home. The oddest thing was that they decided not to take anything with them to the new bungalow except my mother's 'best company' crockery – not a single stick of furniture, no clothes other than the ones they wore, hardly any mementoes or family photographs, most of which they left behind in boxes in one of the empty rooms. They simply stepped out of one life and into another. I admired that, even though I did not quite understand it. Across the years, my father had been governed by a set of obscure, unworkable principles, like a kitchen appliance for which the instruction booklet had been lost.

'I don't want to help you, it's too depressing,' said Kath, heading out of the room. 'I'll be next door if you need me.'

'Did he mention me at all?' I called back.

'Just once, after he came out of hospital. He said, "I don't suppose I gave Chris any reason to love me."'

'He really said that?'

'He knew he'd never get around to telling you. He felt he'd left it too late for that sort of thing.' It was typical for our family to have set a time limit on a declaration of feelings.

There wasn't much to sort out. A couple of distinguished-service medals that had belonged to my grandfather, some cheap tie-pins and tarnished cufflinks, tobacco tins of odds and ends, insurance policies, a spectacularly ugly musical box made by William, and a couple of blown-up wedding photographs. As I looked at them I found myself wondering: had my grandmother really been such a monster? Long after she had died I discovered why she always wore her black boots. One was built up to hide a short leg. Life could not have been easy for her, so perhaps the only way to survive was to be tough. Families often resented an interloper, so it was likely that Bill's sister Doreen, who had been closer to Mrs Fowler, would have been wary of my mother, with her refusal to join in the small talk and her stuck-up manners. The alliances and enmities were all so subjective, but they still coloured how we felt about the past and affected who we were in a variety of subtle and unexpected ways.

There was one wedding photograph I had never seen in the house before. It showed my father standing next to a handsome, muscular young man dressed in the kind of smart grey suit that Bill was later to adopt. He was being handed his wedding ring, but there was something about the pose that was too private to be entirely comfortable.

'Who is this?' I asked, wandering into the lounge to show my mother the picture.

'Oh, that was Jack, your father's best man. He doted on you. We used to call him your Uncle Jack, although he wasn't a relation. Those two used to be inseparable.'

'I'm surprised I don't remember him.'

'He died when you were little. Bad lungs.'

'He's very good looking. Far more your type.'

'Oh no, I don't think so.'

'You didn't tip your hat at him, then?' I joked.

'No, Jack wasn't interested in the ladies, not in that way. He was a confirmed bachelor. Your father was fond of him, and took it very badly when he passed away so early in life. They knew each other from work. Jack collected antique glass. He had a flat in Bayswater. Your father would always stand him a beer or two. They were thick as thieves.'

'Did you go to his funeral?' I asked, a faint question nagging at me.

'No, and neither did Bill. His mother wouldn't let him. She'd heard something, you see, and put her foot down. It wasn't mentioned in those days, you just avoided certain people. You probably remember how she could be.'

A shadowed piece of my father moved into the half-light.

'He burned my poetry book,' I said.

'Well, he had a thing about poetry, he didn't think it was manly. That was his mother's doing. They lived their lives along very strict lines. There were things that were appropriate for a man to like, and things that weren't. I fought hard for him, but I knew I'd lose out either way. She tore her son into a terrible bundle of contradictions. She tried to make him stay away from Jack. You don't know what it cost him to get married at all.'

She paused in the doorway, unsure if she should say anything more.

'He didn't understand you, Chris. But I think perhaps he was envious. On the night before he died, Bill and I sat in the garden – he felt too hot in the house – and we had the oddest conversation. He pointed above the trees to a distant star – he always had incredibly good eyesight, even at the end – and asked if I thought there was life on other planets. I told him I didn't know. "What if we were living on the last star left in the sky?" he suddenly asked. "We'd be all alone. It wouldn't matter any more what anyone else thought of us." Well, I could hardly be expected to think of an answer. I wasn't prepared for him suddenly showing signs of curiosity or regret. Then I remembered what he had been like when we were courting, the wild ideas, the plans for the future.'

I thought of my father standing in the darkness on Blackheath at the age of seventeen, firewatching as phosphorescent bombs left angel-trails across the night sky. The distant glowing fires that turned the air around him acrid, the warning shouts from indistinct figures, the rumours and stories of death and dying. It must have seemed like the end of life, just as his was starting. His mother had told him to remain at home, where it was safe. She had been frightened of losing her only son. No wonder he had been so afraid to take any chances after that. He had been barely more than a child himself when war had broken out, and had remained the same age ever after.

That was why he always stood at the window, I thought. *He was imagining life among the stars, thinking of what might have been.*

'I suppose he thought he could get away from his past. It would have been an escape for both of us. Except that it could never happen.'

'He couldn't leave her.'

'Of course not. He needed her to feel reassured about himself, and she played on it. I think at heart he was a good man, but he wasn't a good husband. Lord knows he tried hard enough. I have to take my share of the blame as well. I should never have married him. Whenever he saw you and I conspiring together, it must have made him feel worse about his own mother. I suppose he thought I was doing the same thing to you.' She sighed, rising to make a fresh pot of Brooke Bond. 'I loved him in my own way. You can always find a way to love someone if you understand them. I'll miss him. Well, there you are. What's done is done.'

It was the last word she had to say on the subject.

35

Accidental Examples

My old school friend Simon was getting married, and wanted me to be his best man. After a whirlwind romance that lasted a mere twenty-two years, he and his intended, Kate, threw caution to the wind and rushed into betrothal, perhaps because their children had shamed them into tying the knot before somebody died.

It took a lot to get me down to Somerset. In the intervening years I had rarely been spotted outside the M25.

'So,' I said when I arrived at Simon's front door, horrified to find mud and what appeared to be some kind of horse ordure on my newly purchased Prada boots, 'I hear you finally became a custom car designer.'

'And you became a writer. Didn't you start with horror stories?'

'Yeah, no matter what else I write, satires, drama, social comedies, that's what they're going to put on my tombstone.'

'I can't believe how many books you've written. And yet nobody I know has ever heard of you.'

'Well, occasionally I get lucky, but mostly I'm mid-list.'

'What does that mean?'

'It means I'm one of the legion of writers out there who get respectful reviews and a steady readership, but never tap into current chattering-class obsessions.'

'Sounding a bit bitter there, mate.'

'I'm very happy,' I promised him.

'From what I've heard, your stuff's just too weird. We're ordinary families down here. We like our Harry Potters and Jeffrey Archers.'

'I thought you would.'

'I was sent a newspaper cutting about you. Those crazy elderly detectives you write about, Swan & Vesta.'

'Bryant & May. I write the Bryant & May mysteries.'

'Yeah, those are the ones.' He grinned. 'Bryant & May? Quite a match, eh?'

'Right, haven't heard that one before.'

He leaned forward, lowering his voice, looking very serious. 'Look, you might have to tone it down around here. The locals aren't much struck on Londoners with weird ideas, especially ones who reckon they're creative.'

That sounded familiar. I smiled to myself. When my first published tale featured the end line *Vengeance sits on the left hand of God*, I realized I had written a horror story just like the ones I had read as a child, although there were no ghouls or ghosts in it. For years, fiction had remained something I did in my spare time, like building galleons out of balsa wood or repairing clocks, an alternative to watching television. Now it was my livelihood. When people meet me, the first thing they usually ask is 'What have you written that I've read?', a question which presupposes some level of psychic ability. For the record, the second question is always 'Do you write under your own name?' because an amazing number of people think authors' names are made up.

'You could probably shift a lot more books if you wrote like Jeffrey Archer.'

'Probably.'

'Still, I guess you're just grateful to be published at all. I mean, who reads any more?'

Novels, I was told by one publisher who had rejected my work, were commodities sold like tins of biscuits, and the sweeter the taste, the more you could sell. But to me, the most important thing was that they had to contain fresh ingredients, not recycled ideas from other people. I realized now that my mother had been trying to tell me this for years; I had simply not been listening to her.*

Still, I had delayed. I had been afraid to try, and risk failure. I remembered my father angrily snapping off the volume dial on his transistor radio while listening to *Movie-Go-Round* because an actor had said that performing required an act of courage. Courage, said Bill, was still working on the roads at sixty-five, spreading tar even though you knew it was giving you lung cancer, as his own father had done. Courage wasn't mincing about on a stage or fiddling with a pen.

But in a way that Bill could never understand, it was. For years I was sure that if I failed as a writer, there would be nothing else left for me. If I could not achieve the one thing in life I tried hardest to do, it would be tough living with the loss of my dreams. How many people set out to change their worlds, only to find themselves in a state of perpetual downward revision and disappointment?

Over the years my list of favourite books had changed. These days it contained peripheral novels, tomes that fell outside the critics' canon of greatness. High on the list

---

*It's commonly said that the English write as if their mothers are reading over their shoulders. See the dedication in Russell Brand's autobiography.

was Keith Waterhouse's *Billy Liar*, because Billy's story acted as a warning and a reminder to me of the path not to take.

It took me years to build up the courage, but I finally stepped on to the train of opportunity that Billy Liar had let pass, and attempted my own novel. The size of the task dawned on me when I entered my flat and saw that it had turned yellow – the lounge floor and all the windows were covered with scribbled Post-it notes, like the exposed ramblings of an unsettled mind.

The main thing was not to think about the task in terms of success or failure. Writing came naturally, but writing well did not. It was like speaking a foreign language: you could never afford to stop concentrating for a second.

I added parts of myself to the stories, trawling for scraps of half-buried memories, like shaking seasoning into a stew. The things I recalled eventually allowed my characters to become both predictable and unknowable. It was like attaching a hundred coloured strings to push-pins, and sticking the pins all over a huge map, then plotting the trajectories and intersections of all the bits of string. And after I did it once, I did it again and again, until it started to make a vague kind of sense.

'Yeah, I've been meaning to write a novel,' said the unimpressed cab driver who dropped me back at the station. 'I just haven't had the time to get around to it.' He made it sound like mending the guttering or putting up a birdhouse, a tiresome chore anyone could handle if they owned a decent toolkit. I did not believe it was something you could simply choose to do. Most of the writers I knew did it because they had no choice at all in the matter. In that sense it was like supporting a hopeless football team or being a kleptomaniac.

The most articulate child I ever met was a pretty little girl called Athena, who grew up in her mother's steam-filled restaurant in North London, and who helped out in the evenings by serving at the tables and talking to the customers about themselves, before falling asleep behind the counter where the dishcloths were stored.

The most doomed boy I ever met went to an incredibly posh school in Westminster, where he was surrounded by every possible aid to becoming 'creative', supplied by an angry, determined, media-obsessed father he dared not fail.

From this I realized that it didn't matter if you grew up in a house with hardly any books, or if you behaved so differently from your parents that everyone thought you must be a stranded foreign-exchange student. You could still pop up like a pavement weed and prove impossible to stamp down, just as a young chef might appear in a household that survived on microwaved food, or an artist could rise from a home that only had The Green Lady on its walls.

An invisible, inconsequential family, marking time together in a small, hospitable neighbourhood, like a Reader's Digest condensation, only with more swearing and unconscious cruelty. Nothing the Fowlers ever did made any difference at all to the universe, the world, England, London or even Westerdale Road, and yet they were the product of a particular time, and therefore became accidental examples of it. People complained that everyone's lives were too open now, but for too long they had been closed so tightly that no one could draw breath.

Back at my parents' bungalow, I studied the photograph of my father. Bill was thirty-five when he married, but looked careworn and much older. The strain of his paradoxical life showed in the creases on his face. My fingers traced the contours of his knobbly skull, wondering what he was thinking in the picture.

I'm sorry I didn't know you, I thought. *The fault was mine as much as yours. I got lost in my books. I should have bothered to find out who you really were.*

Kath and I sat side by side, sipping strong dark tea from fat white mugs. The delicate red and gold cups, the bone-china cake-stand and side plates she had kept for best had been the only items to survive the cull, tucked away and taped shut in cardboard boxes, in the tacit understanding that they would probably never be used to entertain friends and neighbours. The civilized social life my mother had been promised in the magazines, all dainty doilies and conversations about literature, had failed to materialize. And yet she had found contentment, after a fashion.

A few days after Bill's funeral, the neighbours tentatively knocked to see if the coast was clear, and brought her little things they thought she might like. It was as if they half expected Bill to come back, like a Hammer Films zombie, and throw them all out. Slowly, the front room was opened up to guests, just for a mug of tea and some biscuits, a shop-bought fruit cake, the shy delivery of a bunch of flowers, but it brought Kath back to life.

She remained my greatest critic. After finishing one of a series of books I had written, she closed the cover with a final pat and said, 'Well, dear, I think you've mined out that particular seam.' And yet one day, when we quietly sat in her bungalow, she said after a thoughtful silence, 'You know, when you first got published, I felt that I did, too.' Beyond that, she wouldn't be drawn on the subject.

As I drove away from the house, my mother stood at the door, smiling and waving until she was lost from sight. The curse of youth, I thought, was the determination to ignore the past; the curse of age was a desire to remember it. I was interested in understanding what had gone before, but Kath preferred to switch on the television and drown out old memories. Why shouldn't she? She had earned the right. On the day I cleared out my father's clothes, I had finally come to understand why I should love him. It was a shame that the realization had taken so long.

At home that night I climbed on to the bed and reached to the top of my wardrobe, pulling down the last few remaining notebooks, which were now covered in layers of grey dust. At some point I had stopped writing in them, and now I wanted to remind myself when that was.

Even though I had switched to writing short stories, filing film reviews had been a hard habit to break. They peppered the pages so much that it was possible to provide an exact date for each book.

I found I had stopped filling them in on the very day I had left Cyril Villa to go and live alone. It seemed that those early, hopeless attempts at writing had not been signs of individuality at all, but of dependence and frustration. The blank pages that followed were the real signs of freedom.

Even though my father's death had placed a full stop on one page of my life, the rest of the book would continue onward, each sheet as bare and white and wide as the horizon, waiting to be filled with words that might one day glimmer like stars.

'I don't know who he is,' Bill had said of me plaintively. 'There's nothing in him I recognize.'

I am my mother's son. Just as you were yours. But I finally became myself. I wish you could have, too.

Time, I thought, for just one final list. Thinking back to all of the years of advice that my mother and the librarian of the East Greenwich Public Library had given me, for no other reason than to hope I would improve myself, I set down my own list of writing rules:

My Rules for Writing

Fiction means you can make things up.
Don't be ashamed of embarrassing yourself.
Stories don't have to be biographies.
Ask yourself what your hero really wants.
Be prepared to think the unthinkable.
When you imagine your story can't go further, go further.
You don't always need to explain why people do things.
Crisis moments are better when they're completely still.
Some of the best stories occur because the hero is slow to correct a mistake.
Everyone has the same feelings; they just think differently.
Leave room for your characters to breathe.
You have to love something about your hero.
Always keep the story moving forward.
Characters who contradict themselves are more human.
You don't need to spend six months on a trawler to write about a trawlerman.
Dialogue is not conversation.
It's better to do than to describe.
Life is a mess to which fiction brings a shape, which is why it's called fiction.
There's a difference between being realistic and being believable.
Make sure that something always remains hidden.
What your hero thinks he wants might be different from what he needs.
Nobody knows why people fall in love.
Believe what you write, even when it's all made up.

No matter how deeply hidden, there will always be
   love.
Always love.

I had reached the bottom of the page.
   No longer ashamed of the notebooks I had hidden for
so long, I put them out on the shelf, for all to see.

36

The Sovereignty of Words

If life is a series of locked doors you must find ways to open, books provided me with the first of many keys. But when I was ten, they were also my private shame. I was embarrassed to be seen carrying them everywhere I went, but couldn't help myself. If I had walked around the streets clutching a football to my chest, or a bicycle pump or even a shoe last, no one would have made fun of me. Books were things I seemed to be forever hiding. I stuffed them under beds and on top of cupboards, tucked them up my jumper and even hid them inside the brick air vent in the front garden until I could safely smuggle them upstairs. They gave too much away about me, and – as adults were always saying – the money spent on a book could be spent in other far more useful and practical ways. 'You could have bought a puncture kit for that,' my father had once said when he saw the price of a book. But all through my childhood I had a secret I could barely acknowledge, which was that if I had to make a choice between buying a book or buying a shirt to keep out the cold, I would always have chosen the book. I was sure that if this secret was revealed, it would make me look weak and stupid in the eyes of others. It was a long time before I began to suspect that it might actually make me stronger.

After I had my first novel published, I felt there was something I needed to do.

I went back to Westerdale Road on one final visit. I walked along the same street, retracing my steps from where the little orange brick house had stood, towards the East Greenwich Public Library. The sky was the colour of a bus driver's socks, it was raining lightly and the street lights were just coming on. The road was as empty as it had ever been, but judging by the dozen or so road signs along its way I could tell it now prioritized vehicles, not people. No children played on these pavements any more.

This time, I was not going to the library to borrow books. I was going to give some back. I was taking a few of my own favourite novels, from *Scoop* to *Orlando* to *The Crystal World*, from *Gormenghast* to *The Stirk of Stirk* to *The White Cutter*. I was just going to walk in and quietly leave them on the shelves, correctly alphabetized, to repay in some small part the debt I owed, in the hope that another ten-year-old child would find them there and begin to read.

This time, as I walked up the street with my armful of books, I realized I had nothing to hide. The printed page had not imprisoned my thoughts but had given them shape and set them free. Instead of shrinking away until they were invisible, the books in my hands seemed to grow plumper and lighter with every step I took. Each book had a different voice, and each voice could be distinctly heard. Some were yellowed and tinged with obsolescence, others were as stinging and insistent as they had been upon first reading. And there were new voices that had never been heard before, the memories of those who had been overlooked or ignored, now newly empowered by paper and print. These writers could be discovered with the rest – although you still had to be directed to them. The library directed children by encouraging them to browse. Without it, I would never have found the books I loved.

It seemed that as I walked the words expanded, signing themselves on the glittering damp air above me, doubling and folding like musical harmonies or sharp and shimmering drips of paint, reflecting their rainbow colours on the houses all around until the entire sky of lowering cloud was filled with sentences and phrases and quotes and descriptions of every kind, spiralling and exploding in every direction. The words became all the emotions they represented, laughter and argument, pleasure, exhilaration and endless, boundless delight.

Faced with such a cacophony of imagination, the rational brick-and-concrete world could only crumble and fall away like burned paper, blackening and drifting from view. The sturdy, sensible Victorian houses of London, branching out across the suburbs like concrete cilia, could not contain the force of these flimsy pages. Surrounded by this heuristic army, I wondered how I could ever have really been afraid of anything at all.

With the precious cargo in my arms, I headed through the rain towards the welcoming lights of the library.